D0866736

Microcomputers in Production and Inventory Management

THE DOW JONES-IRWIN/APICS SERIES
IN PRODUCTION MANAGEMENT

Microcomputers in Production and Inventory Management

Thomas H. Fuller, Jr.

DOW JONES-IRWIN
Homewood, Illinois 60430

This book was set in Times Roman by Eastern Graphics.
The editors were Mary Lou Murphy and Jane Lightell.
The production manager was Irene H. Sotiroff.
The designer was Tim Kaage.
The drawings were done by Horvath and Cuthbertson.
R. R. Donnelley & Sons Company was the printer and binder.

ISBN 0-87094-930-6

Library of Congress Catalog Card No. 87–70920

Printed in the United States of America

1 2 3 4 5 6 7 8 9 0 DO 4 3 2 1 0 9 8 7

The future of North American industry depends upon the effective and innovative use of every resource. This is especially true of that most versatile manufacturing tool—the microcomputer.

For decades, manufacturing professionals have generally relied on traditional methods of control, from cardex systems to large mainframe computers. As Tom Fuller points out in his book though, manufacturing planning and control applications may now be innovatively addressed by microcomputers.

Larger companies use micros to extract and translate information from the formal mainframe system into a more flexible and visual format for the users. And, even the smallest companies find micro-based manufacturing systems affordable.

Through his writing Tom shares a broad knowledge of both microcomputers and their applications within the manufacturing industry. His extensive understanding of the vital role of education helps translate the promises into reality, while his knowledge of materials management enables him to relate to the reader specific problems that microcomputers can be used to solve. He presents his insights in a warm and often humorous manner that makes this book good reading, as well as a valuable reference source.

APICS encourages the publication of this type of book to enable professionals in manufacturing planning and control to more effectively and efficiently carry out the day-to-day operations of their manufacturing enterprises. A significant addition to the APICS library and to the body of knowledge, this book should prove informative for both current and future manufacturing professionals.

I highly recommend *Microcomputers in Production and Inventory Management*. It provides new ideas and concepts that will benefit you *and* your company. I know it has offered new insights to me.

> Gordon E. Ellis, C.P.I.M.
> International President, 1987
> American Production and Inventory Control Society

.

They have landed.

Although the invasion in its early phase was as unseen and silent as a submarine, it has now emerged to be as clamorous as D–day.

Personal computers have invaded the world of manufacturing.

In 1982 the *Time* magazine "Man of the Year" was the IBM Personal Computer. Now *that* is getting *too* personal!

LOOK AT THE BENEFITS

The master scheduler of a small Midwest bicycle plant has traded in the green columnar pads of his former schedules for a personal computer (PC or microcomputer or just micro—by the way, Appendix B is a glossary of all acronyms used in this book). A production planner at Ford gives up on his trusty calculator for a TRuSty micro and builds plans in a day that used to take two analysts a week. The accountants have turned in the green eyeshades and arm garters for electronic spreadsheets. A revision to the budget that used to consume two working days and a mile of adding machine tape now takes 15 minutes.

The forecaster no longer waits in line at the Data Processing Output Window pleading with the Imperial Keeper of the Information for one more run before tomorrow's quarterly outlook meeting. In the privacy of her family room, she builds the revised model of her markets and prepares the report, the graphs, and the viewcells for the presentation.

The receiving clerk in Liege, Belgium, has exchanged the old clipboard for a glowing red wand that reads bar codes in less time than it used to take to click the ball point pen into action. And the inventory record 100 meters distant is adjusted simultaneously—*très vite!* In southern England a network of micros exchanges order information, inventory data, and shipping notices between remote locations at 50 times the speed of "ringing the bloke up."

BEWARE!

With so much good news spilling over the horizon, can the cautionary caveats be far behind?

Most micro users settle for using only a few functions of the dozens that they could use. A surprising number of users are on their second system. The first just didn't pass muster once they really loaded their work into it. *One fifth* of all micros are completely *abandoned* by their users—largely due to poor planning, poor training, and poor management. The vast majority of micros operate as isolated islands that call out to be joined together into a coherent network of productivity and cooperation.

No single tool holds so much promise for improving the productivity of today's manufacturing professional. However, the potential for confusion, incompatibility, unreliable data, uncontrolled proliferation, and frustration looms equally large.

The executive or manager faced with acquiring or controlling a department or division of micros faces a bewildering array of issues—security, compatibility, coordination of application selection or development, data integrity, training, documentation of procedures, and data communications. The list of potential suppliers of systems, programs, and services is even more bewildering.

HELP IS ON THE WAY!

The purpose of this book is to help manufacturers make better use of these promising tools. No single volume can satisfactorily plumb the depths of the many convergent areas of knowledge required in this field. Entire books are available (and useful) on many subjects included herein —communications, data bases, system selection, training, manufacturing software, and so forth. But this book serves to acquaint the manufacturing professional with these issues to be better prepared to select systems, to plan for their effective use, and to better control their implementation. This book begins, but does not end, the quest for wisdom! Consequently, many channels are suggested for the pursuit of this subject.

The information contained herein has been gathered over the last few years from dozens of corporations and many individuals.

The book is filled with real-world examples and real-world lessons. The author has been fortunate enough to have witnessed the good, the bad, and the ugly in PC installations. Some of the successful companies have gained genuine strategic advantages over their competitors through the use of these versatile tools—advantages that are daily translated into increased market share and profits through radically different methods of managing production systems. Contrariwise, I have seen PCs languish in disuse after the expenditure of hundreds of thousands of dollars in their acquisition and internal promotion.

The effort is made to explain why both happen and what the individual user, manager, or executive can do to secure the former rewards while minimizing the risk of the latter disasters.

The largest part of the book focuses the productivity spotlight on specific departmental benefits. This unabashedly practical section includes specific formulas that can be used by PC users. These are in the form of spreadsheet examples and guidelines—suitable for 1-2-3® from Lotus®, Microsoft Multiplan®, and others. By themselves, such examples make for dull reading. But these are woven into the tapestry of solving daily problems. These problems span, department by department, the spectrum of manufacturing—engineering to forecasting to scheduling to shop floor control to sending the bill.

Examples are offered of effective applications and implementation. Counterexamples of unsuccessful efforts are given as well to alert the wary. The emphasis is obviously on the former, but both are valuable.

THE SETTING

The beginning of this decade marked the first time in history that America's productivity gains—long the bastion of our economic prowess—were negative. Then in 1982, as mentioned above, *Time* magazine placed an IBM Personal Computer on its cover as "Man of the Year." Depending on your perspective, this could be interpreted as an omen of promise or doom.

The following table shows the steady erosion of mainframe turf by the proliferating micros—what mainframe suppliers view as the bacterial attack of the microaggressors! The figures are in dollars, not units, so the actual impact in the eyes of the user community is probably greater than the table indicates.

This means that micros are within a whisker of actually bypassing mainframes in the generation of revenue for data processing manufacturers. The age of the micro has dawned.

TABLE 1   Infiltration of Micros (percentage of total DP market by revenue dollars by year)

	1977	1982	1987 (est.)
Microcomputers	2%	17%	35%
Minicomputers	24	31	29
Mainframes	74	52	36

SOURCE: Lester S. Shindelman and Carter C. Utzig, "Move over Mainframe: Make Way for the Micro," *1986 APICS Conference Proceedings*, p. 467.

It was inevitable that someone (several someones, to be sure) should address the need to harness the potential of the microcomputer to fortify manufacturing productivity. Most companies have such devices in nearly every department. Two thirds are realizing only that meager fraction of their potential represented by word processing and isolated electronic spreadsheets. Significant productivity improvements remain untapped.

PCs have been economically justifiable for a few years now. Recently, it has become affordable to connect them to each other and to central systems. Trends in the areas of software, training technology (like interactive video disks), and system development have proven to be just as significant as the remarkable advances in the hardware technology. These advances open vast possibilities for streamlining the very methods by which we manage and communicate. Some examples of these advances are revealed in the section on implementation.

It is hoped that the guidance given, the examples shared, and the warnings sounded will save the reader some of the faltering steps taken by those who have walked over this trail. I gratefully acknowledge the debt owed to those who have shared these costly lessons. It is squarely in the spirit of APICS's educational charter to make this knowledge available to the widest possible audience so that all may become stronger.

OVERVIEW OF THE PARTS

The book is divided into five major parts.

The first, "Overview" explains the importance of *managing* the company's entry into the arena of PCs. Topics are presented relating to the management of this process, the selection and involvement of key players, and the benefits of doing so.

The next part, "General Productivity Tools," identifies broadly used

generic software available on PCs, its impact on professional productivity in general, and its particular value in planning and controlling
manufacturing. The part includes examples showing how such tools can
increase the productivity of these functions.

The next part, "Implementation," acquaints the reader with various
steps necessary to successful implementation. It develops the theme that
two elements seem to distinguish the most effective manufacturing users
of PCs: commitment to user support (especially training) and networking the PCs to each other and to the central operational (planning and
control) computer system. Both of these elements of success raise the
initial cost of PCs, but both pay more than commensurate dividends.

The largest part, "Departmental Benefits," is a collection of specific
examples, case studies, anecdotes, explanations, common sense, and
practical wisdom of PC use in a variety of settings from forecasting to
shop floor control. The case studies, examples, discussions, questions,
and answers are usually specific to the professionals in these departments.

Finally, "Follow-Up Information" lists just that—where to get more
information, software, installation help, and so forth—for the industrial
PC user, influencer, or manager.

READER'S TRAIL MAP THROUGH THIS BOOK

The author has the utmost respect for the Reader's scarcest resource—his
or her time. Therefore, I suggest that the reader may not wish to avail
himself (or herself—my use of the masculine always assumes either
unless specifically noted) of every section. The following Trail Map
serves as a pocket-size guide to this volume—to speed the reader to the
destination of job-enhancing knowledge with the fewest number of de-
tours, scenic overlooks, or switchbacks. These intriguing diversions are
ever available if later interest impels their revisiting. Happy trails!

General Manager:
   Primary: Chapters 1, 2, 9.
   Secondary: Chapters 3–8.
Operations Manager:
   Primary: Chapters 1, 5–8, 9–18 (as applies).
   Secondary: Chapters 3, 4.
MIS Manager:
   Primary: Chapters 1, 3–8, 9–18 (as needed).
   Secondary: The rest.

Departmental Micro Coordinator:
  Primary: Chapters 1–8, 9–18 (as applies).
Departmental User:
  Primary: Chapters 1, 3, 4, 6, 9–18 (as needed).

ACKNOWLEDGMENTS

It is but fair (though inadequate) to acknowledge the great tangible and intangible support rendered in the development of this book. My involvement with APICS in general and this book in particular would never have borne fruit without the generous support of my former manager, John Rioux. Gord Ellis and Charlie Mertens were valued cheerleaders when I was convinced that the goalposts were out of reach—and backing away! Don Fogarty and Tom Brown were most helpful in patiently reviewing and offering comments on the manuscript in its roughest form. Gene Crepeau and Sam Tomas provided valued comments that further strengthened this effort. The many manufacturing professionals who have explored this field and shared their hard-won lessons have made a more significant contribution to these pages than can be acknowledged in these few words.

Finally, this volume owes much to my wife—patient transcription of garbled dictation, clarification of obscure explanations, simplification of jargon, the removal of several failed attempts at humor (but a few slipped through), and constant encouragement. To her, to the two little micro programmers with whom we share our life, and to my parents who taught me to inquire and to persist, this book is gratefully dedicated.

Thomas H. Fuller, Jr.

CONTENTS

PART ONE

Overview

_____

CHAPTER ONE

Introduction and Basic Management Issues

This chapter acquaints the reader with the issues of most general interest regarding the microcomputer (or PC). It explains the widespread applications of micros in the world of manufacturing, illustrates how they may become even more productive, and describes various *changes in thinking* necessary to secure the principal benefits of these tools. It begins to answer the question, "How do I get my money's worth out of the micro?"

The major benefits of micros are *not* secured by treating them like little mainframes on our desks. Some companies have erred in the opposite direction by going hog-wild with enthusiasm—and have paid the price of relearning much of what systems people learned from mainframes two decades ago. To be successful, some rethinking is needed.

This point is so important that I use it to introduce a technique used throughout the text to call attention to items especially worth remembering. These are the NOTAble BENEfits of this book, which can be abbreviated NOTA BENE. This is the first:

NOTA BENE

_____

There is limited benefit in the microcomputer until the user adopts a change in routine, sees the task at hand differently, or gains an applicable new vision of the situation whose solution is sought.

_____

AN EXAMPLE

A true story of inventory intrigue and marketing machinations will illustrate this point.

The general manager had given the brand new product manager a very simple request. "Take a look at what we have in finished goods inventory and compare it to what's selling. Find out if some items have been 'forgotten' by the market. Then let me know what I should ask marketing to promote, discount, or else write off."

What a chance! Imagine the opportunity to tell marketing something! Especially via the boss!

Earnest in analysis and eager to please, the product manager scanned the various reports that were conscientiously fed to his department on a weekly, biweekly, and monthly cycle. Although there were fewer than 500 products, the stack of reports was over two feet high. After a few hours of bleary-eyed gazing into the green prison bars of computer output, he realized he was no closer to identifying the potential promo items than at the evening's beginning.

He was staring at reports that looked like this:

Inventory Analysis

Item Number	Description	Sales last 12 months						Total
G12345	Wrapping paper	12	16	34	11	61	. . .	
G23456	Folded 14" bags	7	43	12	32	9	. . .	
G34567	. . .							

Stock and Location Analysis

G12345	. . .

And on and on.

This was not helping.

It occurred to him to load all these products into an electronic spreadsheet on a nearby personal computer (it actually belonged to another department, but they were long since home). Next, he made a new column to the right of all this "information" that figured the average sales over the last 12 months. Hmm, he pondered, that at least shows what's moving.

He then created a column called NUMBER OF YEARS TO SELL STOCK ON HAND by dividing the quantity on hand by the average monthly sales times 12: Quantity/Average monthly sales × 12. Some products only had a fraction of a year on hand. Some had more than a year. Some had a lot more than a year. He then sorted all the products by this last column. This brought the slowest turnover items to the top of the chart.

How simply may germinate the fragile seed of *vision*! He was beginning to uncover a pattern.

These slow moving items at the top of the chart were obviously the prime candidates for promotion—depending on why they were turning over so slowly. A look at longer term sales histories and a quick calculation of potential profit revealed half a dozen items that filled the bill in all respects. He *saw* what he needed to do. The next day he gave a summary copy of this spreadsheet to the general manager with his recommendations.

The general manager also *saw* the need and thanked the new product manager. Marketing did promote the products, and they sold pretty well.

We all recognize there are a lot of ways to uncover useful information in the forest of data that most of us face. We all have our favorite reports, inquiries, and retrieval tools. However, the above story illustrates the ready utility of the PC. This immediacy, combined with its low cost and relative ease of use (more on that later) can make the personal computer (PC), or microcomputer, as indispensable to the manufacturing professional as his ID badge.

A quality control supervisor needed an analysis of tolerances and control limits on a candy batching operation. In less than an hour she put such an application together on a micro. A payroll clerk wanted to calculate and distribute a decreasing-rate overtime payroll. This took hours to calculate every week. On a PC, the application took about 45 minutes to develop. It cut the payroll clerk's expenditure of time by two thirds, eliminated errors, and yielded some handy productivity reports that did not exist before.

A PAUSE FOR THE WOLF AT THE DOOR OF PC PROMISE

However, [paraphrasing the Yankee farmer] if you're so smart, why aren't you rich?

Why is so much of this fertile field for white- and blue-collar productivity lying fallow? Why are a fifth of all PCs simply abandoned? Why are two thirds used for relatively limited functions—isolated spreadsheets and word processing? As handy as these functions are, they represent only a sliver of the potential functionality. Why are the vast majority of PC users disconnected from the main founts of information that could double or triple the PCs' value?

Later in this chapter several reasons for these shortfalls are introduced. But this much can be shared right now. The reasons are only *partly* (about one third) technical. They are *mostly* a matter of sound application of basic principles of systems development, and people care. Much more needs to be said and will be said to fill this in, but first let's understand this phenomenon of *vision* or *insight*. What is its relation to the process we call decision making? This may well be at the center of the PC revolution we are witnessing.

REVOLUTIONS IN THE WAY WE WORK

In history it seems that most revolutions—not the political variety but revolutions in the way we work—have sprung up in the wake of particular new tools. These in significant measure (usually unexpectedly) led to such a change in the work and tasks of a particular phase of society that this shift was later called a revolution.

Examples abound.

In the 18th century, James Watt made significant advances in the mechanism of regulating steam power. These major improvements harnessed steam power for a wide range of industrial applications. It can be said that this technology fueled the industrial revolution. In a similar manner, Eli Whitney's cotton gin and Cyrus McCormick's reaper paved the way for the agrarian revolution that currently enables a handful of farmers to feed much of the world. The revolution in space exploration was largely propelled by Robert Goddard's research in liquid and solid fuel rockets.

It may well be these tools were a product of their times—that in some sense they would have been invented by somebody given the needs and culture of their era. The accumulating demand for the tools perhaps gives rise to an inventor who bears them into the world. The mother whose name is Necessity cares little which inventor plays the midwife. Whether such tools actually *cause* the revolution or merely *coincide* with the revolution will be the subject of future historiography and is not germane here.

A revolution is going on right now that is exactly germane. It is going on in the community of users of information systems. The revolution is in the way these users *view* this information. It is following on the heels of the widespread introduction of the microcomputer—the new tool that is actuating the revolution of this hour.

We can remember not so many years ago when the grandfathers of today's micros—tractor-strength mainframe computers—were first introduced into manufacturing applications. For more than a decade we merely used the tractor like a diesel horse—the computer just sped up the manual processes of the past. Statistical reorder points, economic order quantities, machine loading, and a variety of such venerable techniques were accelerated to two thirds the speed of light with perfect memory in exponentially growing storage. It became possible to recalculate new economic order quantities (EOQs) for thousands of parts between lunchtime and the midafternoon coffee break.

It was nearly a decade later that pioneering practitioners experimented with *significantly different approaches* to managing inventory —approaches that would have been unthinkable without the power of storage and calculation that the computer offered. The techniques converged in material requirements planning and, later, manufacturing resource planning.

One of the pioneers of that pregnant era, Joseph Orlicky, made an observation that is hauntingly prophetic of today's user of the micro.

> The breakthrough, in this area, lies in the simple fact that once a computer becomes available, the use of such [older] methods and systems is no longer *obligatory*. It becomes feasible to sort out, revise, or discard previously used techniques and to institute new ones that heretofore would have been impractical or impossible to implement. It is now a matter of record that among manufacturing companies that pioneered inventory management computer applications in the 1960s, the most significant results were achieved not by those who chose to improve, refine, and speed up existing procedures, but by those who undertook a *fundamental overhaul* (my emphasis) of their systems. The result was abandonment of techniques proven unsatisfactory and a substitution of new, radically different approaches that the availability of computers made possible.[1]

If the word *computer* is replaced with *microcomputer* in this quotation, might we not conclude that the great gains of our era will come from those who leapfrog the data processing techniques of their peers? This does not suggest a wholesale abandonment of proven techniques such as MRP, MRP II, Just-in-Time, and so forth. But it does call for a rethinking of the assumptions involved in planning and control. It calls for recognizing the estimates, guesses, and hedges permeating our systems. And it calls for the vision to seek out better methods.

When radically different technologies come along, there is a tendency to shoehorn them into the outlines of familiar concepts. For exam-

---

[1] Joseph Orlicky, *Material Requirements Planning: The New Way of Life in Production and Inventory Management* (New York: McGraw-Hill, 1975), p. 4.

ple, the first motor-driven vehicles resembled horseless buggies. The first aeroplanes looked like gliders. The first jet planes looked like propeller planes. (This is why the wings tore off when they broke the sound barrier!) The first motion pictures were made as plays acted on a screen. In each case there was no real progress until the inventors/developers adapted radical design changes.

NOTA BENE

They who drag the baggage of past notions, pressing to board the onrushing train of progress, are doomed to be left waiting at the station of mediocrity.

Of course, Don Fogarty's reply has its place, too. They who drop everything to leap aboard the train without checking its destination may be disheartened when they arrive.

Orlicky, referring to the systems of the 40s and 50s, wrote in another prophetic passage:

> These methods and systems had been devised in light of the information-processing tools available at the time, and they suffered from a lack of ability to correlate and handle data on the massive scale required. This *constraint of the tools* [his emphasis], which affects the efficacy of methods and systems, also governs the way people look at things, perceive problems, and formulate solutions to these problems at a given point in time. The constraint of the tools is reflected in the thought and literature of an era.
>
> The introduction of computers into production and inventory control work represented a sudden increase—by orders of magnitude—in the power of available tools. In the late 1950s the constraint of the tools was lifted and a new era began.[2]

Again, in our era, the constraint of the tools has been lifted—and again not by niggardly degrees but by orders of magnitude. Are we as prepared to change our approaches by the same margin as those winners of the last revolution in manufacturing methods? Time will tell.

THE INVASION OF THE MICROS—REPRISE

Of course, it was a bit hard to hear the march music of the new era of the 80s for all the side shows and the carnival barkers.

---

[2] Ibid., p. 258.

To wit, the micros' first real successes were as—how humiliating —video games.

By 1986 the world's best invader of "Space Invaders," Sonny Shum of Victoria, British Columbia, racked up a score of 29,090. For those of you who were wondering if this craze has any relevance to industrial automation, you will be glad to know that Jim Jung of Santa Ana, California, captured world honors on "I, Robot" with 818,684 points.

By 1984 more than 5 billion quarters had been poured into microprocessor-based videos. Silicon Valley had finally discovered the "Philosopher's Stone" that had eluded medieval alchemists. They were turning sand into—if not gold—at least silver.

The processing power of the first computer—ENIAC—filled two stories, covered 15,000 square feet, and weighed 30 tons. Forty years later this much computational horsepower fits under your airplane seat. Actually, the raw processing power lives on a chip smaller than your watch. A PC is 20 times faster than ENIAC.

These changes in the technology of pushing numbers through electrical paths have occurred over a stunningly brief interval that has also witnessed great changes in the business of production and inventory control. As the work force has steadily shifted from the foundry to the office, it was natural that the tools would follow suit.

The American Production and Inventory Control Society (APICS) has grown from its first member in 1957 to more than 60,000 today. It has prospered largely by the simple philosophy of teaching its membership and the manufacturing community at large how to get better at manufacturing. It has fostered the sharing of ideas, and the development of a broad body of manufacturing knowledge. It has developed widespread tests to measure assimilation of that knowledge. It encourages the correlative professionalism of today's manufacturer. The competitive pressures from the emerging unified world economy challenge every one of us to think better, plan better, control better, and execute better.

The need is to extend this professionalism to the rapidly emerging world of microcomputers.

MICROCOMPUTERS IN MANUFACTURING

Microcomputers have now proliferated in nearly every aspect of business and virtually every function of manufacturing—from design idea to warranty work. In 1960 there were only 5,000 computers in the world. Now—with a very generous definition of processor (including the little brains at work in cars and such like)—there are 50 million! Boeing has more than 5,400 PCs installed, and the number grows every day.

In 1986 there were about 10 million PCs in offices, which worked out to about 15 PCs for every 100 workers. According to *Future Computing* (quoted in the 1986 APICS Conference Meeting of the Microcomputer Applications Special Interest Group), this will swell to nearly 30 million by 1990—40 PCs per 100 office workers. Currently about 6 percent are connected to some local area network. It is estimated that by 1990 40 percent will be.

Various other surveys predict that the number of microcomputers will increase by rates ranging as high as 50 percent per year. The more skeptical observers suggest that the growth is cresting. But still the questions remain:

Why are these flooding the world of manufacturing?

How are they being used?

Will microcomputers replace "dumb" terminals? (One small manufacturer in Florida only uses micros for terminals—more than 50 at last count!)

Are the promised gains in productivity true numbers or the fanfare of marketers and devotees (who probably believe in UFOs and the Loch Ness monster as well)?

Why are 20 percent abandoned after brief experimentation?

Is it true that most are greatly underutilized?

Can they be better used and, if so, then how?

What part should management play in harnessing the potential benefits and minimizing the risks?

This slim volume cannot address every aspect of this phenomenon, but it can offer some practical guidance and a useful sampling of solutions that have worked for many manufacturers. These guidelines spring from the applied knowledge of actual companies ranging in annual sales from barely a million dollars to billions—companies whose products range from peanut butter to autos to aircraft carriers and from children's cassettes to 10-ton turbines. These experiences were gathered through the generous sharing of those in every walk of corporate life—corporate presidents to clerks—from three continents.

This volume also includes several descriptions of what has failed. A production manager once said, "If you learn from your mistakes, then I must be a genius since I have made so many." This book can't promise genius, but it may save a few bumps along the road.

An effort is made to organize the information as a job aid to executives, managers, and both staff and line professionals.

WHAT DIRECTION WILL PCs TAKE FROM HERE?

Personal computers, individual and clustered workstations, microcomputers—the monikers are legion—have been on the market for nearly a decade now. In a report published in January of 1986, Fredrick G. Wiffington and Oscar H. Rothenbucher of Arthur D. Little predicted that the dumb terminals of the world (that is terminals that are not readily user programmable) are on the wane. They are going to be increasingly displaced by what they define as intelligent terminals—terminals that are operator oriented, user programmed, and clustered. In virtually every case, they are talking about microcomputers.

They also observe that dumb terminals, intelligent terminals, and word processors are coalescing into the *multifunctional workstation.* This concept is illustrated by the IBM 3270 Personal Computer AT™ and by the Unisys B25 and B28 lines.[3] Such devices can be linked to one another with local area networks (LANs) or connected to other systems using telecommunications facilities.

The *multifunctional workstation* requires software which includes office automation, information processing, and a host of productivity aids (see Chapters 3 and 4, for example). The expectation is that they will eventually handle images (like video) and voice as well. One of the suppliers I work with has a micro that takes the order over the phone, digitizes each second into 24,000 bits of electronic data, and stores it on a hard disk until it can be transacted. Just imagine—a phone recorder for only $5,000!

The multifunction workstations are expected to displace the desktop computers in the market as time moves on—perhaps by 1990. The dumb terminal has already reached what marketing types call "a mature position" (that means sell your stock) and will be rapidly declining in market share. Intelligent (programmable) terminals may well continue to grow in numbers for the next several years, becoming passe only in the mid-90s. Above the maelstrom of these aging technologies, the multifunction workstation will be growing vigorously through the end of the decade and by that time should be the dominant device clustered at the end of our networks.

---

[3] Unisys is the company formed by the union of Burroughs and Sperry.

WHAT'S IN STORE FOR THE COMPUTER USER OF THE FUTURE?

The computer user of the late 80s and 90s will expect to write letters, prepare financial spreadsheets, schedule his days and years, read his mail, and send memos—all from the comfort of his workstation. He will expect to link to other users in the same department or in other departments or—through public data networks—in other hemispheres. This is all accomplished through that selfsame intelligent workstation.

This approach is already realized in some firms, including a few manufacturers (more about them later). Telecommunication costs are not cheap, however. The talk continues about the coming reduction in communications costs, but it hasn't arrived yet. One is reminded of similar promises from the emerging nuclear industry. In the 1950s there was talk of electric power "too cheap to meter." I'm still waiting for Boondock Electric to take the meter off my wall because the electricity is "too cheap to meter."

Even given the dearness of long distance phone lines, the attractions and genuine justifications of integrating operations will increasingly impel the acquisition of desktop computers, word processors, office automation devices in general, and certainly terminals that can talk to each other.

There is little reason to doubt that many so-called knowledge workers—planners, analysts, managers, and others—will have such a device on their desks (or in their briefcases). Just as steam invaded every major machine shop and McCormick reapers invaded every sizable wheat field, can't we expect a comparable revolution today as these versatile devices permeate every department in the plant?

Isn't this technical advance just as likely to incite a revolution in the way information is gathered, analyzed, and reported—a revolution in *decision support systems*—a revolution in how we *envision* the problem and hence, in how we *solve* the problem?

HOW DOES THIS AFFECT THE MIS GANG?

This is unquestionably causing a stir in the relationship between the individual end users of the information and MIS (management information systems)—those responsible for the storage and maintenance of that information and the application systems in central computers.

Rather than feel threatened by the micro invasion, those with experience in systems methodology can be of great value in guiding and supporting this transformation of work methods. They certainly could save much of that fifth of all the personal computers abandoned by their users. They could organize the training and networking of users (not to mention their workstations) that would enable much more fruitful use of these devices.

A very large number of those unabandoned micros are used for nothing more than isolated spreadsheets and word processing.

NOTA BENE

If users were *trained* to do more and if they *understood* the value of doing more with their systems, most would *do* more.

They may begin to reap the enormous potential that these remarkable devices have to facilitate accurate decision making, clearer views of the activity of our manufacturing businesses, and a stronger grasp of the underlying issues and trade-offs.

WHERE DOES THIS BOOK FIT IN THIS GRAND SCHEME?

It considers a small part of that revolution. It introduces some of the key elements involved in the selection, acquisition, implementation, and use of such microcomputers in the specific field of production and inventory control.

Within this slim window itself are vast opportunities for the improvement of our daily tasks and better coordination with other users. A few examples will serve to introduce the breadth of the topic as well as to give some specific indication of the types of benefits derived from applying some of the simple principles that are offered in this book.

There are excellent texts available on many of the operational aspects and the technical applications of these systems, and I will refer to these from time to time. The follow-up information section in the back of this book includes lists of additional information on this subject. Many specific systems will be presented as they provide value to the manufacturing subjects of interest to us.

Throughout the book appropriate case studies are drawn from actual manufacturers who have applied these workstations for the solution of their problems. Let's start off by introducing one of those which will be expanded later.

Karl Schmidt was involved in inventory and production planning for the Chassis and Axle Division (six plants) of the Ford Motor Company. He received forecasts for several different car models and needed to allow for the common parts associated with the axle and chassis assemblies of these cars. This was necessary to identify current inventory holdings and then to calculate the production needed to meet the forecasts. This was factored across several plants for each model. Allowances were made for transfers between the plants, and the schedule was developed.

This plan was redone every month. Karl estimates that the two people involved in performing these calculations expended approximately 30 hours *each* to build one of these monthly plans, or 60 labor-hours per month.

This same application was set up by a systems analyst for Karl on a small microcomputer using an *electronic spreadsheet* (a term to be explained in Chapter 3). A number of things happened. First, because the microcomputer did the calculations, they were more accurate, fewer mistakes were made, and much less time was spent correcting mistakes. Second, only a couple of numbers needed to be changed each month—not the entire plan. Of course, these few changes rippled throughout the entire spreadsheet. But a change in such a case is no longer threatening—the rippling is all done automatically. Third, and most significant, the introduction of this flexibility in the calculation process allowed the consideration of "what if" alternatives that could not reasonably have been tested otherwise.

Many iterations of the plan could be viewed in a matter of minutes. This greatly improved Karl's ability to fine-tune the inventory requirements and production schedules. It allowed him to project further into the future because the calculations could easily be extended for several months. This longer planning horizon simplified the task of determining longer term material and capacity requirements of these plants. This, in turn, opened the way for developing better plans, which led to more economical acquisition of materials and allocation of manpower.

The entire process was reduced from 30 hours each for two people to 10 hours of work by one individual. This is a reduction from 60 labor-hours to 10 labor-hours per month with an increase in accuracy, flexibility, and an extension of the planning horizon as well.

It would be hard to convince Karl that this wasn't a well-justified system. By almost any calculation of return on investment the savings of 50 hours 12 times a year (a total of 600 labor-hours) easily justified the $2,000 for this particular workstation. As a matter of fact, it would have been completely justified in the first year of usage.

This story has been repeated thousands of times in the world of manufacturing planning and control. The explosion of these devices is surprisingly recent. Most have been sold in the last few years. And with one curious exception, very few data processing or manufacturing pundits predicted the surge. That exception, by the way, was a writer (now lost to the author's memory, alas) in *Boy's Life* (the official magazine of the Boy Scouts of America). This clear-eyed prophet predicted 25 years ago that by the 1980s computers would shrink to desktop size and be common features of every office worker. With vision like that, he should be my broker!

The reasons that underlie the surge are simple enough:

1. Many of the workers in the manufacturing arena have developed increasing professionalism and sophistication in the last two decades. The American Production and Inventory Control Society and its international affiliates may justly claim some credit for this. Other groups, such as the Society of Manufacturing Engineers, the Association for Statistical Quality Control, the Institute of Industrial Engineers, and the American Purchasing Managers Association, have also contributed to this development. This advancement has led to the collection, review, and analysis of increasing volumes of data. As well, the number of such "knowledge workers" has steadily increased relative to the purely clerical workers.

2. This demands higher productivity of the white-collar work force. The productivity yardstick for such workers is something like "wise decisions per hour." Reasoned decisions often rest upon the intersection of appropriate information and insightful judgment. The micro can be a natural catalyst for joining these two elements.

3. This type of decision-driving information and/or insight lends itself to sharing with others in networks, visual displays, and group presentations. Thus, the newfound knowledge is readily communicated to those who must implement the decisions. The micro is seen to be one response to the general demands of these times for better managers, communicators, and implementors at all levels.

4. This work force demands more efficiency in many of the support areas that constitute its environment—letter writing, filing, report preparation, scheduling, mail, documentation, and so on. More effective use of the time and energy of both line and "overhead" staffers contributes to

profits. One frustrated manager said that 90 percent of the controllable cost in a fighter jet built at his plant was paperwork. In many plants the need is urgent to tame these paper tigers.

5. Simultaneously with the above four developments, a backlog was building up at the door of the mainframe system. Often these systems were initially purchased to automate financial applications such as payroll, general ledger, and accounts receivable. Too often the operational demands of the plant were still "outsiders" to the financial "homesteaders" on the MIS farm. Application backlogs ran from several months to several years in many MIS departments. Beyond this was the "hidden backlog" where the frustrated users had surrendered without a fight. Enter the micro which promised the proverbial "chicken in every pot"—information processing on every desk. Every user is now the master of his own destiny.

6. Finally, the economics are getting too good to resist—at least on the surface. Microcomputing has declined in cost by about 20 percent per year all this decade. It shows no sign of quitting. The software is also a bargain. Database software for a typical mainframe may run over $100,000. Several strong databases for micros are less than $1,000. For under $2,000, there are micro databases that can be shared by multiple users.

Lest all this good news make the esteemed Reader giddy with enthusiasm, allow me to once again throw the cold water of reality on the subject. *Distributed* data processing has the potential to place keen tools in the hands of knowledge crafters. *Dispersed* data processing invites disaster. The successful companies in this arena have had to do battle with the forces of chaos and disintegration. Since these enemies seem to wear the same costume for nearly every contest, it behooves me to identify them to the wary Reader, to wit:

1. *Loss of data integrity.*   Picture this scenario: The numbers presented at the morning planning meeting are concise, clear, easily understood, and supportive of decision X. The graphs are stunning, and the logic is compelling. However, Alvira Murkberry—CPA and resident destroyer of the underprepared—points out from his seat next to the radiator that the numbers happen to be wrong! Another promising young career goes down in flames.

2. *Training incomplete, late, or disjointed from user needs.*   This system is really nifty, but only Hortense Sliderule (MIT summa cum loudness) is getting anything done with it. Joe Supe, who runs the ship-

ping dock, can't get to first BASIC with it. There's another abandoned PC for the record—a $2,000 doorstop. Don't laugh. I have seen this!

3. *Security.* This coin has two sides—lost and found. One type of security problem involves making sure that useful data (and the time and thought that produced it) are not *lost* through electrical, systematic, or personal *gotchas*. The other problem is to make sure that this useful data is not *found* by someone else's Hortense Sliderule.

4. *Disintegration.* Information that is only on one PC can be neat, even somewhat valuable. But to gain organization-driving, decision-making, and economy-producing *power*, sooner or later you have got to get the PCs together. Exceptions (to confirm the rule) are few. This may involve getting the network's arms around the mainframe as well. Unless some sound planning, disciplined execution, and purposeful direction have preceded this need, the potential for confusion and frustration is staggering. It could make the Tower of Babel look like a symphony.

WHAT IS THE ANSWER?

Actually, there are several answers. The nature of the answers will be strongly influenced by the organization's current position along the path toward systematization. Let me explain.

Most organizations do not enter the arena of PCs through a logical sequence of events such as by surveying all their needs, analyzing the offerings of the market, and then buying the answer for all their users. These systems, instead, emerge gradually, in unpredictable and unexpected ways. There is no single correct answer but rather a mix of answers which evolve with the sophistication and needs of the user community. Besides, even if this diversity were not the case, I don't know many managers smart enough to clearly define the key issues and needs of three years from now. And besides that, the more your people really get their hands on these tools, the more serendipitous applications they will uncover.

The winning strategy, then, is not to try to manage the details of each user's individual encounter with the PC but to manage the *environment* within which these highly individual encounters will grow. The farmer doesn't manage each kernel of corn. He plows, plants, fertilizes, sprays, and reaps—he is managing the environment (and the quality) of the kernels, not the kernels themselves.

The wise PC administrator is providing appropriate hardware, software, connectivity, data availability, discipline, support services, problem solvers, occasional handholding for the needy, training, and links to outside (fertilizing) agents such as user seminars. This micro husbandry will change in character as the organization evolves through the various *phases* of implementation.

These phases have been addressed in several ways and with great thoroughness elsewhere. See, for example, *The Micro Mainframe Link* by Perry, "The Information Archipelago—Maps and Bridges" by McKenny and McFarlan, and others. These are all in Part Five—"Follow-Up Information." We might distill this broad subject into the following *four phase descriptors*—which will be used throughout the book as reference points for the progression from first experimentation forward:

1. *Experimental.*   Let a few of the fanatics try them out. Bring up some word processing. Create a few spreadsheets. Try different brands in the more adventurous departments.

2. *Individual.*   The users (several now) are quite competent at the above functions. The systems are all standalone—that is, they cannot directly share data or functions. Often though, diskettes with such files are passed around. This requires a measure of consistency in both hardware and software.

3. *Departmental.*   The users within a department (or many departments) are now "within earshot." Disk files, printers, and plotters may be shared by local area networks (LANs). Joint applications may include office automation, databases, scheduling, and so forth.

4. *Organizational.*   The PCs become utilities. Most users of the organization are connected in the manner described in the departmental phase. Most importantly, the organizational data is now part of the network. All planning and control functions are integrated in this network of mainframe and micro-size computers. Applications span the spectrum from memos to artificial intelligence.

These are certainly not absolute lines of demarcation. Other authors use phases such as experimentation, standalone, network terminal, workstation,[4] project initiation, experimentation, control, technology transfer[5] and others.

Before explaining the phases, let me observe that appropriate management evolves as the phases emerge. Here is another:

---

[4] William E. Perry, *The Micro Mainframe Link: The Corporate Guide to Productive Use of the Microcomputer* (New York: John Wiley & Sons, 1985), p. 70.

[5] James L. McKenny and F. Warren McFarlan, "The Information Archipelago— Maps and Bridges", *Harvard Business Review*, September/October 1982, pp. 109–19.

NOTA BENE

Too much control early in the evolution of micro systems tends to stifle the evolution and developmental process.
Too little control later on forfeits the great benefits of integration, support structures, and transferability of lessons learned.

As McKenny and McFarlan sagely observe, "Organizations change much more slowly than technology." Management methods must change at a rate between these two.

The most successful management culture will, in many cases, be the least noticeable. The tools should be taken for granted by the users. Like utilities (heat, water, light), they become evident only when deprivations or barriers occur.

GOOD MANAGEMENT OF PCs IS LIKE GUIDING A MEANDERING BROOK

The author knows a robust stream that wends its way through a number of farms as it unthinkingly seeks out the Atlantic. Some of the farmers have made no effort to curb the creek—every spring it invades their yards, pastures, and a barn or two. Some farmers—taking a second type of approach—have dammed it up entirely to create large but sadly stagnant ponds. Others—the wisest—seek to confine it to well-carved banks— thus the stream is channeled but retains its flowing, living character.

The wild and unmanaged stream corresponds to a lack of management control and MIS involvement in the phases of micro evolution. Brands proliferate, applications vary from desk to desk, and no one can talk to or learn from anyone else. The waste and frustration overshadow the modest gains in speeding up clerical tasks.

The dammed-up stream corresponds to overcontrolling (possibly by MIS) in the first two stages of development. "We have standardized on the Grunch 9000 Microcomputer, the Lemon spreadsheet, and the Bizorsky database, and only certified gurus can write programs." The ideas stop flowing from the users, application needs and training requests pile up, discouragement sets in, and after a while, the scene looks a lot like the logjam at the application backlog window that the PCs were supposed to alleviate.

The ideal is suggested by the well-carved banks. It is more than just a level of management interest halfway between the extreme poles just described. It involves the continuing commitment from company leadership, a PC steering committee drawn from MIS and using departments, and an implementation team from MIS and other departments. It will necessitate the discipline of settling on a very few styles of micros and application packages—enough to accommodate the genuine differences in user needs but few enough to permit thorough training and support. This style of PC management channels without restricting. It offers guidance but avoids the stifling fiats that breed stagnation. It allows discovery and experimentation by the more adventurous users but manages the PC environment for the larger community of settled users.

The following chapters investigate the differing needs and applications that characterize this pathway of evolution. The Trail Map at the end of the Preface will be a useful guide through the rest of the book. The next chapter in this first part ("Executive Reporting") serves up a selection of applications for the under-info-nourished senior decision maker.

The rest of you will just have to make your own way (using the Trail Map, of course)!

CHAPTER TWO

Executive Reporting

The right information at the right time is nine tenths of any battle.

Napoleon[1]

This need of the right information at the right time characterizes more than French armies on the move. The success of a manufacturer—or any other organization—requires accurate information in front of the right decision makers at the right time. Executives of many companies are often dissatisfied with the quality of information received, its accuracy, and its relevance to decision-making.

NOTA BENE

Few things can advance the career of a middle manager as rapidly as presenting reliable, insightful, and relevant information to senior management.

This chapter sketches several useful principles of gathering information for the senior executive, methods to present it meaningfully, and the place of microcomputers in this activity.

For a nice counterexample to the above ideals, consider this fictional but all too prevalent scenario:

Our hypothetical top executive starts work at 7:30 at a breakfast meeting with two staff members to discuss production and inventory levels. Most of the remainder of the morning is given to a decision regarding

---

[1] Quoted in Ron L. Skelton, "The High-Tech Express," *Datamation,* December 1985, p. 110.

the acquisition of a company with a hot sales record but not enough capital. Lunch is occupied with three product managers competing for attention in order to introduce major new product lines. "Chief, the market is begging for this." "We are way out in front of our competitors on this one." "If we don't move this month, we can kiss the Christmas season good-bye."

After lunch, the plant supervisor wants to justify a reorganization that increases his span of control, the movement of key personnel to important new positions, and so forth. The executive turns him down for now.

And so it goes.

Finally, the unavoidable chore must be faced—plowing the paper field. Observing the great volume of paper that crosses the imposing walnut desk every day, this executive is hardly ready to face a mountain of irrelevant financial details that have no bearing on the key decisions facing her. Yet she is liable to discover that most of the "reports"—which are supposed to illustrate and summarize for her the state and story of the business—are little more than coagulations of stale numbers generated as a by-product of operational systems and forwarded to her to advance some group manager's cause or concern.

BETTER DECISIONS REQUIRE BETTER INFORMED DECIDERS

The dynamic changes in today's world of manufacturing require key decision makers to constantly reappraise their situations. Those who would achieve excellence in management do so by managing a little better each day. This often means being better informed each day. This is analogous to the demands on the army general continuously reassessing his moves over the terrain, his deployment of troops, the corresponding moves of the enemy, and his allocation of resources.

Colonel J. R. Boyd has made the observation that modern military strategies have greatly compressed the typical cycle of the command officer.[2] That cycle is described as *observation, orientation, decision, action*. The success of a military officer depends on continuously cycling through this process more rapidly than his enemy. This same type of cycle applies to the management of large organizations, especially those involved in manufacturing.

---

[2] Quoted by Dennis Long, "Command and Control Restoring the Focus," *Military Review,* November 1981.

One has to continually observe the activities of one's own organization and competitive organizations and then develop a mental, conceptual model of these. This conceptualization is the orientation phase. Next come the decisions about the appropriate deployment of resources, organization, products and so forth. Finally, actions are directed that implement those decisions. This continual cycle requires leadership which translates its vision into the day-to-day activities of the corporation.

Contrast the earlier hypothetical scenario with the following actual case:

This senior executive actually starts about an hour and a half later than our hypothetical friend above. (This is not common for senior executives by the way.) Although the computer salesman might declare otherwise, this more civilized arrival time probably has little to do with his possession of a more civilized reporting system.

After a brief meeting, he sits down at his desk to assess the company's position. He turns on his microcomputer. After entering the appropriate identification and password, he is presented with a menu of 148 reports. As would the reader of a newspaper, he moves quickly to a few favorite reports—sales versus forecast for a newer division, actual production versus plan, total number of employees per division and personnel movements, and key financial ratios and trends.

These reports are all presented in an electronic spreadsheet called Microsoft Multiplan® (more about that in Chapter 3). This enables him to "play" with the numbers. For example, he might ask the micro to sort the sales by all districts to highlight the best performers. He might call the top district sales manager and compliment him on the job he's doing, even mentioning the actual numbers (as of yesterday at the close of business).

Any of these reports can be arrayed on the micro in a number of predefined, colorful graphs. (Although he could create other graph formats in a couple of minutes, he prefers not to—that's why he hires sharp people!) He sends a note (on the micro) to one of his division heads to check two of the reports before their 11 o'clock meeting.

The information is actually maintained on a very large mainframe system. The top executives of this manufacturer (which sells more than a billion dollars per year) all use microcomputers. Each is connected (clustered) to the others to support mail and scheduling between the execs, and the cluster is connected to the mainframe. Every night summary information and special data are extracted from the mainframe files and downloaded into the micros (which happen to be a different brand than the mainframe).

He marks a few of these reports for later printing (by the DP staff). He wants a snapshot of the balance sheet and rough financial statement for his next meeting, so he prints that off immediately on the attached printer. On second thought, he also prints the graph portraying plant productivity for the last several weeks. (When you live in the corner office on the top floor, you get a graphic printer if you want one!)

It is important to understand that the value of this reporting system is only tangentially related to the presence of clever micros. The more important factors include some of the issues that were raised in the first chapter—(1) data integrity and reliability, (2) management savvy in using the data along with seasoned judgment, and (3) sound management of the data processing resource. This recognized, we will defer until later (chapters 5–8) the identification and illustration of the elements of success in these areas. For now, let's consider the elements of more civilized executive reporting.

THE SIGNIFICANCE OF VISUAL PRESENTATION OF INFORMATION

Recently, while 37,000 feet above the Atlantic, I had a chance to visit the pilots of a B747 jumbo jet in their cockpit. It was like being inside a computer or, more accurately, a video game! The area was filled with lights, switches, meters, and displays. Why? Is this what we pay a pilot to do? Actually, yes—we pay the professional pilot for decisions. Although life-and-death decisions are thankfully far apart, in the event of a crisis these decisions need to be made in very short time cycles. How can we possibly prepare pilots for this?

Consider the presentation of information to the pilot. It is *highly visual*. The instrument panel is filled with go and no-go lights, gauges, digital readouts, little pictures of the aircraft and engines, and so forth. When the chips are down, the pilot can assess a rapidly shifting situation with *glances* instead of *stares*. That little difference can make the whole difference.

NOTA BENE

If we expect our executives to more quickly orient themselves to new or dynamic business situations, why not offer them a more visual display of what's going on?

Isn't this the reason that study after study demonstrates that meetings with significant visual messages more often reach satisfactory conclusions, and in less time? It makes sense.

I have had some fun making this point to audiences. When I detect skepticism on the subject, I offer the following test to the group. I explain that I am going to give them a test with only two questions—actually the same question asked twice. I will give them two chances to examine reports on the planned load of a typical critical workcenter. The two reports are shown in Figure 2–1 and Figure 2–2. From the reports, they must determine if the workcenter is overloaded and, if so, in what periods. The catch is that I give them only three seconds to see the reports on the overhead projector.

It is hardly surprising that virtually no one can pick the information out of the first report, but everyone sees the bright red "overload" sections of the second. But, you might object, this is irrelevant—no one in real management situations has to comprehend a report in three seconds. No, but it is *shocking* how quickly the brain loses interest if the eye is not getting the message—I suspect that this happens in *seconds* more often than we admit. The average TV show presents new scenes or changes in scenes every few seconds. They have learned this lesson well.

HOW EXECUTIVES GET INFORMED

John F. Rockart analyzed the four general methods by which chief executives obtained their information.[3] Although the technology of information processing has changed a great deal since then, the executive's need for sound information and the basic principles of management have remained interestingly constant. He classified these as the (1) by-product technique, (2) the null approach, (3) the key indicator system, and (4) the total study process.

By-Product Technique

The by-product technique is the method most widely used by manufacturing companies today. As the title suggests, relatively little attention is actually paid to the information needs of senior executives as the operating systems are implemented. The systems tend to be implemented around

---

[3] John F. Rockart, "Chief Executives Define Their Own Data Needs," *Harvard Business Review*, March–April 1979, pp. 81–93.

FIGURE 2–1   Load Profile for Excello Machining Center

Machine No: XC747

Week No:	47	48	49	50	51	52	53	54	55	56
Begin date:	2/1	2/8	2/15	2/22	3/1	3/8	3/15	3/22	3/29	4/5
Scheduled Hr	160	160	160	160	160	200	200	200	200	200
Utilization	0.79	0.79	0.79	0.79	0.79	0.84	0.84	0.84	0.84	0.84
Efficiency	0.95	0.95	0.95	0.95	0.95	0.95	0.95	0.95	0.95	0.95
Net Capacity	120	120	120	120	120	160	160	160	160	160
Load (Std Hrs)	97	94	80	130	115	125	170	145	148	178
Load Percent	81	78	67	108	96	78	107	91	93	112

FIGURE 2–2 Excello Machining Center Load Report

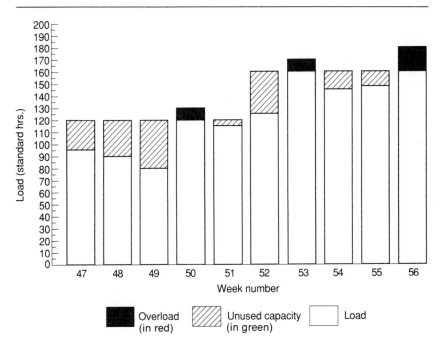

the accounting, scheduling, and controlling necessities of the manufacturing firm.

As a *by-product* of the computer systems thus operating, a certain amount of information, sometimes summarized, sometimes printed out by exception conditions, sometimes interesting, is generated. This is then compiled and distributed to the senior executive on a daily, weekly, or monthly cycle. One of the problems with such information is that its orientation toward accounting or, less often, scheduling requirements rarely reflects the real information needed by the executive to better orient himself to the dynamics of the business and to be prepared to make better decisions about this business. Also, this format makes it very difficult to ask the "what if" questions that the fertile executive thought is ever hatching.

One of the other difficulties in all such executive reporting systems is the natural and unnatural "filtering" that operates on the paper flow. Much of the information that ends up on the executive's desk represents what some subordinate felt was most important for the executive to see. A great deal of such filtering is genuinely needed to protect the exec from immersion in inanity. And, after all, the senior manager has to trust his staff to be alert to prevent the misuse of this selectivity.

Nonetheless, some possibly embarrassing data never makes it to the desk in the top corner of the glass castle. In other cases subordinate managers exercise their successes and deflate their failures. This all too often results in rather unreliable conduits to move the informational by-products to the walnut desk.

As Rockart observes, though, the whole logic of by-product reporting has the paper processing tail wagging the information dog. He says, "This approach is, however, understandable. Paperwork must be done and clerical savings can be made by focusing on automating paper processing systems. It is necessary to develop this class of data processing system to handle day-to-day paperwork. However, other approaches are also necessary to provide more useful management information." To this end, enter the null approach.

Null Approach

The null approach essentially develops around the great disappointment often associated with the by-product executive reporting technique. In this case, the observation is made that the typical executive really can't depend on these computer-generated reports for his real information needs.

In most cases, the chief executive spends very little time analyzing these reports. Even those reports that are read are often regarded superficially. The real flow of information to the chief executives tends to come by word of mouth from trusted advisors, pricey consultants, peers, and friends. Some additional (largely external) information is derived from data services and the media.

The world in which the chief executive makes decisions is a very fluid one. Every day brings news of new competitors, new moves by old competitors, market stirs, financial shifts, and political groundswells. Set against this turbulent backdrop, his daily information needs are far too changeable to be built into any operational system. This argument justifies the pursuit of soft and speculative data, hearsay, gossip, word-of-mouth tips, and so forth in order to really stay abreast of the constant changes.

There is some validity in this argument, but there are also some hard quantitative data that is fundamental to running the business and to recognizing its current state. Probably the most valid conclusion here is to recognize the need for some informal information to be supplied by word of mouth.

There is certainly an equivalent, if not greater need, for clear, hard, systematic data that can be analyzed and perhaps more efficiently gathered through the use of personal computer based reporting systems. The PC can summarize mainframe systems data in efficient ways while retaining the flexibility in presentation and the versatility of "what if" considerations. This is the executive version of having your cake and eating it too.

Key Indicator System

One of the areas where the personal computers can be most effective is in the key indicator system. This, in many ways, draws upon the utility of the by-product technique but recognizes the fluctuations that drive report readers to the null approach.

In the key indicator system, the executive makes the effort to identify those specific factors that are most likely to contribute to the success of his organization. A second element of this particular approach is exception reporting. This involves the selection of key discriminators to report by exception rather than reporting all of the elements involved in the business. After all, an executive's (or manager's) scarcest resource is time. The key indicator approach lets him focus on the particular projects, product lines, sales trends, and ratios that are most likely to indicate key changes or to necessitate decisions.

A stunning (and early— 1976) example of this approach is at Gould, Inc., developed under the direction of Gould's chairman and CEO, William T. Ylvisaker. The system includes a console allowing him to select from about 75 categories of reports. As reported by *Business Week,*

> Gould is combining the visual display board, which has now become a fixture in many boardrooms, with a computer information system. Information on everything from inventories to receivables will come directly from the computer in an assortment of charts and tables that will make comparisons easy and lend instant perspective.[4]

More recently Unisys has used a cluster of microcomputers in its plants to develop displays and graphs of production plans, inventory levels, and performance to plan. These displays and graphs can be fed from

---

[4] "Corporate 'War Rooms' Plug into the Computer," *Business Week,* August 23, 1976, p. 65.

the micros to large television monitors as a routine part of production planning and performance review meetings.

I expect that micros and associated display devices will become as common in board offices and conference rooms as ice water and bobbing heads. In fact, such highly visual presentation methods may reduce the latter.

Total Study Process

Rockart describes this method, developed by IBM and others, as a reaction to the widespread use of the by-product method. Total study is perfectly described by its name. A very large sample of line, staff, middle, and senior managers are interviewed to determine the needs for information. This may include as many as 100 individuals in some organizations. The effort is made to identify areas of overlap and duplication.

Typically, a summary report is developed from this analysis outlining the information needs for all key players, the degree to which these needs are being met, and the areas requiring new systems or the integration of existing systems to provide these needs. Also, typically, the solutions involve the purchase of more hardware (memory, mainframes, micros, and so forth) and software. Then it is possible to develop a plan for implementing these systems.

This comprehensive process of needs assessment, sweeping the company from the top down, can yield useful insights into missing, redundant, and ineffective systems. In too many cases, however, these studies tend to be dominated by special interests that lean more toward paper processing, cleaning up existing systems, and justifying hardware and software.

Rockart states that he has never seen a total study team that genuinely gave top priority to executive reporting. I confess that this desired perspective has been rare in my own experience as well, but I have seen a few teams that did so. One example was the team that designed the cluster of microcomputers described as the second example (the real case study) in this chapter.

The total study process can also be highly consumptive of time, people, and money. If the biases of the investigation team are known from the start, and if they are in concert with those paying the bill, this method can be of value. It is probably too expensive to be done more than once or twice per decade.

SUMMARY OF EXECUTIVE REPORTING METHODS

Given the diversity of information that senior executives need, it is likely they will continue to receive it from a wide variety of sources. However, several key points can be made. The companies that have carefully thought through the "critical success factors" (Rockart's phrase) stand the best chance of getting useful cogent information to the top office. There are typically only three to six *critical* success factors for a firm. Some examples of such factors in different industries are:

1. Electronic technology firms: Advanced engineering, short lead times, strong purchasing support (high purchased content makes this critical to gaining competitive costs), sufficient market share to achieve economical volumes.

2. Food processing firms: New product development, effective distribution, advertising success.

3. Automotive firms: Strong dealer organization, tight quality and cost controls, short lead times, strong purchasing performance integration of design and manufacturing engineering.

Once these critical success factors have been identified, the MIS staff can be given the guidance necessary to implement systems that support these information goals. Microcomputers have proven most effective as the final delivery tools of this information for the reasons outlined in the second case study—flexibility in (1) retrieving the information, (2) manipulating the data, and (3) presenting it in highly visual ways.

WHAT SHOULD THE EXECUTIVE DO TO SECURE THESE RESULTS?

As is so often the case, much comes down to good leadership skills and clear communications with the operational departments and the MIS folks. W. B. Foss offers several concrete steps (from which the following are drawn) that can help:[5]

1. Talk to the MIS manager. Establish the reporting and microcomputer needs of senior management. Show there is a commitment to such systems.

---

[5] W. B. Foss, "Top Managers: What Do You Expect from EDP?" *Business Quarterly, University of Western Ontario,* Summer 1979.

2. Form a steering committee to guide the entry into networks of micro and mainframe systems. This should consist of both user departments (master schedulers, planners, and department heads) as well as MIS gurus.

3. Give the systems people the business exposure they need to be responsive to the users' requirements. This can include cross-training users on micros and MIS representatives on production management. It can also include promotions and reassignments among these various disciplines. It also means that both information users and information providers should be on the implementation teams. The responsibility for the success of the implementation should rest with both "parties to the contract" as it were. Since turnabout is fair play, user analysts for the MIS team may be drawn from the user departments. This may be on a temporary, part-time, or full-time basis.

4. Set information goals and objectives for the MIS manager. Let him have a long-term plan to support the long-term plans of the organization. Make it clear that he is not trapped in a dead-end or frustrating career. Give him opportunities to advance professionally (within the firm and through professional societies).

5. Define clear lines of responsibility for departmental relations with MIS. This can be hammered out by the steering committee mentioned above, but the procedures and responsibilities should be written out and understood by all. This document should address such things as the development and implementation of new systems (micro, mini, and mainframe), maintenance of existing applications, training, security, and so forth.

By resisting the temptation to bypass the formal communication and information systems ("Say, Joe, could you put some statistics together on market share?")—by insisting, within reason, that MIS deliver the goods—the senior executive can set the leadership example that will strengthen the use of such systems for everyone in the organization. This will mean, sometimes, that the executive must learn a bit about the micro himself (at least enough to select the reports and to posit the "what if" to the spreadsheets). It will require attending a steering committee meeting a couple of times a year. The rewards in effective information systems far outstrip the inconveniences.

Many universities offer courses and seminars for the executive that can provide further information on these topics. The author is aware of such seminars at the London Business School, the University of Michigan, the University of Virginia, and others. Several of the firms that sell the systems offer such courses—AT&T, Unisys, and IBM, among them. Finally, the training sources and techniques developed in Chapter 8 may prove useful even for the executive.

CONCLUSION

Let me close this chapter by recasting the earlier analogy between flying an airplane and running a business. Instead of the huge 747, we will consider a single-engine four-seater.

I took my first flying lesson a number of years ago in just such an airplane. Unbeknownst to me, on that particular Saturday morning rare patches of fog had elected to haunt the tidewater estuaries. Having logged all of eight minutes of lifetime flying experience, I vanished into one of these fog banks. After a few foggy minutes without any visual references, I had the increasingly disconcerting feeling that the airplane was *not* flying level—in fact, I was convinced we were noticeably tipped toward the right.

On the instrument panel of this particular plane was a small picture of the plane that showed it to be flying perfectly level—banked neither to the right nor left nor gaining or losing altitude as we cruised blindly through the fog. I remained convinced that the airplane was unquestionably tilted to the right. As I attempted to steer the craft so that it felt level, I noticed that the little picture of the plane on the instrument panel indicated that we were actually tilting to the left. The instructor snickered but said nothing. Once we popped out of the fog, it became clear that the instruments were right and that I had been wrong.

After a few more incursions into the fog back along the river, I gradually developed a certain confidence in that little picture of the airplane on the instrument panel. I had to admit that it was a far more reliable indicator of the actual activity of the aircraft than the constantly misleading sensations emanating from the pilot's seat. With a great deal more training than I have yet had, pilots gain great confidence in the instrument panel and eventually become certified in flying solely by instruments. As weather conditions prove unreliable, this is the only safe approach to guiding an aircraft. The kinesthetic (I think this is Latin for "seat of the pants") approach is just not reliable.

The time has passed when we can run our companies by "the seat of the pants"—by occasional plant tours, by sporadic conversations with a coterie of trusted associates, or by brutalizing our subordinates. These practices have not vanished entirely yet, but successful corporations have discovered that sound reporting systems are vital. Not only must the information be gathered but it must be reliable—accurate, consistent, and useful. And it must be presented in a manner that supports the deeply human processes of observation, orientation, decision, and action.

The world of manufacturing has evolved too far and too fast to long support the outdated management styles named above. Today, the times demand that we must fly by the instruments—the numbers generated by our manufacturing planning and control systems and visualized, perhaps, on our micros. The flexible and highly visual systems described briefly in this chapter and further developed in subsequent chapters will be the "instrument panels" for tomorrow's winners in the manufacturing arena.

When is the best time to develop such systems? Sooner is necessarily better than later. Why wait until the storm hits to learn to use and trust the instrument panel—or to start assembling the instrument panel! Have you ever tried to work a screwdriver in a hurricane?

The time to begin assembling such systems is now. The remaining chapters can help. Happy flying!

PART TWO

General Productivity Tools

CHAPTER THREE

Electronic Spreadsheets—Simple but Powerful Tools

By far, the largest number of microcomputers in manufacturing applications are being used for electronic spreadsheets and word processing. A fraction are being used for other applications. In larger companies, 96 percent of microcomputers are at least used for spreadsheets. Figure 3–1 illustrates the distribution of microcomputer applications in large corporations.

A larger fraction could probably be used very profitably for other applications. But no matter how you slice it, spreadsheets—simple but powerful—are the center ring of the micro circus. That's where the attention is most often, and that's where many of the applications described in Part Four—"Departmental Applications" (Chapters 9 through 18) are found. Often, a more sophisticated application begins with prototypes developed in spreadsheets or databases.

PURPOSE OF THIS CHAPTER

This chapter serves to acquaint the newcomer with the concept and rudimental techniques of electronic spreadsheets. If the reader is already familiar with such spreadsheets (for example, 1-2-3® from Lotus®, or Microsoft Multiplan), he will probably want to skim the applications at the end of the chapter or skip it altogether. It's his book after all, and he is welcome to stay with us if he desires. But most of this chapter is devoted to the spreadsheet tyro (novice).

We name the better known spreadsheet packages, also called worksheets, for illustrative purposes only. We explain some of the salient features which distinguish packages. Evaluative information concerning these offerings can be gained from Part Five—"Follow-Up Information."

FIGURE 3–1   Microcomputer Applications in Large Corporations

Invoicing (13)	
Order entry (13)	
Customer history (18)	
Electronic mail (32)	
Inventory control (42)	
Personnel files (48)	
Accounting (52)	
Business graphics (68)	
Word processing (92)	
Spreadsheet (96)	

0 10 20 30 40 50 60 70 80 90 100

Percent of micro usage

SOURCE: Newton-Evans Research Company (*PC Products Magazine*, June 1986), p. 9.

We will build a few elementary spreadsheets step-by-step to develop some understanding of them. We will gradually increase the level of complexity until the clever Reader has an elementary grasp of the methodology. This should be enough to send him or her off to create a few to impress the boss tomorrow morning!

The specific and unique techniques of any particular software must be eschewed in this discussion because any worthwhile spreadsheet package includes a tutorial that is far better suited to teach its particular methods and tricks. Rather, by the end of this chapter, the savvy Reader should begin to recognize the flexibility of these tools and visualize extensions of this concept into his own spreadsheet package—and more importantly —his own workplace.

SPREADSHEETS ARE QUICKLY LEARNED AND WIDELY APPLICABLE

The techniques used here have virtually unlimited applicability in many arenas of manufacturing. In the first day of class after explaining the methods and uses of spreadsheets, I have had manufacturing professionals develop actual usable spreadsheets for the following:

Simple master production schedules.
Payroll with decreasing overtime premiums—so-called Chinese overtime.

Quality control charts with limit points, control points, averages, and standard deviations.

Production plans with associated resource requirements plans.

Forecasts with exponential smoothing and seasonal decomposition for groups of items.

Production downtime reports.

And many others.

In nearly all cases these were individuals who had no prior knowledge of programming, nor any particular experience with computers. In all fairness, they did possess three key ingredients that seem to characterize all the successful users of spreadsheets: (1) They knew their particular application thoroughly and understood how to perform it manually. (2) They were willing to try something new without prejudice and with a minimum of apprehension. (3) They had someone at hand (namely, the instructor) to answer the occasional questions that arise with such a new tool.

All three of these are important ingredients. However, this is not to say that these spreadsheets cannot be learned on one's own. Some individuals do. Engineers, accountants, and, rarely, a marketer will buy one of these packages and run off with it into all manner of useful areas. Generally, though, a few questions will emerge that will stump the neophyte but can be answered in seconds by the in-house "hot line," an instructor, the department PC coordinator, or the firm that sold the system. We will hear more about this in Part Three (Chapters 5–8) "Implementation."

In one particularly enterprising class, I had two wise guys who used an electronic spreadsheet to create a real time material requirements planning (MRP) routine with bills of material, lead-time offsets, gross-to-net calculations, and lot-sizing logic. It took them most of two nights and pretty well ruined them for any other learning for a while. (By the way, I don't recommend such an approach to microcomputer MRP. If you have more than a few dozen part numbers, systems much better than spreadsheets are available.) However, it does hint at the versatility of such software and the speed with which a newcomer can gain a useful skill on the system.

FIRST, A WORD ABOUT THE MOST POPULAR SPREADSHEET SOFTWARE

The last time we looked, there were 46 well-identified, critically reviewed, demonstrable, salesworthy spreadsheet packages available. This does not include the many integrated spreadsheets (discussed below) nor the many variations that may exist under one spreadsheet brand name.

You could do worse for your stock portfolio than to have invested a few grand in the Lotus Development Corporation (overlooking the Charles River in Cambridge, Massachusetts) five years ago. They broke all manner of corporate records for starting up a company. The largest selling single piece of application software in the history of silicon is 1-2-3 from Lotus. VisiCalc® actually was the first such package, and it did very, very well also. Many imitators and refinements appeared in the wake of VisiCalc, but Lotus ran off with the prize.

A word of caution is in order. This prodigious marketing success does not mean that Lotus is the only choice for the prudent shopper. More Chevrolets are sold than Volvos each year, but both cars have their champions. Second place in the spreadsheet race—again referring just to marketing prowess—probably goes to Microsoft Multiplan. (Microsoft is the same company that wrote your MS-DOS® operating system.) I have used both spreadsheets extensively and a few others to a lesser degree. I have a preference but will decline to state it, since I would be hard-pressed to really prove one better than the other before a jury of my peers.

Integrated Systems

There is an interesting class of spreadsheets that are integrated into a whole "desktop environment" of software. These integrated packages usually include four principal application elements, namely:

Spreadsheet—as we have described.

Word processor—more on this in the next chapter.

Database manager—for creating your own files and building your own inquiries and reports on them—also covered in the next chapter.

Network—to link a number of PC users in order to share the above three items and to share hardware such as hard disks, printers, and graph plotters. More on networks in Chapter 7.

Such integrated packages allow easy movement from one function to the next. For example, an inventory clerk might create a spreadsheet showing potential excess stock, write a memo calling the manager's attention to the problem, graph it, store the critical items in the database, and then send the entire package to the manager's PC with the network routines.

Also, such packages attempt to be consistent in the use of the screens and keyboards. For example, all screens within one integrated system may display status information at the bottom of the screen and choices at the top left, use function key 1 for help and function key 10 to leave the program.

Although this may seem like "the foolish consistency" that Emerson deplored as "the hobgoblin of little minds," it actually can be a great help to the newcomer. Even the experienced user will find the regularity conducive to more comfortable and speedier working habits. The same keys always respond in the same way. This uniformity of key usage is not the case for the wide variety of applications in today's PC market. In fact, even some of the integrated packages are less than completely consistent, but the effort is strong enough to be of some value.

Obviously, these considerations apply to the user who has a regular need to work among all the various functions and to transfer data among these different functions. The best known of these integrated packages is Symphony® from Lotus®. Other well-known ones are Framework (from Ashton-Tate) and SMART.

None of these has yet found the degree of market acceptance that the specialized packages have. It is often suggested that when all four of the above functional areas (spreadsheet, word processor, database, and network) are forced into the mold of one operational scheme, none has the "room to zoom"—the freedom to excel.

Another Approach—Systems Integrators

For this reason some vendors—such as Unisys (using Context Manager to oversee the team of packages)—have chosen to gather strong players in each position (Microsoft Multiplan spreadsheet, Professional Word Processing, MicroRIM database) into a more federal approach. Such packages are classed as *systems integrators*. Topview® (from IBM) also falls into this latter category. These could not properly be described as integrated systems, but, rather, they integrate a number of applications into a reasonable working environment.

The use of keys and screens is not as consistent, but each application is quite strong. Also data transfer can be a bit more awkward—some codes and formats need to be converted. These integrated systems will be further discussed in the next chapter.

The two philosophies will probably converge—the integrated systems will be competitive with the single function systems. Meanwhile, the single functions systems will grow more consistent in their transfer of data and use of the keyboard as they find useful confederations under systems integrators like Unisys's Context Manager and IBM's Topview.

NOTA BENE

The forces of natural selection among micro users will eventually favor more integrated approaches over fragmentary approaches.

The great need to streamline training and user support combined with the great usefulness of sharing information among these systems should impel this ultimate convergence.

ENOUGH WITH THE APPETIZERS. LET'S GET INTO THE MAIN COURSE

As promised, we will embark on a journey through a series of spreadsheets that build gradually. Let us postulate the following scenario. An inventory analyst has been asked by the controller to develop a prediction of what the overall level of finished goods inventory will be by the end of June. The date is now January 2.

In the bygone era of green eyeshades and arm garters, he (back then it almost certainly was *he*) would have created a bookkeeping spreadsheet on a green columnar pad that looked a lot like Figure 3–2. The eight totals—two at the right and six at the bottom—would have been calculated by whatever mechanical contrivance he had. True to form, new numbers would be given to him by the production people and the sales team at least three times during this process. This is why these spreadsheets are always done in sharp, but erasable, pencil. The sheet would actually have included the same calculations for all 10 product groups (only one product group is shown here) and down totals ("footers") for all six months. This means that the changes in either production plans or sales plans could require the recalculation of *86 totals*. And this is a highly simplified example!

Note that this situation is about as far from the insightful query of "what if?" as it can be. With the reappearing of the production planner with a note in his hand, our noble but anguished inventory analyst doesn't ask "what if?" but "what next?"

FIGURE 3-2 A Sample Spreadsheet for Inventory Planning

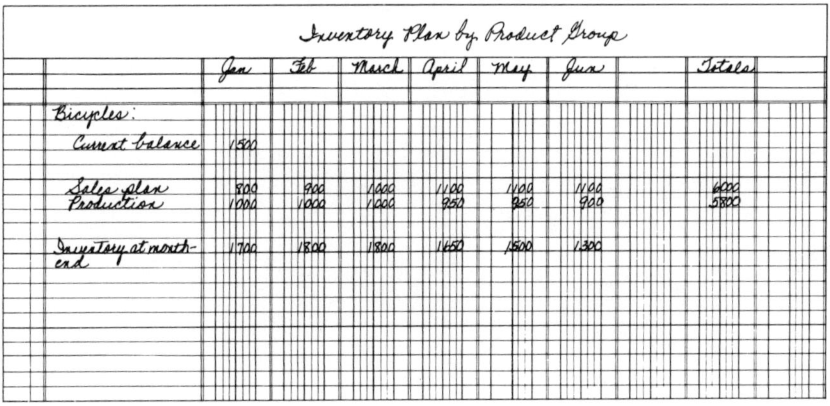

Inventory Plan by Product Group

	Jan	Feb	March	April	May	Jun	Totals
Bicycles:							
Current balance	1500						
Sales plan	800	900	1000	1100	1100	1100	6000
Production	1000	1000	1000	950	950	900	5800
Inventory at month-end	1700	1800	1800	1650	1500	1300	

What's an Analyst to Do?

Having just taken delivery of his new Grunch Brothers Model 9000 microcomputer, our protagonist has the microcoordinator for the department—Bill Cursor—load the requisite system software and the latest in spreadsheets. He finds out how to turn the system on, fire up the spreadsheet, and perform a few other fundamental commands to avoid doing violence to his files—the fruits of his hours. Now he is ready to build his first spreadsheet, and he decides to redo the inventory planning spreadsheets that have been done manually for so long.

Upon typing in the start-up commands, he is presented with an empty spreadsheet like the one shown in Figure 3–3. Note that the row numbers and column letters do not usually show up on printouts. They are printed here to make this explanation easier. Each cell is identified by its column letter and row number—the top left one is A1; the bottom right one is H18. He moves the cell pointer to the C2 cell and types "Inventory Plan by Product Group." The extra letters spill over into the next cells. This is fine for the top heading line but won't work for the side headings. Therefore, he enlarges the whole column of A cells from its current width to about 14 letters wide, which should give him enough room for the side headings.

Next, he types the side headings into cells A6, A8, and A10 through

FIGURE 3–3   A Sample Spreadsheet for Inventory Planning

	A	B	C	D	E	F	G	H
1								
2								
3								
4								
5								
6								
7								
8								
9								
10								
11								
12								
13								
14								
15								
16								
17								
18								

FIGURE 3–4   A Sample Spreadsheet for Inventory Planning

	A	B	C	D	E	F	G	H
1								
2			Inventory Plan by Product Group					
3								
4		Jan	Feb	Mar	Apr	May	Jun	Total
5								
6	Bicycles:							
7								
8	Current Bal							
9								
10	Sales Plan							
11	Production							
12	Inventory at							
13	month-end							
14								
15								
16								
17								
18								

FIGURE 3–5   A Sample Spreadsheet for Inventory Planning

	A	B	C	D	E	F	G	H
1								
2				Inventory Plan by Product Group				
3								
4		Jan	Feb	Mar	Apr	May	Jun	Total
5								
6	Bicycles:							
7								
8	Current Bal	1500						
9								
10	Sales Plan	800						
11	Production	1000						
12	Inventory at							
13	month-end							
14								
15								
16								
17								
18								

A13. Finally, he types the abbreviations for the months in cells B4 through G4 and the word *Total*, in cell H4. Now his spreadsheet looks like Figure 3–4. So far, he has only typed into the cells. Now he must type some numbers into other cells.

He moves the cell pointer to cell B8 and types the current inventory balance for bicycles, namely, 1,500. Flushed with this newfound success, he fills in the number of bikes that marketing plans to sell in January—800—into cell B10 and the production target for bikes in January—1,000—into cell B11. The company is overbuilding slightly in January because the market always picks up sharply in the spring. With pride and sincere admiration, he now examines his spreadsheet which currently looks like Figure 3–5.

Forming Formulas

So far, he has only entered words and numbers. The spreadsheet has acted as little more than an overpriced typewriter. True, if he had made any mistakes, he could make the corrections easily before printing. But he hasn't printed anything yet. The next step begins the process by which the spreadsheet is going to earn its keep.

FIGURE 3–6   A Sample Spreadsheet for Inventory Planning

	A	B	C	D	E	F	G	H
1								
2				Inventory Plan by Product Group				
3								
4		Jan	Feb	Mar	Apr	May	Jun	Total
5								
6	Bicycles:							
7								
8	Current Bal	1500						
9								
10	Sales Plan	800						
11	Production	1000						
12	Inventory at							
13	month-end	1700						
14								
15								
16								
17								
18								

He wants the spreadsheet itself to figure out the inventory balance at month-end. He tells it to do this by entering a *formula*. Now before you panic, let me point out that a formula in a spreadsheet can be quite simple. In this case, he types:

$$+ B8 - B10 + B11$$

The spreadsheet interprets this as "take the number in cell B8, subtract the number in cell B10, add the number in cell B11, and show the resulting number in the cell where the formula is—namely, B13." Presto calco—the spreadsheet looks like Figure 3–6. Now if marketing walks in the door with a new forecast of, say, 750 bikes, our inventory analyst merely types 750 over the old forecast of 800, and the month-end balance immediately changes from 1,700 to 1,650. This makes changes a lot less threatening—which is much of the reason for the breathtaking marketing success of these packages.

Please recall that the formulas used in this example are not meant to represent any particular spreadsheet package. They actually happen to work for 1-2-3 from Lotus and for a few other systems, but their purpose here is purely expository. The esteemed Reader is urged to verify any application of these techniques with his own system before trying to type these formulas into that system.

FIGURE 3–7   A Sample Spreadsheet for Inventory Planning

	A	B	C	D	E	F	G	H
1								
2				Inventory Plan by Product Group				
3								
4		Jan	Feb	Mar	Apr	May	Jun	Total
5								
6	Bicycles:							
7								
8	Current Bal	1500						
9								
10	Sales Plan	800	900	1000	1100	1100	1100	6000
11	Production	1000	1000	1000	950	950	900	5800
12	Inventory at							
13	month-end	1700	1800	1800	1650	1500	1300	
14								
15								
16								
17								
18								

The analyst now types (or enters in computer parlance) the sales and production numbers for February through June in columns C through G. He could type in formulas to calculate the inventory balances for each month. But he doesn't. Being smarter than the average inventory analyst, he just types a single formula in cell C13:

$$+ \; B13 \; - \; C10 \; + \; C11$$

This amounts to: January's ending inventory minus February's sales plus February's production. Immediately 1800 appears in cell C13. Now he simply copies the formula into cells D13 through G13. The spreadsheet will create a nearly identical copy of the formula for each of these four cells, but it will adjust the formulas to the cell position. Thus, the formula in cell D13 will look at C13 month-end inventory and add the plans for March.

This copying (and automatic adjusting) occurs with just one command and takes about 10 seconds with any properly bred spreadsheet. It also guarantees that if you have one correctly working formula, you will have several correctly working formulas. We have all heard about quality assurance through repetitive process control for the plant. This is quality assurance through repetitive process control for the keyboard crowd!

Naturally, the month-end balances appear for the remaining months. Our stalwart analyst quickly types formulas for the sales totals and production totals in cells H10 and H11. By the way, it is not really necessary to type the cell names like B10 through G10. Usually, you just move the cell pointer to the cell in question. It's like saying: "Add this one [move the pointer] all the way through this one [move the pointer], ENTER." The spreadsheet will fill in the proper cell names. The spreadsheet now looks like Figure 3–7.

The reader may conclude at this point that this is somewhat better than just a word processor. After all, it has performed a few calculations, and it does allow the fast replication of a working formula, which is quicker and more accurate than the pocket calculator. But there must be more.

Indeed, there is. Remember that our noble defender of the stock has completed his calculations for only one of 10 product groups. But he has convinced himself through a few minutes' observation and testing that these formulas are correct. This is a vital step.

NOTA BENE

The builder of spreadsheets should expend as much care in verifying that the formulas are complete and that the logic is sound as an application programmer would in testing a new program.

The spreadsheet does much to make verification easier. (1) If the pointer is used to delineate the items to be summed or compared, the verification is visual and immediate. The pointer is either sitting on the right number or it isn't. (2) It is very easy to create verifying entries (balancing totals, cross-footers, and so forth). If these fall out of balance, an error exists somewhere. (3) If a formula works correctly for one column, it can safely be copied to a hundred other columns with no risk of deterioration.

Understanding the care implied in the last paragraph and the benefits of replication, our analyst now copies the entire rectangular section outlined by cells A6 and H13 into a new section below his current work. His screen now looks like Figure 3–8. To add the second product line, he only needs to change the heading from bicycles to tricycles and to enter the figures for tricycles. The logic of totaling and calculating the month-end balances is preserved flawlessly. Just as quickly, he can create a section for each of the remaining eight product lines. (We will only show the

FIGURE 3–8 A Sample Spreadsheet for Inventory Planning

	A	B	C	D	E	F	G	H
1								
2				Inventory Plan by Product Group				
3								
4			Jan	Feb	Mar	Apr	May	Jun	Total
5								
6	Bicycles:							
7								
8	Current Bal	1500						
9								
10	Sales Plan	800	900	1000	1100	1100	1100	6000
11	Production	1000	1000	1000	950	950	900	5800
12	Inventory at							
13	month-end	1700	1800	1800	1650	1500	1300	
14								
15								
16								
17	Bicycles:							
18								
19	Current Bal	1500						
20								
21	Sales Plan	800	900	1000	1100	1100	1100	6000
22	Production	1000	1000	1000	950	950	900	5800
23	Inventory at							
24	month-end	1700	1800	1800	1650	1500	1300	
25								

first two here.) Finally, he creates the grand totals by moving the pointer to B28 and entering +B13 + B24. Then this is copied to the next five cells to the left with one command, and the spreadsheet is complete—resembling our Figure 3–9.

Actually, few spreadsheets are ever "complete" if by that we mean that no further refinements are available as the thought of the user expands. Refinements are always possible! Besides, the ease of adapting the spreadsheet to changing situations is one of its chief attractions.

For example, the current spreadsheet now offers all the information that the original pencil-and-paper version did, but would more information be helpful? How about some cost data? How about "dollarizing" these figures to express the value of inventory on hand according to current plans?

In Figure 3–10, we see that the average cost has been typed into cell B7 for bikes and into B18 for trikes. Then the cell pointer is moved to

---

FIGURE 3–9   A Sample Spreadsheet for Inventory Planning

	A	B	C	D	E	F	G	H
1								
2				Inventory Plan by Product Group				
3								
4		Jan	Feb	Mar	Apr	May	Jun	Total
5								
6	Bicycles:							
7								
8	Current Bal	1500						
9								
10	Sales Plan	800	900	1000	1100	1100	1100	6000
11	Production	1000	1000	1000	950	950	900	5800
12	Inventory at							
13	month-end	1700	1800	1800	1650	1500	1300	
14								
15								
16								
17	Tricycles:							
18								
19	Current Bal	1225						
20								
21	Sales Plan	2180	1800	1650	1400	1575	1550	10155
22	Production	2000	2000	2000	2000	2000	2000	12000
23	Inventory at							
24	month-end	1045	1245	1595	2195	2620	3070	
25								
26								
27								
28	Total Units:	2745	3045	3395	3845	4120	4370	
29								
30								

B15 to type the appropriate formula using the following symbols: +B13 (this is the inventory at month-end), * (this means multiply), and B7 (this is the cost). Thus, the formula is:

$$+B13*\$B\$7$$

The formula immediately calculates that the current cost of inventory is $45,526 and displays this value.

Warning—this paragraph gets a bit technical and can be skipped if confusion arises. The dollar signs in the cost cell mean that the cost will always be found in this cell. If the formula is copied to other cells (and we

FIGURE 3–10 A Sample Spreadsheet for Inventory Planning

	A	B	C	D	E	F	G	H
1								
2				Inventory Plan by Product Group				
3								
4		Jan	Feb	Mar	Apr	May	Jun	Total
5								
6	Bicycles:							
7	Avg. Cost	26.78						
8	Current Bal	1500						
9								
10	Sales Plan	800	900	1000	1100	1100	1100	6000
11	Production	1000	1000	1000	950	950	900	5800
12	Inventory at							
13	month-end	1700	1800	1800	1650	1500	1300	
14								
15	Cost of Inv.	$45526	$48204	$48204	$44187	$40170	$34814	
16								
17	Tricycles:							
18	Avg. Cost	14.05						
19	Current Bal	1225						
20								
21	Sales Plan	2180	1800	1650	1400	1575	1550	10155
22	Production	2000	2000	2000	2000	2000	2000	12000
23	Inventory at							
24	month-end	1045	1245	1595	2195	2620	3070	
25								
26	Cost of Inv.	$14682	$17492	$22410	$30840	$36811	$43134	
27								
28	Total Units:	2745	3045	3395	3845	4120	4370	
29								
30	Total Dollars:	$60208	$65696	$70614	$75027	$76981	$77948	

will do this next), then this cost cell stays the same even as the others are adjusted to correspond to the different positions.

This is called an absolute reference because it does not change when copied to other locations. This is best explained by examining what would happen if we did not do this. The formula is in cell B15. If this formula were copied to cell C15, the formula would change to +C13*C7, but there is nothing in cell C7, so the multiplication product would be zero. By making the reference absolute (with the dollar signs), the copied version becomes +C13*B7, which is just what we want. We now copy this formula to the next five cells to the right. By doing the same to the tricycle and adding a new total line in row 30, we end up with the spreadsheet in Figure 3–10.

What If?

What if sales increase? What if production plans are reduced? What if costs go up? Any one of these scenarios can be introduced into this spreadsheet in as little time as it takes to enter just the changes. All the formulas would recalculate new values, and the analyst can immediately assess the impact on inventory units on hand and dollar value of inventory. If the spreadsheet includes graphics (most do), a line graph of inventory in units, dollars, or both can be drawn to more visually depict trends, peaks, troughs, and turning points.

NOTA BENE

The ability to immediately determine and evaluate the impact of changes—both actual or suggested—is one of the keys to the remarkable usefulness (and success) of spreadsheets in manufacturing applications.

Another aspect of the use of spreadsheets lends enchantment to their use in the eyes of many of their users. The logic of the above example is very clearly spelled out in every cell. To determine the new month-end inventory balances, we take last month's balance, subtract planned sales, and add planned productions. To get the costs, the units are multiplied by the average cost. The numbers for the entire calculation are visible to the whole world. A well-constructed spreadsheet should take advantage of this "transparency" of purpose. This means the user should *avoid* burying hidden assumptions in secret cells far from the results or concealing strange and mystical variables in long complicated formulas.

One of the great frustrations of some computer-generated reports is that the results are *not obvious* from the information given. It would be hoped and it should be expected that any knowledgeable reader could reconstruct the results from the data available in the report. But in many cases this is impossible. This not only leads to *confusion* on the part of those reading the computer reports but to *distrust* of the reported information. Well thought-out and well presented spreadsheets usually make their logic and their assumptions clear to the reader of the output and certainly to the user of the spreadsheet.

This clarity of logic and assumption has two serendipitous benefits. First, the user tends to trust the information. It is not usually hard to verify the figures, and such understanding builds trust. Second, the assumptions and logic of the spreadsheet are available to the user who therefore can alter them if this improves the usefulness of the information being considered. This does require the ability to interpret the formulas (like the several that we have shown here). And a certain care is prudent to avoid destroying working formulas by copying numbers over them or by careless alteration of them. The adaptability is highly useful overall.

For example, in Figure 3–10, the inventory values are shown for the two product groups. It is obvious from the spreadsheet that these are figured at average cost and that these costs are not assumed to change over the six-month period being considered. Suppose these assumptions are not acceptable to a subsequent user of this spreadsheet. Suppose the engineering and purchasing people have developed a series of cost changes for the next six months. It is easy to add a cost line (see rows 7 and 18 in Figure 3–11) to the spreadsheet that shows the differing costs each month and to use this new data to calculate the inventory investments. Figure 3–11 shows an example of this. This rather significant change to the assumptions and conclusions of the spreadsheet was made in less than a minute. And again, the logic of the new calculation is patently manifest to the next user or viewer of the spreadsheet.

NOTA BENE

The logic and assumptions of a spreadsheet should be obvious and understandable to the user. This builds credibility in the results and facilitates adaptation of this logic and these assumptions to make the most intelligent use of the information.

FIGURE 3–11 A Sample Spreadsheet for Inventory Planning

	A	B	C	D	E	F	G	H
1								
2				Inventory Plan by Product Group				
3								
4		Jan	Feb	Mar	Apr	May	Jun	Total
5								
6	Bicycles:							
7	Avg. Cost	26.78	27.10	27.25	27.40	27.80	28.00	
8	Current Bal	1500						
9								
10	Sales Plan	800	900	1000	1100	1100	1100	6000
11	Production	1000	1000	1000	950	950	900	5800
12	Inventory at							
13	month-end	1700	1800	1800	1650	1500	1300	
14								
15	Cost of Inv.	$45526	$48780	$49050	$45210	$41700	$36400	
16								
17	Tricycles:							
18	Avg. Cost	14.05	14.20	14.30	14.40	14.55	14.55	
19	Current Bal	1225						
20								
21	Sales Plan	2180	1800	1650	1400	1575	1550	10155
22	Production	2000	2000	2000	2000	2000	2000	12000
23	Inventory at							
24	month-end	1045	1245	1595	2195	2620	3070	
25								
26	Cost of Inv.	$14682	$17679	$22809	$31608	$38121	$44669	
27								
28	Total Units:	2745	3045	3395	3845	4120	4370	
29								
30	Total Dollars:	$60208	$66459	$71859	$76818	$79821	$81069	

AN EXAMPLE IN A MAINFRAME COMPUTER PLANT

It is hardly surprising that Unisys Corporation uses Unisys microcomputers in its Los Angeles plant where large (million dollar) mainframe computers are assembled. Nonetheless, their uses of electronic spreadsheets are ingenious and useful enough to be included in our discussion of spreadsheets. This rather extended example illustrates the application of spreadsheet techniques to a variety of plant functions—manpower scheduling, labor efficiency, utilization, productivity reporting, quality control, and others. In fact, the users feel that the use of the spreadsheets (with graphics) completely justifies the systems.

More important to the valued Reader, this example illustrates the benefits of letting the levels of management closest to the actual operations gain the mastery of their fate. The system makes them responsible for analyzing their individual workcenters (called zones in this plant), for recognizing the need for corrective action, and for taking that action.

In the language of the original objectives of the Management Control System (as it is known in the plant), the system was to:

> Provide management and supervision with refined additional information necessary for more effective control of individual production departments (i.e., printed circuit board assembly, final assembly, system test, etc.) thereby controlling the total operation of our manufacturing facility. Desired improvement will be achieved by prompt corrective action on any operation irregularities highlighted by MCS (Management Control System). By recognizing these operating irregularities, prompt remedial action could be taken by management to correct these off-schedule conditions. In addition, management could place the proper degree of responsibility on supervision who, in turn, could more readily appreciate the problems and responsibilities of their departmental functions.[1]

The plant was off to a good start by following the first rule of successful use of spreadsheets—or any systems. They knew the application cold. They also recognized the need to involve the front-line supervisors in the design and operation of the system. The next task was defining the standards by which production could be evaluated. These were called reasonable expectancies (RE). It was a measure of the work that could reasonably be expected of a qualified worker (in the absence of interruptions

---

[1] Don McNally, "Building a Management Control System from Multiplan Graphics," *Business Micro World*, March 1984. This example and spreadsheets are reprinted with permission of *Business Micro World* © 1984 Publications and Communications, Inc.

FIGURE 3–12   Daily/Weekly Operations Report at Unisys

Unisys Corporation
System Manufacturing Group
Pasadena Plant

Daily/Weekly Operations Report

Management Control System

Week Ending   12/18/8X
Zone 29   Card Shop

	CREW			LABOR HOURS				PERFORMANCE						
	2	3	4	5	6	7	8	9	10	11	12			
Day	Auth	Plan	Actual	Planned M.S.	Direct	Absent	Memo O.T	Avail. Hours	M.S. Hours	Direct Hours	Prod. Hours	% EFF.	% Util.	% Prod.	Total Lost
										9-10		12/11	11/9	12/9	File
Mon	42	33	31	49.5	235.6	0.0	41.4	277.0	22.5	254.5	236.9	93%	92%	86%	
Tue	42	33	31	42.0	235.6	2.2	39.6	273.0	22.5	250.5	235.9	94%	92%	86%	
Wed	42	33	29	49.5	220.4	3.0	36.2	253.6	22.5	231.1	225.4	98%	91%	89%	
Thr	42	33	31	42.0	235.6	4.7	43.2	274.1	22.5	251.6	229.0	91%	92%	84%	
Fri	42	33	30	42.0	228.0	4.6	40.6	264.0	22.5	241.5	218.9	91%	91%	83%	
Sat	42	22	28	20.0	212.8	5.0	212.8	207.8	22.5	185.3	162.7	88%	89%	78%	
Sun															
TOTAL	252	187	180	245.0	1368.0	19.5	413.8	1549.5	135.0	1414.5	1308.8	93%	91%	84%	

such as meetings, downtime, parts shortages, and so forth). These reasonable expectancies were developed for each particular workcenter and operation.

Each individual worker monitors his own output against these REs. At the end of the day these are summarized by the supervisor for the whole department into the spreadsheet shown in Figure 3–12. Notice that the supervisor only needs to enter data in the cells within the dark lines. In fact, the other cells can be "locked" to prevent their accidental alteration. Reading across the columns of this figure, information is entered concerning:

The number of workers (authorized, planned, and actual in columns 1 through 3).

The hours worked (note that column 6 is simply the actual crew times 7.6 hours/day; column 7 is the hours absent; column 8 is the overtime hours worked).

Available hours (column 9)—this is calculated by planned direct hours (column 6) − hours absent (column 7) + overtime hours (column 8).

Non-scheduled hours (column 10)—hours lost to meetings, downtime, and other interruptions.

Production measured in hours (column 12)—this is based on the reasonable expectation (for example, if it "should" take 20 minutes to
assemble a memory card and the workcenter has assembled 210,
this amounts to 210 * 20 minutes or 70 hours).

By the time these columns have been filled, the clever spreadsheet
has already calculated some interesting information. For example, down
totals for the week are summed. Columns 11 (direct hours), 13 (efficiency), 14 (utilization), and 15 (productivity) are calculated for each
day. The formulas are abbreviated above each column. For example, the
column labeled "Efficiency" shows the formula "12/11" (which is a short-
hand notation for column 12 divided by column 11) which is production
divided by direct hours expressed as a percent.

Next, the supervisor fills in the Weekly Lost Time Summary Report
(Figure 3–13) which shows exactly where and how production time was
lost. Work centers are listed down the left side and explanations (machine
down, material short, and so forth) are listed across the top. Then the
Weekly Non-Scheduled Report (Figure 3–14) is completed listing the
time that is not scheduled for production due to meetings, training, pre-
ventive maintenance, and so forth. Note on this report that the actual non-
scheduled time is compared with the planned non-scheduled time. The
planned non-scheduled time was originally entered in the spreadsheet
shown in Figure 3–12. This column of data is simply copied from that
sheet into this one (Figure 3–14); hence, it does not need to be reentered.

Nearly all spreadsheet packages allow some sort of copying from one
sheet to the next. Such an "external copy" can be identified as a "linked"
sheet. This means that whenever sheet 3–12 is changed, the corresponding changes are linked to sheet 3–14. Therefore, the two spreadsheets
can never get "out of sync." Changes in the one will always be reflected
in the other. This may not appear to be much of an advantage to a user in
the first and second phases of microcomputer development (as discussed
in Chapter 1)—Phase 1—experimental and Phase 2—individual. However, if and when the user matures to Phase 3—departmental or Phase
4—organizational, such considerations are very important because many
users may be drawing from common data. It must be kept "in sync."

This Unisys plant could be considered in the third phase of microcomputer implementation. Since the micros were actually linked across
departmental lines and everyone from management to the supervisors

FIGURE 3–13 Weekly Lost Time Report at Unisys

Unisys Corporation
System Manufacturing Group
Pasadena Plant

Weekly Lost Time Summary Report

Management Control System

Week Ending 12/18/8X

	Mach. Down	Matl. Short	Work Inter.	Proc. Prob.	Re-work	Test Inter.	Sched. Change	Mfg. Defect	Replac Parts	On Job Train.	Screen ing	Excess Debug	No Asg Work	Wait. Supp.	Self- Repair	Other Zone	Total Zone
Card	3.5	3.0	2.9	2.0	7.0												18.4
40-2	2.0		1.0		0.5												3.5
43				1.2			0.7										1.9
Mod		0.2															0.2
FF	0.1			2.1	0.5												2.7
CT	1.0	1.0		0.8					0.1								2.9
SysT	2.3	1.2									2.1	0.5			1.7	2.0	9.8
Insp											0.6						0.6
Store		0.5															0.5
Recv				1.4												0.0	1.4
Re/In		1.5								0.1							1.6
Ship	0.8		1.5	1.4	1.2											0.3	5.2
Totals	8.9	7.7	4.4	6.4	10.6	1.4	1.2	0.7	0.0	2.0	0.1	0.5	0.0	0.0	1.7	2.3	40.7

Zone	Area
29	Card Shop
40	Cabling
42	Sub-assembly
43	Final Assembly
FF	Fault Finder/Open Short (44)
CT	Card Test (44)
SysT	System Test (54)
Mod	Mod Center (60)
Insp	In-Process Insp (10)
Store	Stkrm/Recv.
Recv	Receiving
Re/In	Receiving Inspection
Ship	Shipping (95)

Employee Cost at Hourly Rate:

Zone	Lost Time		Hrly. Rate		Total
29	18.4	x	5.67		104.3
40-2	3.5	x	5.67		19.0
43	1.9	x	5.67		10.8
Mod	0.2	x	5.67		1.1
FF	2.7	x	5.67		15.3
CT	2.9	x	5.67		16.4
SysT	9.8	x	5.67		55.6
Insp	0.6	x	5.67		3.4
Stores	0.5	x	5.67		2.8
Recv	1.4	x	5.67		7.9
Re/In	1.6	x	5.67		9.1
Ship	5.2	x	5.67		29.5
Opportunity		--------->			276.1

were united in a common network of micros, an argument could be made that they were in Phase 4. But since no mainframe was a part of the network, and the network resided largely within the operations division of one plant, Phase 3 is probably more descriptive.

Since so many users are observing a common pool of information (a

FIGURE 3–14   Weekly Report of Non-Scheduled Hours at Unisys

```
Unisys Corporation                                         Week Ending   12/18/8X
System Manufacturing Group          Weekly Non-Scheduled Report
Pasadena Plant
                                    Management Control System
                                    ---------- ------- ------
```

ZONE	Lead Time	Scheduled Meetings	Training	ECN	Material Rwk/1stAr	Maint./Handling Filing		Planned Non Sched	Actual Non Sched
	50.0			5.0	5.0	1.0	X	210.0	61.0
29___Card Shop - 1	10.0		1.0	5.0		5.0	X	12.0	21.0
29___Card Shop - 2	10.0				2.0		X	40.0	12.0
40-2__Cable & Sub Assy.	10.0				0.4	1.0	X	40.0	11.4
43___Final Assy.	10.0						X	6.0	10.0
60___Mod Center	10.0	2.0					X	5.0	12.0
44___Fault Finder	10.0			2.0	1.0		X	5.0	13.0
44___Card Test	15.0					1.4	X	57.0	16.4
54___System Test - 1	5.0						X	19.0	5.0
54___System Test - 2	10.0	2.5			0.5	0.5	X	10.0	13.5
18___Inspection	4.5				1.0		X	5.0	5.5
11___Stockroom	10.0		1.0			0.5	X	0.0	11.5
13___Receiving	25.0		1.6	2.0			X	0.0	20.6
15___Receiving/Inspection	1.2						X	0.0	1.2
95___Shipping							X		
___TOTALS	170.7	4.5	4.6	8.4	9.5	3.4		409.0	222.1

database of a sort), it is quite important that the various spreadsheets keep in mesh with each other. They must maintain a reliable and consistent relationship between such items as planned and actual non-scheduled hours. The linked copy feature of Microsoft Multiplan accomplishes this. Other mechanisms can offer this to greater and lesser degrees in most spreadsheet software.

Now back to our story. The plant is guided by the philosophy, "Quality begets productivity." Therefore, the quality team enjoys a natural link to this network of micros. The inspection department records the results of its several in-process inspection stations on the form shown in Figure 3–15.

FIGURE 3–15 Quality Data Record at Unisys

Unisys Corporation
System Manufacturing Group
Pasadena Plant

Visual Inspection Data Sheet

Week Ending 12/18/8X

Zone 29 - Card Assembly

	Component Inspection			Solder Inspection			Final Inspection			I.C. Inspection			Daily Totals		
	Qty. Insp.	Qty. Reject	Defect/Qty.	Qty. Insp.	Qty. Reject	Defect/Qty.	Qty. Insp.	Qty. Reject	Defect/Qty.	Qty. Insp.	Qty. Reject	Defect/Qty.	Total Insp.	Total Reject	% Reject
Mon	473	5	5	279	8	8	180	2	3	172	0	0	1104	15	1%
Tue	364	5	5	318	10	10	118	1	1	119	0	0	919	16	2%
Wed	353	8	8	259	1	1	272	1	1	115	1	1	999	11	1%
Thr	268	5	5	321	0	0	79	5	5	130	0	0	798	10	2%
Fri	231	0	0	257	0	0	260	0	0	64	1	1	812	1	0%
Sat	250	10	10	300	1	4	300	0	0	100	0	0	950	11	1%
Sun															
TOTALS	1939	33	33	1734	20	23	1209	9	10	700	10	10	5582	72	1%
% Reject		2%			1%			1%			1%				
Avg. Defects/Bd.		1.0			1.2			1.1			1.0				

Management Reports

The data from the four preceding spreadsheets is gathered together into the Weekly Summary Management Report (Figure 3–16). This report is yet another spreadsheet that gathers its figures by the "external copying" feature named earlier. For each of the 14 work centers, management sees a weekly summary of scheduled hours, production, absentee hours, overtime hours, efficiency, utilization, productivity, and reject rates. Also, these are summarized for the whole plant.

Virtually all spreadsheet packages include readily accessible graphics. Several graphs have been predefined for this management report, but it takes only a few minutes to create others. To access predefined graphs, the user names the graph and presses four keys—G(raph), L(ine), P(lot), and Go. Management has found several graphs particularly useful. Figure 3–17 shows a line graph prepared for each of the work centers comparing productivity, efficiency, and utilization on a week-by-week basis. In this

---

FIGURE 3–16 Weekly Summary Management Report at Unisys

Week Ending   12/18/8X

Unisys Corporation
System Manufacturing Group   Weekly Summary Management Report
Pasadena Plant

Management Control System

Zone Area	LABOR HOURS Planned M.S.	Planned Direct	Absent	Memo OT	PERFORMANCE Avail. Hours	M.S. Hours	Direct Hours	Produced Hours	QUALITY % Eff.	% Util.	% Prod.	% Reject
Card	245.0	1368.0	19.5	413.8	1549.5	135.0	1414.5	1278.9	90%	91%	93%	1%
Card-2	30.0	722.0	15.0	0.0	674.0	15.0	659.0	617.0	94%	98%	92%	
40-2	48.0	280.0	0.0	48.0	306.4	13.0	293.4	285.6	97%	96%	93%	2%
43	48.0	360.0	0.0	0.0	342.0	25.0	317.0	307.0	97%	93%	90%	1%
Mod	18.0	512.0	19.0	9.0	512.7	10.5	502.2	489.0	97%	98%	95%	
FF	25.0	152.0	0.0	0.0	114.0	4.3	109.7	102.6	94%	96%	90%	
CT	75.0	494.0	30.0	0.0	352.0	20.0	332.0	324.4	98%	94%	92%	
SysT	45.6	722.0	45.0	25.0	686.6	15.0	671.6	641.0	95%	98%	93%	
SysT2	15.2	722.0	15.0	0.0	674.0	15.0	659.0	617.0	94%	98%	92%	
Insp	10.0	370.0	7.6	45.5	425.5	20.0	405.5	340.0	84%	95%	80%	
Stores	5.0	225.0	0.0	0.0	230.0	10.0	220.0	211.0	96%	96%	92%	
Recv	5.0	65.9	0.0	13.9	89.9	9.0	80.9	77.9	96%	90%	87%	
Re/Ins	50.0	153.4	23.4	0.0	242.6	10.0	232.6	226.0	97%	96%	93%	
Ship	1.2	360.0	0.0	0.0	342	25	317	307	97%	93%	90%	
TOTALS	621.0	6506.3	174.5	555.2	6541.2	326.8	6214.4	5824.4	94%	95%	89%	

(demonstration) example, we can readily observe the trends for Zone 29—the card assembly workcenter. Drawing upon the previously accumulated inspection data (Figure 3–15), the quality rates can be compared visually to the productivity rates. The philosophical link between the two is thus tested in the crucible of actual results. This graph is shown in Figure 3–18.

To ensure that a clear supervisory perspective is maintained and that follow-up is not overlooked, a running five-week analysis of lost time is prepared using both comparative bars (Figure 3–19A)—which show the lost time trend for the workcenter—and stacked bars (Figure 3–19B)

FIGURE 3–17   Graphic Management Reports at Unisys

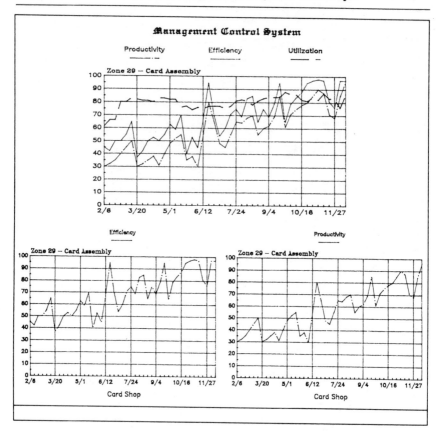

—which portray the accumulated lost time of the last five weeks for the workcenter. A pie chart is created to illustrate the distribution of causes of lost time (Figure 3–19C).

A guiding rule of graphics is illustrated here. The charts are made easier to read by the consistent use of color (although this is not evident in the black and white reproduction). For example, lost time due to material shortages is always shown as green; lost time due to rework is always shown in light blue, and so forth.

NOTA BENE

The essence of useful graphics is *simplicity*—supported by consistent use of color, clear comparisons, and self-explanatory labels.

FIGURE 3–18   Card Shop Percent Rejected

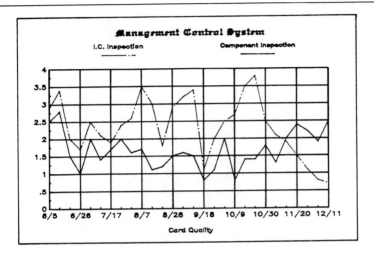

Finally, the line graph in Figure 3–20 takes the lost time information for the last 30 weeks and calculates the dollar cost of this lost time. A user reports,

> By following up from week to week, we can readily tell which areas are being addressed, where action is needed, and in turn, a remedy for these bottlenecks. [The system] is not a panacea for all production ills; however, it does give us tremendous insight as how to more effectively run our production floor. By posting such results throughout the production floor for everyone to see, we receive some very important by-products of graphics. As a result, we have identified our action areas in an easy-to-read format and can readily determine from week to week if benefits were received from corrective action or what type of action is warranted. Perhaps more importantly, MCS, with the aid of graphics, has created an awareness—an awareness for both management and production to see where we are going, where remedial action is needed, and ultimately, a quality product without compromise.

CONCLUSIONS FROM THIS CASE STUDY

These are obviously proud words from a satisfied user, but what made this micro system successful? Several lessons can be learned from this case. (1) The system was clearly developed with appropriate input from the users on the production floor and the users in the management offices.

FIGURE 3–19A   Card Shop Lost Time (Hours)

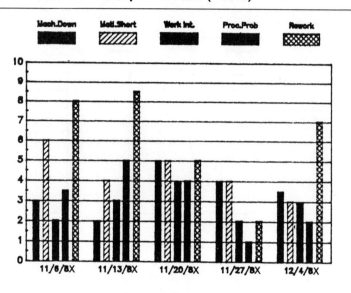

FIGURE 3–19B   Card Shop Lost Time (Hours)

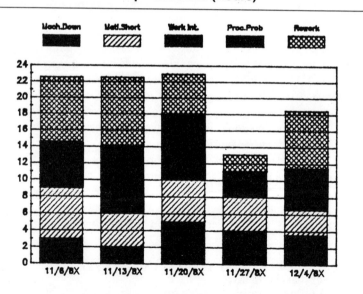

(2) The system is transparently simple. It has been described in the last few pages practically in its entirety. (3) The fact that it was built out of a series of linked spreadsheets makes it extremely easy to maintain and to adapt.

FIGURE 3–19C Card Assembly Lost Time

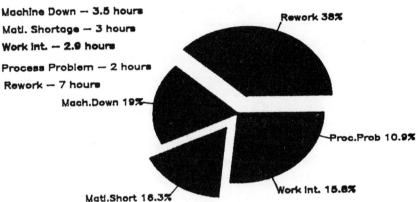

𝕸𝖆𝖓𝖆𝖌𝖊𝖒𝖊𝖓𝖙 𝕮𝖔𝖓𝖙𝖗𝖔𝖑 𝕾𝖞𝖘𝖙𝖊𝖒

Week Ending 12/4/83

Machine Down — 3.5 hours

Matl. Shortage — 3 hours

Work Int. — 2.9 hours

Process Problem — 2 hours

Rework — 7 hours

Mach.Down 19%

Rework 38%

Proc.Prob 10.9%

Work Int. 15.8%

Matl.Short 16.3%

FIGURE 3–20 Dollars Lost Due to Lost Time

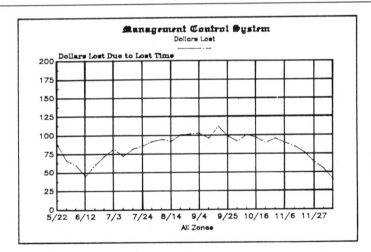

The fact that the many B20s were all networked together must not be undervalued. This linkage not only saved the tedious and highly error-prone work of reentering the data from the various departments but allowed the users to share information vital to other departments. Thus, the quality team is aware of manpower loading, production results, and the costs of rework. This helps them make better informed decisions about the resolution of quality issues. By the same token, the production planners are similarly aware of quality issues. Moreover, the entire plant is increasingly aware of production bottlenecks and can work together to streamline the flow of products through the plant.

NOTA BENE

No microcomputer is an island unto itself. Great benefits can often be gained by linking it to other micros and to the operating planning and control systems.

Although individual PCs can certainly provide a variety of useful results, many companies discover that the largest benefits derive from the linking together of the PCs to each other and, when applicable, to the mainframe systems. After all, that's where the vast preponderance of the data is. The subject of how to further this linking is the subject of another chapter.

CHAPTER FOUR

Other General Productivity Tools

In the last chapter we explored the most widely used productivity application among all PC users—electronic spreadsheets. Once the benefits of these fine work savers are under the clever Reader's belt, and even after the initial microenchantment has mellowed, a wide variety of other applications await the community of PC users. Many useful functions—involving spreadsheets, databases, and specific application programs—are explored in Chapters 9 through 18.

Before doing so, it is useful to investigate several other general productivity tools. This class of software includes such handy items as office automation (word processing, scheduling, electronic mail, and such) and other productivity aids such as databases, electronic publishing, and presentation graphics.

GENERAL PRODUCTIVITY ISSUES AS RELATED TO MANUFACTURING

The literature of micro productivity includes books by the hundred, monthly magazines by the score, buyer's guides by the dozens, information services, on-line service bureaus, and consultants by the hour. It is certainly not our purpose to reproduce this great resource herein but merely to identify several of these areas for the edification and broadening of the esteemed Reader. Furthermore, a few specific examples are offered (as always) to illustrate how particular companies have applied these methods to problems of manufacturing.

OFFICE AUTOMATION

How much paper does your firm generate in the course of a year? How much paper flows in from suppliers, customers, the government (at all levels), and professional organizations? How much paper flows out in the form of letters, promotions, invoices, and so on? Figure 4–1 summarizes a study of one industrial firm conducted a few years ago.

Of the staggering mountain of paper generated by this fairly typical firm, 75 to 80 percent was *internal to the firm*—just the memos, engineering documents, catalogs, purchase reqs, and notes of daily business. In fact, 60 percent was internal to the firm's headquarters office. Of the totals for the typical sales office, 60 percent is internal (15 percent to the sales office itself, 45 percent to headquarters). Interestingly, 10 percent of the mail that comes to the sales office goes right to archives with no other action being taken. In one year the sales office had 20,500 pages (5.5 million words) languishing in archives. Imagine what forests were sacrificed to meet this demand for fiber! Closer to home, what effect does this logjam (literally as well as figuratively!) have on the quality of communication and decision making.

If your company has never done a study of this nature, it might be well worth the time. The results may be startling. It forces the question: "Can we do better than this in our internal communications?" What systems are failing us that we need a shady grove's worth of tree pulp to make the point? Often the answer is as simple as poor communications within the firm, lack of standardized procedures, overuse of computers or microcomputers, (abuse is probably more accurate than overuse), and excessive detail relative to the decisions being made and the people being informed.

How do microcomputers fit in?

Actually, they can appear on both sides of this problem. Without a modicum of discipline, overzealous "mikers" (users of microcomputers) can generate more paper in a good afternoon than was earlier possible in a week. However, with a bit of wisdom (see Chapter 8) and a mile or two of wire (more on this in Chapter 7), they can do much to reduce the paper mountain. This wisdom includes: sound training, operational discipline, wise attention to the development and use of forms and reports, entry of information at the point of the information's origin, reporting of information to the point of need (into a spreadsheet, for example), and the networking of micros to the central system. The central system may simply be the center of office automation including file storage and retrieval, word processing, maintaining schedules for staff and managerial personnel, and many other services such as those addressed in the balance of this chapter. Even better is to have the office automation system also

---

FIGURE 4–1 Yearly Document Handling in a Large Firm

Headquarters
| Number of documents handled | 66,000 |
| Number of pages | 792,000 |

Typical sales office
| Number of documents handled | 1,200 |
| Number of pages | 15,000 |

Incoming mail at a typical sales office
| Number of telexes | 2,960 |
| All types of incoming documents | 6,400 |

SOURCE: Dimitris N. Chorafas, *Office Automation, The Productivity Challenge* (Englewood Cliffs, N.J.: Prentice-Hall, 1982), p. 96.

linked to the central operating system where the production, inventory, marketing, and financial systems dwell. Every one of these practices can help manage the paper tiger.

Economics of Office Automation

According to Chorafas it is difficult to assess office automation in general or word processing in particular without some sense of the economics of office activities.[1] He offers some enlightening figures on the capitalization of the office in 1982. In the United States only 9 percent of the population manufactures products for the whole 220 million. Another 3.5 percent produces the agricultural products for the entire population. The rest of the work force (roughly 60 million) are engaged in the so-called service sector. The remarkable productivity of the first two sectors has been made possible by technology and investment. The average manufacturing worker has $25,000 of capital investments supporting him. The average agricultural worker has about $35,000 behind him. The average office worker has $2,000 to $4,000 behind him. This may include a typewriter, calculator, possibly some DP services and a terminal, a desk, a chair, and a trash can. It is not surprising that this sector is less productive.

---

[1] Dimitris N. Chorafas, *Office Automation, The Productivity Challenge* (Englewood Cliffs, N.J.: Prentice-Hall, 1982), p. 7.

NOTA BENE

Office work costs all sectors of U.S. business over $200 billion. Productivity payoffs abound in this sector just as much as they do in the plant. Conversely, poor office systems can do just as much harm to our morale and our wallets as poor plant systems.

Although whole books exist on ways to lower these costs by automating this sector, let me share a few useful comments on the subject insofar as it relates to the microcomputer in manufacturing. Although the typical user of such systems may have acquired them for production and inventory control, it is also likely that some of the following functions can profitably be used as well. Therefore, it is useful to gain a working acquaintance with such subjects.

Word Processing

Foremost among these functions is word processing. This refers to the daily creation of memos, notes, letters, statements of policy, quotations, and so forth that constitute much of office life. The author's first use of microcomputers was for word processing—eventually learning and using eight different word processors. As with spreadsheets, there are preferences, but the reasons are not of great import. Again, too, the best sellers are not, in my estimation, the most desirable, but such is the convoluted web of marketing.

A wide variety of institutions and magazines offers comparisons of the word processing software—*Datapro, Data Decisions, Computerworld, PC Week*, for example. For high volume stenographic work some of the more sophisticated features are of genuine importance—features such as synchronized and snaking column handling, table of contents generation, address and data merging, paragraph numbering, and such. For the occasional professional user, I find the needs are simpler—easy movement of text among one or several documents, easy-to-use formatting for printing, spelling verification and hyphenation, recalling of often-used phrases, and convenient recovery methods in the event of a system failure or a sudden attack of overwhelming dumbness.

As an aside, the last feature is still somewhat of a rarity among today's offerings. The word processor used for this text (Professional Word Processor™) actually protects me from such dumbness as leaving a letter half typed on the screen to run to a meeting while a well-meaning friend turns the system off. In fact, I have had the power fail after an afternoon of work. As soon as power is restored, the system recovers all the work. You may only need this once or several times a year, but it is nice when you do need it. Ask anyone who had the office bigfoot kick the plug out after about three hours of work on a report!

The other features named above are pretty well standard. In the field of word processing software, one soon discovers a phenomenon of the crowded competitive market called *features poker*. The logic is akin to that of a poker game. The first player enters the arena with a particular array of features. The next player in the same market cannot very well offer less, so he attempts to offer the same array plus a feature or two such as search and replace and spell checking. The next player meets the search, replace, and spell checking, and raises by address merge. The fourth player meets search, replace, spell checking, and address merge, and raises by snaking columns. Now the betting comes back around to the first player who has to meet the current offering or fold his cards.

And so goes the logic of features poker. Theoretically, no active vendor can afford to fall greatly behind the offerings of any other. However, there are, in fact, quite significant differences among the several frontrunners. Some are significantly easier to learn. Some are significantly more versatile. Some have much more to offer the stenographic user who makes the effort to master the software. A few offer excellent recovery in the event of electrical or operator lapses. In light of the logic of features poker, how can this be?

NOTA BENE

The logic of features poker does not actually require all vendors within a particular market to offer the same level of features and utility. It only requires them to *appear* to do so and to appear to do so to enough prospective buyers to retain a reasonable market share.

Therefore, it behooves the prospective purchasers of word processing (or any other package) software to investigate thoroughly, to accurately assess their real needs, to talk to real-life comparable users, to verify the service available, and to assure themselves that the system does the most needed functions in efficient ways.

Ask yourself, "What do we do the most of?" Make sure the system does this easily and well! This is, of course, true for nearly any software for the micro (or any system). Chapter 5 discusses the elements of acquisition and implementation in further detail.

Other Elements of Office Automation

As with word processing and with all microcomputer applications, it is important to keep a perspective on the big picture when considering the use of PCs. The overarching goal is not to get the letter to Mr. Bigbags by Friday but to become more productive, more effective, and more excellent in the large and small elements of our business endeavors—the office filing routine to the renovation of the factory. This is rarely achieved without a systematic approach to these endeavors. This often includes changing the nature of our MIS systems, integrating the micros into the operating systems, and enlarging the support services available to the end users.

Taken in this context, a fertile field of office automation improvements is available to the PC aspirant. This includes several that will be amplified later such as databases, computer-aided publishing, integrated systems, and remote workstation services. It also includes such mundane activities as maintaining calendars and scheduling meetings for a department. This is actually quite handy for keeping track of everyone, for keeping people informed, and for finding free time for committee meetings. It, too, is much more useful in the network setting.

Electronic mail is another such application. Letters and memos are "typed" on the micro cum word processor and transmitted along with graphs, spreadsheets, and reports, to the intended recipient. Whether that person is present or absent, the message and information is received and stored. Upon the individual's return, the message is read, filed, discarded, or answered.

One study estimates that only about one in three business calls actually reaches the intended individual. In the majority of cases the line is busy, the person is busy, or the person is absent. In many cases the information offered or required could be shared with a few sentences. This also avoids having to remember to retry in the event of failure to make contact the first time.

My current company conducts business on several continents. This is true of many firms these days. As such companies have discovered, besides the usual problems of making contact (busy, absent, and so forth), there is the additional challenge of widely differing time zones. ("Does anyone know what time it is in Tokyo?" "Yeah, Joe says its about six, but he's not sure if that's A.M., P.M., yesterday, or tomorrow.")

We maintain a number of "mailboxes" in Public Data Networks (PDNs). These can be addressed from nearly any phone in the world (via a computer). Our contact in Tokyo merely dials up our mailbox name, plugs in his laptop micro, and sends the memo over the wires. In the morning, we check the mailbox, discover his message among others, and retrieve it into a micro for reading, filing, or retransmission to others. Electronic mailboxes can include a wide variety of services such as special mailing lists ("my department," "managers," "sell" for the marketing department; "the loan arranger" for the finance department). If a firm has evolved in their microcomputer implementation as far as Phase 3 or Phase 4 (departmental and organizational linkages), then they are ready to consider the benefits of electronic mail.

OTHER PRODUCTIVITY TOOLS

A wide variety of other office automation tools are available, and many more loom on the horizon. Systems are available for filing and retrieving by author, date, word, phrase, or even by near match. An enormous variety of data services are available for everything from accounting information to news services to encyclopedias to matchmaking! Soon data services will be combined into networks that also handle phone (voice) processing and video (and other image) processing. The office of 1995 will scarcely be recognizable to today's office worker. And we may find that the ratio of capitalization to expense will fall more nearly in line with the figures for the plant and the farm.

In the next few sections we will explore a few general productivity tools that could as well be called office automation. After all, most plants have appendages that could be called offices, and many manufacturing professionals spend more hours than they care to admit behind what could be called a desk. It is in this spirit of inclusivity and with the hope that some will prove useful that these work savers and thought multipliers are offered for the treasured Reader's consideration.

Integrated Systems

Integrate—verb. 1. To make into a whole by bringing all parts together; unify . . . (Latin *Integrare*, to make complete, from *integer*, whole).[2]

---

[2] *American Heritage Dictionary* (Boston, Mass.: Houghton Mifflin, 1981).

The concept of *integrated systems* was actually introduced in the last chapter since some were outgrowths of spreadsheet programs. As the above definition suggests, the underlying purpose is to present a complete system of functionality to the PC user. The fact that most were such spin-offs of very popular silicon best-sellers has made this unification a bit awkward in practice.

Symphony from Lotus was a natural extension of 1-2-3 from Lotus. Framework (from Ashton-Tate), on the other hand, grew out of their dBASE® database software. In fact, Ashton-Tate recently acquired one of the most popular word processing programs—Multimate (itself an off-shoot of Wang word processing). The hope is that all of this will fold into one tidy unified presentation to the user. But this does illustrate the challenges of trying to integrate the parts while maintaining the integrity of each.

One of the few integrated systems that actually emerged as an integrated system is Smart (from Innovative Software). It includes the usual elements of such ilk (spreadsheet with graphics, word processor, database, and networking programs). It also includes a calendar service that extends forward and backward for many years. As the microcomputers begin to talk together and as users discover the expansive utility outside their initial application, the single-purpose stars like dBASE and 1-2-3 must grow in the direction of integration to continue to prosper.

Telecommuting

Cheryl Sullivan writes about the "30-second commute":

> Most days, it takes David Fleming 25 minutes to commute from home to office. But then there are the blissful mornings when it takes only 30 seconds. He walks from the bedroom to the living room-cum-office, plunks himself down in front of his Macintosh personal computer, and joins as many as 100,000 other Americans who "telecommute" to work.[3]

In fact, she estimates that as many as 7 million of the U.S. work force of 100 million use computers (nearly all are microcomputers) for work at home.

The author has actually indulged in all three principal methods of such telecommuting and herein shares them with the Reader who finds himself comfortably ensconced in his favorite chair next to the fire, hot

---

[3] Cheryl Sullivan, "Computer 'Magic'–30-Second Commute," *The Christian Science Monitor*, August 26, 1985, p. 1.

chocolate at the elbow, and who would savor nothing more than conducting the rest of his business career from that chair.

Alas, I must note that nearly all of these telecommuters also spend the majority of their time at the office. We are not quite ready—culturally or administratively—for the complete lack of office contact and exchange.

Nonetheless, here are three methods for telecommuting:

1. "Carry me back to the ole office." A luggable (such as the best-selling IBM clone, Compaq—portable only by virtue of a handle and concealed keyboard, like the portable TV sets of the 1950s, but still better than staying at work) is brought home, worked on, and returned to the office in the morning. As a variation on this theme, a laptop (or briefcase) micro like the Tandy 200, NEC Multispeed, or Toshiba 1100 can be used even while in a car, train, plane, or hotel room. When returned to the office it is unloaded into the resident micro or mainframe. Finally, the worker may have a micro at home that matches the one at work. The president of a midsize shipbuilding and repair firm does his financial planning on his coffee table in his den. (His comments on the utility of micros for managers are offered below as a NOTA BENE.)

2. "Reach out and touch some CPU." The micro can be connected to the office mainframe, and work can be done on the mainframe. In such a case, the terminal is essentially used like a smart terminal. A modem (internal or external device for converting computer bleeps to phone line warbles) is required in this arrangement. Hewlett Packard has many of its best troubleshooters solve computer problems all over the world using this method. The "bug shot round the world" can be handled from the comfort of the favored armchair.

3. "The best of both worlds." The work can be done on the micro at home, in the air, or pool side. Then the phone link is established, and the work is transferred at about 50 times the speed of expert typing to the office system—either micro or mainframe.

We will see more of this in the coming years. And this can be good. It allows a degree of flexibility in ordering our lives. Let us hope it also brings the discipline to prevent the intrusion of the office into the cherished times of home life. This balance will secure the real benefit.

Databases

A few years ago it was quite rare to hear of a microcomputer user running his own database management system. Databases were relegated to the horsey mainframes, and the database management software alone could weigh in at around $100,000. Now more than half a million PCs are running dBASE (the top seller). The total cost of hardware and software to run dBASE is a mere 25th of that figure. The total number of micro database users is in the millions.

Why the change? First, PC hardware has rapidly evolved in capability. Most systems sold today sport fast (16 bit) processors, 512 KB of internal memory, and some sort of hard internal disk drive storing 10 to 40 million bytes (characters). This makes possible the development and reporting of a worthwhile amount of data. A floppy-only system rarely stores enough data to be very interesting for the corporate user.

The software also has matured in capability and ease of use. Sharon Rae notes that most micro database users are graduates of 1-2-3 from Lotus who accumulated enough information that the spreadsheet approach became cumbersome, if not impossible.[4] When such spreadsheets are overstocked with names, numbers, relations, tables, and such, they tend to become rather "clunky." This leads to "same-day service on most transactions"—not a pleasant way to stay informed.

Micro databases not only allow the storage and reporting of much larger files but offer significantly more sophisticated methods of handling input and processing of information. For these reasons many database users restrict the development of database procedures to those with at least some systems background. This is not to say that the novice cannot develop such a procedure or application. Many novices could, but the resulting systems might not perform efficiently or predictably or in a way that could be explained to the next person interested in the data.

According to Sandy Austin, Coca-Cola's Houston-based food division offers an example of a healthy database with a few clever "programs."[5] (I use the quotes because these programs are developed without any real use of traditional programming languages.) They purchased IBM Personal Computer ATs and the database package from MicroRIM, R:Base™ 5000. The built-in application writer is called Application Express. The database was developed to store information about individual competitors and their marketing activities in Coca-Cola's markets.

Sheryl Currid, sales system manager, states: "Six months ago our

---

[4] Sharon Rae, "Micro DBMSs in Mainframe Shops," *Business Software Review*, December 1985, p. 41.

[5] Sandy Austin, "Data Options for Business," *Business Computer Systems*, September 1985, p. 81.

sales force was doing analysis on calculators. Now, with the PC ATs, electronic mail, and R:Base 5000 applications in place, we have swept them out of the 15th century overnight." Applications that might have taken weeks with mainframe systems can be developed in hours on the micros.

Although the above case involves the marketing group, notice that the sales system manager was directly involved with the development of the database system. This tends to hold true in many companies. Kent Johnson, president of MicroRIM, notes, "The biggest volume of R:Base 4000 and R:Base 5000 users in our major accounts is in the analytical areas of various company departments. Financial analysts, systems analysts, researchers—the users tend to be people who need to keep track of a lot of data."[6] This pattern characterized the earlier days of the spreadsheets, too.

Database Utilization Case Study—E. I. du Pont de Nemours & Co.[7]

Leon D. Wolf, systems specialist with E. I. du Pont de Nemours, is the personal computer coordinator for the biomedical products division of Du Pont. He serves as the liaison between the firm's information systems department and more than 500 micro users. He is understandably enthusiastic about the PCs in general and microcomputer databases in particular. He notes, "The gains our users get from using micro DBMSs (database management systems) are so obvious that the expenses in most cases aren't worth the effort of justification. They gain back whatever expense is incurred almost immediately."

Applications range from simple name and address files to customer and prospect tracking. One large application tracks customer service calls. Small databases are being handled with 1-2-3 from Lotus. Larger and more demanding applications are being developed by an information resource group within each department with tools such as dBASE II®, dBASE III®, Personal Card Filer (Hewlett-Packard), and Condor (Condor Computer Corporation).

The initial application for all these micros, interestingly enough, was electronic mail. There is a PC for nearly every person in the division. These other applications emerged naturally as the possibilities were grasped by the

---

[6] Rae, "Micro DBMSs in Mainframe Shops," p. 42.
[7] Ibid.

users. Programming has remained under the wing of MIS professionals. This ensures consistent logic and documentation which Wolf feels are vital in a large operation where people move in and out of positions constantly.

The information resource groups (supporting the departments) early decided to require that each individual user justify the system to his own manager, thus keeping MIS out of the justification equation. These justifications are immediate and easy, given that the users have the PCs anyway (for the mail system), and only the cost of the micro database (typically $400 to $800) must be justified. As Wolf observes, micro databases "pay for themselves in productivity so quickly that users gain back their investments right away."

Presentation Graphics

Once a company has discovered the value of spreadsheets and databases, can graphics be far behind? As noted in Chapter 2, there is great persuasive power in well-conceived and well-presented graphics. Over and above the palette of colorful graphs that most such spreadsheets and databases offer is a class of software called presentation graphics. This allows the user to create a wide variety of images ranging from dozens of lettering fonts to animated sequences of pictures to actual video-quality reproductions of photographs.

The widely used Graphwriter™ offers an example of this concept. It emphasizes a broad selection of clever graphs more than drawings and pictures. A sophisticated example of the latter is the Executive Picture Show (PC Software in San Diego). Using either a mouse (a hand-held device that causes the cursor on the screen to follow the device's moves on the desktop) or the usual directional arrows, the user can choose from hundreds of predrawn pictures, 255 colors, and a dozen clever fonts or create his own drawings. The outcome can be photographed to make slides or plotted on paper or on transparencies for overhead projection. With a day or two of experimentation (and a bit of taste in combining colors and images), the micro user can develop very professional-appearing presentations for internal or external presentations.

Computer-Aided Publishing

Just when you thought it was safe to go back into the microcomputer productivity issue again, along comes a totally unexpected justification. Not to mention a new buzzword. The buzzword is *CAP*, and it means computer-aided publishing.

Nearly all companies—including manufacturers—generate certain documents that are meant to be seen by an important circle of people—possibly customers, salesmen, executives, or the public. In times past these have usually been typeset. This creates a more finished appearance than just a typed page. Also, typesetting can reduce printing costs by compacting the text, which reduces the number of pages to be printed.

Many graphics-capable systems have the potential to do this sort of thing—with the right software and the right printer. If your printer is a daisy wheel printer, it does no good to create headlines, bar graphs, and corporate logos on the screen—the printer can only print letters and numbers. The rest of this stunning display is lost (or worse—printed as question marks).

However, many graphics printers (dot matrix with multicolor ribbons) produce everything just named. A laser printer does all of the above well enough to suggest to readers that the document was typeset.

Some specialized systems, such as Apple Macintosh®, Manhattan Graphics Corp., Interleaf, and Xyvision, offer even more to the page designer. One user estimates that the cost per original page of finished manuals for clients has dropped from $10 (and up) to a dollar or two. For example, suppose you publish a 30-page owner's repair manual with each new model of lawn mower. The onetime cost of resetting that manual has dropped from $300 to $30. Obviously, duplicating costs (using an offset press, web press, or photocopier) would not be affected.

It is noteworthy that many photocopy service centers now offer Apple Macintosh micros connected to laser printers. This allows their clients to design the desired layouts on the client's own Apple Macintosh micros. The client then brings the disks storing the layouts into the center for printing and copying. By the way, Chapter 6 includes a unique and dramatic example of how far one British firm took this idea.

WHAT DOES THE FUTURE HOLD IN THIS ARENA?

Besides the many productivity tools explained in this chapter and the last, there is no question that more are approaching. Work is being done currently with micros that can accept voice input and respond with voice (the Texas Instruments home computer—TI 99/4A—for $125 had an output vocabulary of hundreds of words in 1981!).

Already a variety of text scanners (for $2,000 or $3,000) can take typed documents directly into the microcomputer. Full graphic scanning is emerging. Our computers, phones, and desks are melding into a workplace environmental unit—a digital cocoon?—that will perform virtually all of the routine tasks of acquiring and disseminating information.

None of this is going to replace thinking as we know it. More than ever, the need will be for the clear thinkers and doers that observe, orient, decide, and act. The need for good instructors, consultants, and guides will become paramount in the face of this proliferation of opportunities.

NOTA BENE

The explosive emergence of productivity applications but lays the tool at the foot of the carpenter. The great need will continue to be—as it has been in the past—for workers and leaders of sufficient vision, communication skills, and action to build the structures that the tools make possible.

The selection and blending of these technologies will become both trickier and more fruitful as these technical capabilities multiply—seemingly without limit. To provide some guidance to the judicious Reader in these critical waters, Part Three—"Implementation"—has been written.

Implementation

CHAPTER FIVE

Selection and Initial Implementation of Micros

Five centuries ago, Machiavelli offered a timeless warning to those who would implement new systems.

> It must be considered that there is nothing more difficult to carry out, nor more doubtful of success, nor dangerous to handle, than to initiate a new order of things. For the reformer has enemies in all those who profit by the old order, and only lukewarm defenders in all those who would profit by the new order, this lukewarmness arising partly from fear of their adversaries, who have the laws in their favor, and partly from the incredulity of mankind, who do not truly believe in anything new until they have actual experience of it.

This chapter begins the third of the five major parts of this book, namely, "Implementation." Since many fine texts and articles exist on the subject, we confine ourselves to a *useful review* of the salient issues of implementation to support the Reader in his noble quest for excellence in the selection and implementation of microcomputers—ever fending off the enemies of lukewarmness, incredulity, and profiteers in the old order. As always we address the particular concerns of the manufacturing environment and provide case studies within this arena.

REVIEW OF THE CRITICAL SUCCESS FACTORS OF IMPLEMENTATION

As mentioned in Chapter 1, the companies that have proven most successful in implementing micros (PCs) have not tried to manage the details of each user's individual encounter with the PC but to manage the *environment* within which these highly individual encounters will grow. We compared this to the farmer who doesn't manage each kernel of corn. He plows, plants, fertilizes, sprays, and reaps—he is managing the environment of the kernels, not the kernels themselves.

The wise PC administrator is providing appropriate hardware (addressed in this chapter), software, connectivity, data availability, discipline, support services, problem solvers, occasional handholding for the needy, training, and links to outside (fertilizing) agents such as user seminars. These subjects will be addressed in later chapters.

REMEMBER THE PHASES OF MICRO IMPLEMENTATION

The care and nurturing of the implementation moves through the same four phases that characterize the acculturation of the organization into the world of micros. This involves the following four phases:

1. *Experimental.* Earliest experimenters try word processing, various spreadsheets, and other applications. Different micro brands appear in the more adventurous departments.

2. *Individual.* The users (several now) are quite competent at the above functions. The systems are all standalone. Some standardization must emerge for hardware and software. Training is becoming available and important to a wider circle of users and is vital to encourage the less sophisticated users who also have important needs.

3. *Departmental.* The users within a department (or many departments) are connected to each other. Disk files, printers, and plotters may be shared by local area networks (LANs). Joint applications may include office automation, databases, scheduling, and so forth.

4. *Organizational.* The PCs become utilities—like phones, lighting, or plumbing. Nearly all the "knowledge workers" in the firm are wired together. Most important, the organizational data is now part of the network. All planning and control functions are integrated in this network of mainframe and micro computers. Applications span the spectrum from those named in 1 through 3, above, to very sophisticated packages. A high degree of standardization is enforced regarding hardware (perhaps two or three brands), software (perhaps one or two word processors, one integrated system, and several select applications), communications, and management controls.

Please remember, these are certainly not absolute lines of demarcation, and many companies will fall between these benchmarks.

"WE HAVE MET THE ENEMY, AND HE IS US!"

So said Pogo, the swamp-dwelling opossum of the cartoon strip. If we are ever to succeed in turning the situation around to the quotation's original sense of victory—"We have met the enemy, and he is ours," we need to identify this enemy accurately. We take a minute here to review the face of the enemy—the elements of chaos and disintegration that war against the benefits we desire from these systems:

1. *Loss of data integrity.*   This is when the data resident in the micros and the data resident in the mainframe disagree with the cold hard facts. It can also refer to variances in the data (currency) of the figures, the assumptions underlying the data, its source, and those responsible for maintaining it.

2. *Training.*   Too often the training offered is nonexistent, incomplete, available long after the point of need, or disjointed from user needs. This probably causes as many micro failures, frustrations, and abandonments as any other single factor. Even if the hardware is sluggish and the software somewhat awkward, a knowledgeable user can reasonably accomplish useful work for himself and the organization. Conversely, if the hardware is excellent and the software perfectly fitted to the need, but the user is untrained or improperly trained, the system is doomed to fail.

3. *Security.*   We remember this as the coin that has two sides—lost and found. One type of security problem involves making sure that useful data (and the time and thought that produced it) are not *lost* through electrical, system, or personal failings. The other problem is to make sure that this useful data is not *found* by someone who has no business finding it.

4. *Disintegration.*   Information that stands alone on a single PC can be useful. But to gain organization-driving, decision-making, and economy-producing power, sooner or later we have got to get the PCs together. Exceptions are few. This may involve getting the network's arms around the mainframe as well. Unless some sound planning, disciplined execution, and purposeful direction have preceded this need, the potential for confusion and frustration is staggering.

WHAT ARE THE ANSWERS TO THESE CHALLENGES?

The first step is to recognize that the answers will vary nearly as much as the needs of the corporations that acquire such systems. However, some general principles emerge. These principles are based on good old-fashioned sound management as applied to hardware needs, software needs, definition of new (and old) business systems, implementation of these systems, and thoughtful consideration of the human elements of this very significant change in the daily round of office life.

An example in each area will serve to illustrate these considerations. The hardware configuration that was more than generous two years ago is now considered cramped and sluggish and will be considered little more than a toy in four more years. In 1981 I wrote two systems for a Texas Instruments micro—general ledger and invoicing (with automatic pricing, subtotals, profit calculations, and so forth)—all in a total of 16KB (KB means 1,024 bytes—think of 1,024 letters or numbers) of memory and a tape cassette storage system. Today, six years later, no serious business user of a micro gets less than 512K and 10 million bytes of hard disk storage.

Recently the local consultant recommended a million bytes (1,000KB) of memory and 20 MB of disk. Remarkably, costs are not much different even as the capability has soared.

On another side of the acquisition coin is the maelstrom of the market. The competitors both onshore and offshore are driving the prices down month by month. I have actually seen firms hurt by one-year commitments on blanket purchase orders—they end up paying 20 percent or more above the prevailing market prices. Circumspect and flexible negotiating is needed here. Watch ads in the large cities. (New York, Boston, and Los Angeles are veritable hotbeds of such virulent competition.) Don't enter into contracts that freeze features and prices for more than a couple of months. It remains a buyer's market and is likely to continue so for the next few years.

Software operates in a slightly more gentlemanly manner, but smaller companies can be accommodating for a large customer—especially in the area of packaging of systems, training, service, and so on. More information on software choices will appear in the next chapter.

Systems implementation rests on the same foundations as classical systems analysis for mainframes. The pilings don't need to be as deep to reach reasonable decisions, but the planks need to be included in the platform. Failing to make this effort ultimates in solving the wrong problems while leaving the real needs unanswered.

One large manufacturer (over $1 billion per year) decided on the hardware and word processing software without adequate systems analysis. The system acquired happened to do a very poor job with preprinted forms and with envelopes. This turned out to be much of what was done every day. The result was that no typewriters left the building, and the micros fought for the scarce space left over on the desktops. Within a year, I saw micros stacked sideways in remote, darkened closets. The typewriters are still humming away (although I thought I heard a snicker from them occasionally). The moral?

NOTA BENE

Systems analysis is just as important (if not as detailed or lengthy) in micro systems as it is in mainframe decisions. Don't pull the trigger until you have clearly identified the target.

Finally, the human elements of this revolution in office and shop procedures are the most important of all. Without clear policies, training, consulting—a nurturing and supportive environment, the real benefits will be greatly reduced, if not lost entirely. When the boss says, "This is the new typewriter; have at it," even the most faithful office worker may well adopt a long-term strategy of passive resistance that severely damages the flow of work and stifles the otherwise active faculty of problem solving. "Well, I'll use it, but don't expect me to do all those fancy things with it."

Think of the enormous advantage if the individual first encounters the micro sitting beside someone who has worked the same job, who has shared the same fears, and who is now very encouraging (if not genuinely enthusiastic) about the system's use. Think of the advantage of an in-house user's group to support and fortify the new members of the micro fold. "You are not alone, and we can help." (More is said about training in Chapter 8.) These simple and relatively inexpensive actions can make an enormous difference in the success or failure of the implementation.

Now that we have seen both the pitfalls along the trail and some hints of the way around them, we will develop a more definite outline of the key steps.

WHAT ARE THE STEPS TO GOOD MICRO SELECTION DECISIONS AND SUCCESSFUL IMPLEMENTATION?

Actually, selection and implementation are not separate topics. If you have done a good job in the selection, you have already done much to make the implementation successful. The following steps are not exhaustive but are certainly critical to success in reaching both goals.

1. Define the scope and nature of the users' needs and the organization's needs.
2. Investigate the spectrum of current technology.
3. Select the most worthwhile micro applications (costs versus benefits).
4. Develop policies and standards for micro acquisition and use.
5. Organize the implementation and support environment.
6. Develop timetables and budgets for system acquisition.
7. Train supporters, programmers, developers, and users.

The following sections explore these steps and furnish examples of their application.

DEFINE THE SCOPE AND NATURE OF THE USERS' NEEDS AND THE ORGANIZATION'S NEEDS

Systems analysis is no more (or less) than its name implies—analyzing the systems that are currently in place and thinking through the desired systems of the future. The trick is in recognizing that a system (invoicing, for example) may currently look like a dictaphone wired to a phone answerer, clerk, typewriter, calculator, sales catalog, computer terminal, and a trash can in its current state. The need is to boil this all down to the basic issues. As Chorafas points out, it really amounts to asking the following questions:

1. What exactly is to be accomplished (the outputs or objective)?
2. Who (precisely) is to do it, and what steps will be taken to do it?
3. When should this objective be achieved?
4. How will the microcomputer-based system do this work?
5. Where must the results be reported or distributed?
6. Why is this objective desirable?[1]

Documentation of the answers to these questions is important. The information systems department should be thoroughly conversant with the methods of this task. (Just don't let them get carried away—keep the time and expenditure of the analysis effort in line with the cost of the sys-

---

[1] Dimitris N. Chorafas, *Office Automation, The Productivity Challenge* (Englewood Cliffs, N.J.: Prentice Hall, 1982), p. 121.

tems being considered.) It may also prove important to simplify, eliminate, and combine procedures as this analysis reveals such opportunities.

If a certain effort is being expended on reports that do not really influence any decisions nor serve any planning or control purpose, then drop this reporting effort altogether. Simplify before computerizing. Why automate the mess? Seize the chance to streamline—this analysis may yield surprising benefits in its own right. In any case, if this task has been well done, the next is much easier.

If a number of microcomputers have already been acquired (probably being used in an experimental manner), it may prove useful to survey the nature of the hardware, software, and applications currently in-house. *The Micro-Mainframe Link* offers a nice example of the forms that could be used for such a survey.[2]

INVESTIGATE THE SPECTRUM OF CURRENT TECHNOLOGY

It is hard to imagine assigning a more potentially exhaustive task in fewer words than the six that head this paragraph. The technology is racing at breakneck speed toward goalposts that are being moved backwards and sideways regularly. How do you gauge the front-runners? Fortunately, this task can be simplified.

The last part of this book lists a variety of hardware and vendor listing and rating services. This is far from universal, but it will cover many inquiries. Ask your manufacturing peers about the systems that have worked well for them. You might want to get involved in the microcomputer groups in your area (for example, there is a Special Interest Group in APICS just for micros).

There are magazines, books, buying guides, and catalogs filled with useful ideas. Since you will probably want some measure of service, training, support, and guidance, ask other nearby users about these before getting tangled in the issues of chips and KFLOPS. Let these former measures filter out the weak contender that happens to have a grand sales pitch. Colleges, consultants, and vendors of both hardware and software offer a wide variety of introductory courses on this subject. Recognize, too, that the answers to the questions raised in the following sections may well serve to limit the field of consideration even further.

---

[2] William E. Perry, *The Micro-Mainframe Link: The Corporate Guide to Productive Use of the Microcomputer* (New York: John Wiley & Sons, 1985), p. 33ff.

SELECT THE MOST WORTHWHILE MICRO APPLICATIONS (COSTS VERSUS BENEFITS)

Not all cost justifications are created equal. Some tasks are getting done in a reasonably acceptable manner at the present. Some tasks just don't have a great impact on the firm. Ferret out the tasks that have a high payoff in a relatively short time period. It is also useful to evaluate the receptiveness of the personnel involved to new systems and concepts.

The preliminary investigation of hardware and software conducted in step 2 above should give some rough figures for these costs. Maryam Alavi suggests the following checklist of costs with the comment that many first time or smaller manufacturers tend to overlook or underestimate these factors:[3]

1. Hardware costs—purchase or lease: include peripherals such as printers, modems, disk drives, maintenance (could be 10 percent of hardware per year), etc.
2. Software costs—again purchase or lease: include operating systems, communications, and other such "environmental" software items as well as the applications themselves.
3. Facility costs—electrical outlets, electrical surge protectors, noise-reducing printer covers.
4. Staffing costs—clerical and support.
5. Training costs—tuition, travel, staffing, training materials (some might be included with the software).
6. Conversion/installation costs—file creation, input, testing, DP involvement, programming.
7. Supplies and miscellany—paper, ribbons, diskettes (they cost around $4 each—a typical operator will require from 20 to a couple hundred), additional insurance, tables, chairs if needed.

The elements of cost then need to be weighed against potential benefits. Beware of narrowly focusing on the personnel reduction facet of the benefits. This misses the much more important issue of why we are performing the tasks in the first place.

In the example of Karl Schmidt, the production planner, in the first chapter, the obvious savings were in the reduction of his time and that of his associate analyst. This amounted to thousands of dollars per year and was certainly enough to justify the system. However, what is the benefit of producing more insightful schedules for six chassis and axle plants that

---

[3] Maryam Alavi, "Microcomputers & Small Manufacturing: A Strategy for Acquisition," *P&IM Review and APICS News*, January 1985, pp. 30–33.

contain $1 billion worth of inventory? Suppose that the "what-if" cycles and increased flexibility result in improved schedules that just save, for example, one 10th of 1 percent in inventory holdings. This amounts to a $1 million improvement in cash requirements and (at 10 percent carrying costs) $100,000 per year in profit improvement. This is why the whole planning process is done after all. The reduced clerical effort pales in significance beside this objective.

NOTA BENE

Personnel costs are tidier to calculate, but business, functional, and departmental objectives are far more important—even if subject to reasoned estimates instead of hard dollars—in evaluating the impact of new systems.

The ratio of benefits to costs gives a simple but useful quantitative basis for selecting the first applications to be moved to the microcomputers. Qualitative factors should also be weighed. This includes such considerations as probable speed of implementation (the quicker the better—it is useful to build up a strong track record before tackling the tougher applications). Having said this, let me add a warning sounded by Chris Edwards. While it may be wise to tackle the smaller application first, it is just as wise to be sure that the hardware that one commits to will be beefy enough to take on the largest applicational demands when necessary.[4]

For example, if a small manufacturer intended to operate entirely on micros, it would be well to assure that the selected system could handle the most challenging tasks such as material requirements planning or capacity planning even if simpler applications (like general ledger) are first implemented. This may be verified by visits with comparable users or by a benchmark (test of a computer's capability under controlled conditions). Other circumstances that qualitatively influence the selection of initial development are the department's receptiveness to new systems and the degree of existing skill or experience.

DEVELOP POLICIES AND STANDARDS FOR MICRO ACQUISITION AND USE

The manager first entering the brave new world of micros will encounter some strange terrain, stranger jargon, and hoards of helpful strangers ob-

---

[4] Chris Edwards, "Guidelines: Systems Investigation for Microcomputers," *Datapro*, November 1985.

sequiously desirous of putting more distance between him and his dollars. It will prove important to develop policies and procedures for bidding, purchasing, installing, training, protecting, and maintaining the micros.

Let a word of caution be offered about acquisition. The market is hungering for buyers as of this writing and should continue to for the next few years or more. The typical product cycle is four to six months. It makes little sense to wait for some imagined period of tranquility ("I'm holding out till the market settles down.") before choosing the systems that will meet your needs. There will nearly always be good deals available.

Having been forewarned about the maelstrom of marketing, what systems will you permit in the building? Policies run the gamut from "buy whatever fills your bill" to "only the Grunch Brothers 9000 may be purchased here." The former wastes enormous effort when networks, sharing data, training, supporting, and maintaining are considered. The latter deadens individual initiative and prevents the users from "buying into" the corporate objective. Let me offer examples of actual policies in companies that are beyond the experimentation phase and working toward the departmental and organizational phases.

Policy Case One

This firm essentially allows three architectures to exist side by side with very limited communications between these architectures. Wang is used for departments that primarily need word processing; Macintoshes are used for specialty functions such as computer-aided publishing; and IBM and clones (Compaq, Wyse, Tandy) are used by departments requiring a broader range of applications, usually using the integrated system of SMART or 1-2-3.

A minority of maverick users have dBASE III, Multimate, and other applications. Such variations are discouraged (although not prohibited) by the micro systems management, and no support or training is offered in the maverick applications. It is recognized that the individual user may feel well served by a novel package, but the overriding objectives of the organization require strong uniformity.

The Macintosh users are few and support themselves. Two support teams handle, respectively, the Wang and IBM/clone users. Centralized purchasing handles all acquisitions, and the MIS group must endorse all acquisitions. This company has over a hundred micros, and this policy has worked quite well for them.

Policy Case Two

Another manufacturer now has a couple hundred micros. It discovered in the systems analysis that it had essentially two kinds of users: (1) those who wanted a spreadsheet and some word processing and were willing to operate in a standalone environment and (2) those who needed to develop databases and new applications and who needed to be linked together for many daily tasks.

This firm selected IBM Personal Computer XTs™ and ATs™ for the former group with 1-2-3 from LOTUS and a word processor. The vast majority of all the XTs (and clones) are used in standalone settings. The other class of users acquired networks of Unisys B25s, running a few Unisys packages and using MicroRIM R:Base for the database and communications needs. The majority of Unisys systems everywhere live in networks. Therefore, each group of users was capitalizing on the favored environment of the hardware and software.

The flexibility afforded by two or three architectures allows the users a real vote in selection, allows the solutions to fit the needs more accurately, and keeps the maintenance and support task well in hand.

Another tricky area of such policy development arises in the area of security and fraud. Studies do not offer any panaceas but do indicate that most fraudulent losses could have been prevented by such mundane practices as securing systems with passwords, normal divisions of responsibility, and watchful accounting controls.[5]

Micros have the potential for both easier access and greater security. If you really want a file secure, take it with you in the form of a diskette. You may also place it in the company vault. This is especially true for smaller files such as the general ledger, marketing plans or secret formulas. In most cases, passwords should be required to access applications and files. Change them as changes in personnel require and don't share them—one per operator.

Let me summarize the area of policy development by paraphrasing a sample policy statement from William E. Perry:

---

[5] EDP Fraud Task Force, American Institute of Certified Public Accountants, "Report on the Study of EDP-Related Fraud in the Banking and Insurance Industries," 1984.

1. Hardware and software should be standardized (this may include two or three architectures and application programs).

2. An organizational unit (micro systems team) independent of central DP, but drawing upon it for the requisite skills, and drawing upon the user organizations, will be established to oversee and assist in the effective use of PCs.

3. Ownership of all computers, data, programs, and spreadsheet or database templates shall remain with the company.

4. PCs will be subject to all company data controls and security procedures.

5. Appropriate standards should be developed to facilitate interchange of data and programs (addressing both hardware, software, and networking).

6. Standard measures should be developed to evaluate the effectiveness of the use of PCs.

7. These policies shall be implemented under the direction of the manager of the micro systems team, with the support of the general manager.[6]

ORGANIZE THE IMPLEMENTATION
AND SUPPORT ENVIRONMENT

As is suggested by some of the positions and titles mentioned in the above policy section, some organizational changes will be required by manufacturers as they become more extensively involved with micros. During the investigation and experimentation phase, it will be useful to have a single point of accumulation of corporate knowledge. Otherwise, the same lessons must be learned by every department.

In most companies this seems to default to someone in the systems analysis division of data processing or MIS. Although this affords the advantage of skill in such analysis and knowledge in the language and concepts of the genre, it can narrow the scope of the consideration to the technical issues ("Of course, it has the 80386 Intel chip and the 80287 math co-processor chip, but does it run Turbo-Pascal?").

The ideal is someone with both the systems experience (not necessarily expertise) and a sound foundation in operations. If such an individual is not forthcoming, choose one from either background and then add members from the complementary background. In fact, the team should represent members of MIS, operations, and finance. This does much more than just represent a cross section of users and providers; it brings to the team the breadth of perspective to make better recommendations.

---

[6] Perry, *Micro-Mainframe Link,* p. 43.

These supporting elements can significantly improve the quality of the investigation and the subsequent implementation.

At first these assignments need not be full-time. As the number of micros moves from a handful to a few dozen, these will evolve into full-time positions. As the number of micros reaches the hundred mark, it may well become a separate department. This is the core of the eventual support structure. As the number of systems moves beyond the experimentation phase, some instructional or coaching talent may prove useful as well. Also, a general systems steering committee (which is usually in place for MIS oversight and which includes executive-level members) must provide ongoing guidance throughout this development. The steering committee considers long-term issues such as degree of linkage between central DP systems and micros, in-house application development, and policy modifications.

DEVELOP TIMETABLES AND BUDGETS FOR SYSTEM ACQUISITION

It makes no sense to allow micros to be purchased at a faster rate than the users can be trained, supported, and guided. That's why this step is placed after those above. As mentioned earlier, an increasingly wild buyer's market seems to prevail at this point and is expected to continue.[7] Many manufacturers of micros have geared up the plants for high volumes, and the demand has been leveling. As Wiener observes, "If IBM, Compaq, HP, and DEC keep pumping out PCs like there's no tomorrow, one of them may be right." Nonetheless, there are deals to be made.

As these words are written, the IBM Personal Computer AT has been out for over a year. A hot new AT clone that runs 25 percent faster, has 50 percent more disk storage, and a strong company behind it sells for roughly the same list price. This afternoon a financially strong (and widely respected) local dealer offered this promising new system (only out for a few weeks) for 40 percent off of list price for quantities numbering in the dozens. This is a system from a very strong manufacturer and a good dealer. I fully expect both to be in business and healthy for at least the life of the systems—five to seven years—and thereafter. The deals being offered by the boiler-room remarketers would make strong purchasing agents quake! The moral: shop smart, centralize the purchasing of all

---

[7] See, for example, Hesh Wiener, "Stalking the Wilds of the PC Market," *Datamation*, April 15, 1986, pp. 91–92.

micros, and don't commit to prices for more than a few months—"the times, they are a-changing" is the theme music for this market.

TRAIN SUPPORTERS, PROGRAMMERS, DEVELOPERS, AND USERS

As the demands of the firm evolve, the core group of the micro support team will grow. These may be recruited out of the functional areas named above. The training needs will range from one-day seminars to remote classes to college courses. This core group will become responsible for training of the various users in the departments. It is wise to have a *designated micro coordinator* within each department. This may be a stenographic assistant (what we used to call a secretary), an office manager, the newest engineer, or the resident micro enthusiast who already has a system at home.

The training will initially focus on these coordinators. They can serve as links to the whole community of users as the systems proliferate. New releases of software, new training aids, corrections to procedures, instructional and reference materials, and passwords can be transmitted (figuratively or literally) to the whole organization through these individuals. At some point it may be natural to organize a micro user group within the company to build the network of support and encouragement that oils the wheels of the introduction of such new systems.

Case Study: Allegheny International

Allegheny International is a $2.3 billion conglomerate that manufactures a wide variety of consumer appliances and other items. As early as 1978 their MIS group had involved the users in on-line inquiry and reporting systems via a decision support application called Foresight from Information Systems of America, Inc. As B. W. Campbell notes, "By 1980, the in-house time-sharing community had grown . . . to over 400. To be sure, not all of the applications developed were suited for Foresight. Users were so eager to automate their job tasks that they embraced even partial solutions. Unlike many experienced computer professionals, they were willing to use incomplete tools until a total solution became available."[8]

---

[8] B. W. Campbell, "The Planning Side of Success with Micros," *Data Communications Magazine*, October 1984; reprinted in *Datapro Research*, December 1984.

This pattern of learning or prototyping through the short-term solution proved useful for guiding the efforts of MIS, even while giving them time to develop new systems. Since standards were in force, it was not hard to transfer the users over to mainstream systems when they were in place.

These practices were very well suited for introducing micros. Microcomputers were investigated, and acquisition guidelines were published in February 1982. As Campbell notes, "Any standard is better than no standard, or a mixed standard. [MIS] followed the advice they had always preached to users: focus on the application, not the tool."

At this early date the decision was made to standardize on IBM Personal Computers, standard word processing, spreadsheet (1-2-3 from Lotus at first, now combined with Symphony from Lotus), and database applications. It was further decided that a group within MIS would provide the support to the users. The MIS department correctly predicted that the increasing availability of micros would not significantly reduce the load on the mainframe. Even after 200 micros were in place, the mainframe processing load had been reduced by only about 5 percent.

The number of micros grew to 250 by 1984 and is expected to reach 800 in 1986. The number of terminal (Foresight) users has declined from 800 in 1982 to an estimated 400 in 1986. These micros are employed both in the displacement of terminals and for other micro-specific applications.

Data communications are handled through the Irma board (now made by Digital Communications Associates, Atlanta, Georgia), Crosstalk (by Microstuf), and Smartmodems (by Hayes). Because so much of the entry and manipulation of financial or planning data can be done within the PC, the connection time between remote sites and the central systems has been reduced by 90 percent. These costs could be reduced even further by transmitting during evening hours, but users "generally continue to refine their numbers until the last minute before submitting them; in this sense, the process still retains an interactive flavor."

An electronic mail system facilitates usual business communications among the users but also allows the sharing of a considerable library of 1-2-3 from Lotus applications. This includes models for solving financial, marketing, engineering, and other problems. Forecasts are now prepared through the divisions and transmitted to headquarters where they are consolidated and analyzed. They are currently considering programs that will transfer data from mainframe databases to the micros and vice versa.

Case Study: E. I. Du Pont de Nemours & Co.

This case was investigated in the last chapter since much of their work involved micro database managers.[9] It is appropriate to add a few notes here about the more general elements of their implementation. Currently there are more than 500 micro users in the biomedical products division. Support and guidance is provided by the information systems (IS) department. The company standardized on IBM and several compatibles, as well as 1-2-3 from Lotus, dBASE II, and dBASE III, Personal Card Filer (HP), and Condor database manager (Condor Computer Corporation, Ann Arbor, Michigan).

Programming for these systems remains the domain of the info systems group to maintain consistent standards of logic and documentation. Although the original interest stemmed from corporate-wide electronic mail, only about 10 percent of the systems have taken the further step of reaching into mainframe files for data. After all, says PC Coordinator Leon Wolf, "the reason for using a micro DBMS program in the first place is to have local control over a database."

Cost justifications are conducted entirely between the user and the department manager, keeping the IS department out of the decision. Du Pont exhibits more leniency here than Allegheny or the other firms discussed earlier. The Du Pont division averages nearly a micro per individual as a result. Allegheny has many fewer and is very stringent on the criteria for justifying micros. Given the relatively high rate of micro abandonment in the industry (cited in Chapter 1), they want to be sure that the justification, interest, need, and appropriate applications are identified before placing the micro.

CONCLUSION

There are no magic formulas to guarantee the successful implementation of micros in manufacturing companies. The steps outlined in this chapter illustrate guidelines that have proven useful for many. We trust that they will also prove useful to the reader. The elements of successful selection

---

[9] Sharon Gamble Rae, "Micro DBMSs in Mainframe Shops," *Business Software Review*, December 1985, pp. 41–43.

and implementation include not only the steps of this chapter but also sound applications, networking, and integration of the systems and gentle but effective training of the users. The next three chapters address just these issues.

CHAPTER SIX

Application Programs—Selection and Use

Sometime between deciding that a micro would be handy and achieving that exalted status of Phase 4 of microcomputer commitment (organizationwide integration and effectiveness), the micro user has to face the issue of software selection. How does one select among the more than 50,000 offerings of more than 5,000 software firms that are introducing collectively hundreds of new products every month? As mentioned in earlier chapters, the first applications are usually environmental tools such as spreadsheets, word processing, database, and so on.

Most manufacturers will eventually need more micro software than this. For example, it is nearly impossible to run an effective material requirements plan with any combination of the above three. Likewise, they do not lend themselves to invoicing, NC machine tool loading (as an entry to the heady world of computer-integrated manufacturing), inventory control, order processing, and so forth.

Companies who desire to perform such tasks on micros will need to consider application software. Although this chapter on specific applications follows the chapter on system selection and precedes that on networking, all these issues must be weighed jointly to reach successful decisions. As Campbell noted, "Focus on the application, not the tool."

Much application software is purchased off the shelf. Infrequently it may be modified extensively before use. This may be done by the users, by the MIS folks, by the vendor, by a third party, or by some association of users. Some companies write their own software. The list of such authors runs the same gamut as the list of software modifiers.

The issues are many: How do we choose between buying and "growing our own"? To what extent can we trade the convenience of off-the-rack applications for the value of systems tailored specifically to our users' needs? Just how unique are the problems that we encounter in the daily round of business transactions? Can the various applications considered share data among themselves? If not, are we creating disjoint islands of data that will frustrate later efforts toward systems integration? If we elect to buy, where can we find lists of available applications? How do we choose, train, repair, modify, and implement? Is source code available with the applications purchased? If not, how can we maintain the applications as our needs shift? If we write our own, who will write it, document it, train others in its use, and develop it as our needs change?

Here again, many books and articles exist on these crucial issues— several of which are appended in Part Five. This chapter will shed some light on these issues, furnish examples of how different companies tackle these questions, and provide a rather novel case study on one manufacturer's response that resulted in a most positive transformation of their entire business.

SOURCES OF SOFTWARE

Microcomputers have only been around for about a decade, but the software market for micros has virtually exploded. My personal suspicion is that the attic inventors of the 1940s, the closet HO electric train fanatics of the 1950s, the ham operators of the 1960s, and the Heathkit hobbyists of the 1970s are all writing micro software systems in the 1980s. It is a low-capital, fast-moving, and high-potential free-for-all market. Many of the 5,000 companies offering software today will vanish in the next few years to be replaced by even more start-up companies—every one energized by a bold new concept, ambition, and enthusiasm.

The market is awash in more than 50,000 packages. Thousands of these have specific value for the manufacturer. Packages exist today for the following applications:[1]

Inventory control	Shop floor control
Bill of materials	Production control
Order entry/invoicing	Job costing
Forecasting	Fixed assets
Master scheduling	Accounts payable
MRP	Accounts receivable
Capacity planning	General ledger
Purchasing	Payroll
Distribution	Dispatching
CAD	CAM
Statistical quality control	Batch recipe control
Group Technology	Structural design

---

[1] Lester S. Shindelman and Carter C. Utzig, "Move over Mainframe: Make Way for the Micro," *1986 APICS Conference Proceedings*, p. 467.

Energy management	Fluid and piping analysis
Heating, ventilating,	Layout planning
air conditioning	Safety and fire protection
Maintenance management	
Peanut processing	

and many, many others.

What can be done to initiate the search? The basic steps enumerated in the last chapter will help to define the real needs of the users and the relative priorities of the various application areas. Since most new and prospective users of micros are not strongly experienced in computer selection, the steps of research and evaluation of that chapter are valuable. The research may well begin with APICS's Microcomputer Application Special Interest Group. For a few dollars a year, the member is provided access to the investigations of this users group. Local chapters of APICS (American Production and Inventory Control Society), SME (Society of Manufacturing Engineers), APMA (American Purchasing Managers Association), and similar groups are rich repositories of such information. Local retail outlets may well prove useful, but there is great variation in the level of interest, experience, and patience among such stores. Local associations and clubs of PC users offer vast catalogs of applications at all prices (and at all levels of quality—caveat emptor). A number of firms specialize in special markets such as textile manufacturers, confectionery processors, and automotive suppliers. They advertise in manufacturing publications and in the hundreds of micro-related publications that have sprung up recently. These publications regularly review new offerings.[2] Many of these are named in Appendix A, "Lists of Lists," and Appendix C, "Bibliography" of Part Five.

A number of firms have sprung up that offer a matchmaking service between firms with a need and prospective software suppliers. One such is PC Telemart in the Washington, D.C., area. It lets your fingers do the walking through a "software smorgasbord" in special kiosks in computer stores. One merely types in information about features, needs, and price; the system then searches and sorts through thousands of packages to display the best candidates. ITM (Lafayette, California) offers such a service on a floppy diskette. Micro-Information Publishing offers such a service through a toll-free call.[3] It deserves passing mention that all government-

---

[2] *The Wall Street Journal,* March 8, 1985, p. 28.
[3] *The Christian Science Monitor,* November 3, 1983, p. 21.

developed software and much other public domain software is available for free.

By the way, the above services are far from exhaustive (and not verified, endorsed, sponsored, or underwritten by the author). They are merely intended to illustrate the diversity and breadth of means for the enterprising researcher. Perhaps because of the very diversity, most micro users end up relying more upon word of mouth, user groups, industry shows, and magazine reviews (roughly in that order) than all the other sources for their software needs.

If a corporation is prepared to spend thousands of dollars for hardware and software, it certainly seems prudent to spend hundreds of dollars on a few buyer's guides, subscriptions, seminars, and inquiries. This is not a bad investment to assure that the thousands are well spent.

EVALUATING OFF-THE-SHELF APPLICATIONS

Once system needs are identified and a list of possible solutions is presented, how do we compare them to arrive at a final selection? Many of the vendors offer demonstration editions of the software for token amounts to allow a "test drive" of the package before committing to the entire purchase. It is also most useful to talk to a few users who are doing roughly the same things with the target software as you plan to do (same type of processes and similar volumes of transactions and records).

Given the modest level of such expenditures for even a small manufacturer, it is wise not to get carried away with analysis. Nonetheless, the following guidelines are useful in software evaluation:[4]

1. *Ease of installation.*   The software should be designed for self-installation or minimal involvement from your firm's micro support team. It should offer the flexibility to accommodate various hardware configurations, your firm's accounting practices, manufacturing operations, and reporting requirements.

2. *Ease of use.*   The software should allow the novice computer user to quickly move to productive work in a few hours or so (depending on the complexity of the task, of course). The screens and use of keys should be consistent and predictable. Alternate modes of navigating through the system may be available—menus for the novice and com-

---

[4] Dr. Scott Hamilton, "Microcomputer Systems for Small Manufacturers," *1986 APICS Conference Proceedings,* p. 8ff.

mands for the expert, but each should be consistent throughout the system. There should be several levels of on-line help, remembered data (such as dates, part numbers, planner codes) to minimize rekeying, and multiple-use screens (entry, inquiry, report request from the same screen, for example). Movement from one function to the next (for example, inquiring on a part to reporting on expected purchases to sending a shipping notice to the dock) should be obvious and unobstructed. Backup and security features should be largely automatic to protect the new user from himself.

3. *Vendor reputation.*   This refers to the general issues such as financial health, commitment to manufacturing, experience in systems related to your needs, number of installations, and track record in meeting commitments.

4. *Local support strength.*   This is the local issue of who will handle the day-to-day needs as the software is implemented among the users. This may even refer to your own micro support team. Is this an application that they can support in-house? Often vendors will sell ongoing support services, hotlines, and so forth for 10 to 20 percent of the purchase price per year. Outside support may be needed for training, analysis, modification, performance assessment, and so forth.

5. *Availability of education.*   Are there formal classes, self-study materials, computer-based training, or video tapes? Ninety percent of the user community will require specific training to implement manufacturing systems.

6. *Quality of end-user documentation.*   Is it readable, useful, and succinct? It must address the most typical problem areas. Cross-references, indexes, and abundant examples of typical uses are all helpful. Is source code provided for all applications?

7. *Feature content.*   Does it do the things that the users require? Is it flexible and modular to permit the inevitable changes that will arise? Does it handle the highest volume activities in an efficient and comfortable manner? The user may have growth needs (in volumes of transactions or in new processes). Does the software allow room to grow in these directions for the next several years.

8. *Cost and payback.*   Have all costs been taken into account? Usually paybacks are expected within a year or two. Is the cost in line with the expected benefits? If slightly more is spent, can we significantly increase the system's value to the company?

This last question is asked all too rarely by overly cost-conscious buyers. For example, one system that totaled about $16,000 for four users was significantly improved by substituting a laser printer for the letter-quality printer and adding software for graphics applications. This made possible a wide variety of reports and documentation uses. It speeded up letter writing and saved much on outside printing costs. Altogether, this added less than $1,000 to the cost of the system.

NOTA BENE

No purchase decision should be made without asking the question: If we spent 10 percent more, how much greater would be the benefit?

PROTOTYPES AND TRAINING

A hundred years ago shipbuilders would construct a wooden model of a new ship. The 3- to 10-foot-long model would be carefully crafted from fine stock and would represent the hull of the expected vessel in exact scale. This model (a miniature prototype) would then be used for testing the flow of water around the surfaces, the balance and displacement, and the form and fit of major hull elements. It worked quite well and was a lot cheaper than committing tons of wood and steel only to find that the sides did not meet at the stem.

In the realm of computer systems a similar process is often conducted prior to committing vast quantities of manpower, training, analysis, and effort on a major new system. Fourth generation language tools are available on mainframes, minis, and micros for such quick building of prototypes. Even electronic spreadsheets can be used for this purpose.

The idea is to present a screen for input and the capability to create sample reports that will simulate the desired system. The prototype may not include all the necessary logic for dealing with all classes of error conditions, nor may it be capable of handling real day-to-day volumes of transactions conveniently and securely. However, it does allow the users a chance to try on a new application before jumping into the full-fledged commitment. Several companies have used PC-based systems to try out their real needs (versus wants and whims) in MRP II, CAD, and financial systems. The PC can be written off as a cost of investigation (a week of consulting costs more!) and later transferred to a needy department.

In a similar vein such systems have proven invaluable for meeting the training needs of manufacturers. IBM uses a PC-based MRP II system to train its manufacturing people in the many activities of planning, control, inventory decisions, interrelated demands, and simulations of the plant environment. Each student gets to manage his own firm in the PC for several days. This overview of the manufacturing universe within the cozy (and harmless) confines of a PC database better prepares them to work with complexities of mainframe systems at their plants. More will be said of this in Chapter 9.

DEALING WITH SOFTWARE SUPPLIERS

Here is another area where the MIS folks can be a real help. They have been dealing with software vendors for years. Questions about licensing arrangements, source code availability, and concealed costs are well known to most computer professionals.

It is wise to develop some relationship with the local management of the software firm. Recognize that they face economic pressures just as we do. They must amortize the developmental costs of their systems over as large a base as possible while containing support costs. Understanding this helps to build bridges of reasonableness between your firm and theirs. When such understanding exists, they can be of great help in the crunch.[5]

Horst Paul, a Houston-based consultant who has specialized in helping manufacturers install microcomputer applications for the last four years or so, notes that many bargains are available for the deft bargain hunter.[6] For example, many companies will offer special prices for the first few modules of a system. One vendor ran a $99.95 special for the first two modules which normally cost $6,000. Discounts by the thousands are available for buying the hardware and software together from some vendors. For multiple units at one site or within one company there is a myriad of schemes for discounting.

WRITING APPLICATIONS INSTEAD OF BUYING

Some of us recall the classic image of the cowboy on the range who rolled his own cigarettes. There is still something quite American in the notion of individual uniqueness. This occasionally tempts ambitious microcomputer users unwisely to boldly go where no systems analyst has ever gone

---

[5] George J. Miller, "Software Selection: One More Time!" *1985 APICS Conference Proceedings*, p. 703ff.

[6] Horst J. Paul, "'Micro' MRP II User Audit Results: Is It Working?" *1986 APICS Conference Proceedings*, p. 157.

before. It is never wise to take up the tedious and sticky business of programming new systems without a thorough evaluation of what is already available (possibly within the firm).

The phrase "writing applications" is susceptible of many interpretations. There are many degrees of software creation. In a sense the user of a spreadsheet is creating new applications constantly, but these are more appropriately called templates and are much more easily managed. All too frequently, though, they are not well documented nor clear in their logic.

The user of one of the database managers has waded even further into the unsounded waters of software creation. Systems like SMART can actually create a bevy of programs to process the data in the user-defined databases. There are also "environmental" systems such as INGRESS™, Parameter Driven Systems (PDS), and others that permit the development of databases and data-entry screens and the updating of programs without extensive knowledge of the underlying programming techniques. This is why some firms restrict the design of new databases and processing programs to the MIS experts.

Beyond these mild examples are the hobbyist/semipros who develop applications in BASIC for their individual use. Unless disciplined by traditional system methods of design, security, user documentation, and maintenance, such applications rarely outlive the inventor's tenancy in his current position. The next occupant of the position is not usually able to understand the entry of data, processing, and modification of the application and, in the vast majority of cases, discards the program.

The real pros (within and without the firm) program in a veritable alphabet soup of languages such as PASCAL, Turbo-PASCAL, C, CO-BOL, and assembly languages for exotic speedsters. This is an arena for the full-time DP professional and, beyond the interesting case study offered below, is thankfully left outside the scope of this book.

CASE STUDY: MICROS PROVIDING A STRATEGIC COMPETITIVE EDGE IN A GROWING NICHE MARKET—THE MONOTYPE CORPORATION, PLC

Earlier we discussed the possibility of microcomputer systems offering strategic competitive advantage to a company. The Monotype Corporation, operating in Surrey, England, developed a most significant competitive capability in a system linking a network of microcomputers with their mainframe.

In years past Monotype was engaged in the manufacturing of hot metal printing presses, which were sold to thousands of third parties throughout the United Kingdom and overseas. During this period they developed an expertise in developing their own type fonts to be used on this device. "Font" might be defined as the particular style and representation of the letters, numbers, and other symbols of a printed publication. These type fonts included a vast number of specialized characters required by their clients.

In recent years, though, the business of hot metal printing has been completely superseded by the technology of laser-based phototypesetting. To break into this vital new market the Monotype Corporation developed its own system, the Monotype Lasercomp. To give this system a strongly competitive posture, it is offered with a remarkably broad complement of type fonts that are developed internally by the same experts who were designing the hot metal fonts of the past. It is widely felt by experts in this business that Monotype is at the very forefront in the field of font development.

In developing a font capability for their own laser typesetting systems, they have discovered that this capability is of great interest to others in the business of font design and implementation. Monotype captures fonts optically through charge-coupled scanning cameras and loads them in a raster-graphic method onto Unisys B25 micros for modification and refinement. This means that each character of a font is actually manipulated as a series of dots filled into a large matrix. This process might be compared to filling in the squares of graph paper to create, in a very large perspective, the actual character that is desired.

As the font is refined and perfected letter by patient letter, it is stored on the mainframe system. These characters can then be retrieved, modified, and retransmitted to the mainframe system. These can also be printed out for comparison by the type font designers and editors as well as for the client's approval. When the desired copy of the font is finished, the font can be sent to the customer on magnetic tape or on diskettes, or—as is increasingly the case—it can be permanently stored in a small silicon integrated circuit called a PROM (programmable read only memory).

These PROM chips can then be used in laser printers, for example, allowing them to print these different characters. They can also be used by television stations for the creation of subtitles on the TV screen. As well, the Videotex system (in wide use in Europe) uses these. Because of the widely recognized expertise in this market, Monotype has been approached by a number of groups that have special type requirements. For example, if a client desires a modified Cyrillic script, they can call up one of their existing Cyrillic scripts, modify it as desired by the client, and then send it to the client in any of the forms mentioned above.

They also have a very significant capability in Arabic characters and many other specialized character sets. Arabic offers a peculiar challenge in that many of the characters have four distinct forms—dependent on whether the character is alone in the text or preceded, followed, or surrounded by other characters. Thus, each such character requires four unique forms.

For a very close look at the actual type fonts after they have been created, Monotype employs 2,000 line screen monitors that are actually attached to the microcomputers. Of the 40 total microcomputers that Monotype has, about 15 are actually involved in the font editing. The others are employed in somewhat more traditional aspects of office automation including word processing, spreadsheets, and so forth. Of course, all can be used as terminals on the mainframe system.

Security is crucial to the competitive edge at this company. Here again they have taken the basic tools offered by the vendor and moved beyond into their custom requirements. They have a sophisticated series of passwords unique to each of the workstations. To further strengthen security, all of the entries into the system and all transmission of the fonts back and forth are logged into the system for later reference.

Monotype is also involved in the somewhat more sophisticated work of digitizing particular images. A charged coupled scanning camera can actually be coupled to the micro which allows the capturing of any photographic image. For example, logos, letterheads, or a likeness of the general manager can be digitized and then edited.

This combination of Old World craftsmanship and clever adaptation of microcomputer technology clearly has placed Monotype Corporation at the vanguard of this particular business. It also serves as a very interesting illustration of the strategic use of microcomputers. This has given them a capability in their industry that makes them unique—a competitive superiority that separates them from their peers.[7]

CONCLUSION

The various methods and concepts of this chapter cannot be regarded in isolation from the preceding chapters. The considerations of value in se-

---

[7] SOURCE: MONOTYPE Corporation, Mr. David Bridle, Honeycrock Lane, Salfords, Red Hill, Surrey, United Kingdom, RH15JP.

lecting software must be weighed in the scales of expandability, integration into networks, sound cost/benefit ratios, and fitness for managing the business of manufacturing. Whether the demands of the firm call for applications as unique or sophisticated as that of Monotype or as simple as those of the small job shop with one bookkeeper, these principles remain in force.

NOTA BENE

Only as these overlapping goals are simultaneously weighed, can the wisest decisions regarding the acquisition or development of microcomputer solutions be made.

The next two chapters explore the issues of integrating the micros into useful networks and those of training and supporting the growing cadre of micro cogitators. Part Four then addresses the demands of and solutions available for particular departmental applications.

CHAPTER SEVEN

Networking and Integrating Microcomputers

A PLAY IN ONE ACT

The character: You—ambitious middle manager for The Acme Manufacturing Megalith.

The scene: A steamy office at 6:35 on a summer Thursday afternoon. (In the background cheers are faintly rising from Fenway Park. Ironically, the unused tickets to today's game lie crumpled on the floor between your tie and your discarded shoes).

The action: You are frantically typing in the numbers from a report which was generated on the corporate mainframe. You are building an action plan for your product group using an electronic spreadsheet on your trusty micro. Tomorrow morning at 8:30 this plan must be presented to the boss. With the startling clarity of the sun shining after a summer rain, the question grips you:

You: Why can't the stupid mainframe be connected to this micro and download all of this information so that I would not need to retype a report that *was* in a computer into another computer? Then I could spend my valuable managerial time doing the analysis that is made possible by such micro tools as the data bases, the spreadsheets, and so on—not to mention cheering the Red Sox!

Sound effects: A cheer rises from Fenway, beyond the open window, as the curtain falls.

NETWORKING AND THE FUTURE OF MICROS

Why isn't the micro connected to the mainframe where the data is? Why can't the micros talk to each other? Why can't we get the micro on-line to the information service that has the needed data?

The questions are being asked with increasing frequency. Of the roughly 10 million PCs currently in use, less than 1 in 10 is connected either to other micros or to the mainframe of the organization. By 1990 it is expected that there will be at least 20 million PCs installed—possibly 30 million, say the optimists. About 40 percent of those are predicted to be connected to other micros. Furthermore, most of these networked micros will be linked together into mainframe networks.

This means that within the same number of years from the introduction of the IBM Personal Computer until the present, there will be as many networked micros as there are total micros today. The needs for better decision support systems, more efficient offices, and more productive people demand this development. This chapter introduces the general concepts and issues of this business of micro networking.

A study of data processing decision makers conducted in England in 1985 concluded that the *real growth market* was going to be in the arena of PCs and PC networking. PCs are expected to vastly eclipse the growth rates of both minicomputers and mainframes over the same period of time. Consider just the expected purchased-equipment budgets for the next two years. The budgeted purchases for traditional dumb terminals will decline, and the budgeted expenditures for standalone PCs (and PCs that are running terminal software) will continue to increase.

One Florida shipbuilder ordered a mainframe with 54 complete micro workstations and *no other terminals*! He commented, "They don't cost that much more compared to the savings generated by the mainframe systems, and besides, once you've used the micro [running Microsoft Multiplan and word processing], how could you settle for just a terminal?"

In Chapter 5 we saw this same trend at the Allegheny International Corporation. PCs—used both as terminals and as personal computers— had rapidly displaced the use of terminals in connection with the mainframe operations. We also saw how quickly the users were able to work effectively between the two different environments. This was in part due to the strongly supportive MIS organization, good documentation, practice in building flexible prototypes, and familiarity with terminal operations and procedures.

Good training and good people-oriented systems—the basics don't change. The details do change, though, as micros grow into networks.

THE IMPORTANCE OF MANAGING NETWORKS

Recalling the earlier description of the four phases of personal computer implementation, we remember that most firms begin with experimental

FIGURE 7–1   Sharing a Disk and Printer

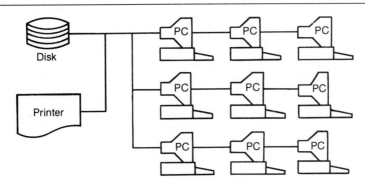

use and then move to increasingly widespread individual use. Therefore, it is ever more important for companies to shape their early micro planning with an eye toward the departmental and organizational phases. The early steps in linking PCs together may be as simple as sharing the same hard disk and printer (as in Figure 7–1).

This allows the users to trade files back and forth *without* having to hand carry the diskette to the next desk. It also economizes on the use of the hard disk and the printer. Why have one for every user in the department, if one of each can meet the whole need? This requires relatively simple hardware and software. As users need to share files and databases simultaneously (as in the case of several PC users drawing upon the inventory database), more sophisticated software is necessary to maintain the integrity of the network and the data.

As we will discuss later, a network that spans a corporation (from coast to valley, from micro to mini to mainframe) involves a level of sophistication in networking software and hardware that is right at the current edge of technology. Some suppliers of PCs have proven more effective than others in developing the networks necessary to organize these PCs into such a cohesive network. It is also important to recognize that the general term *cohesive network* is susceptible to many definitions.

In the course of this chapter we are going to explore different varieties of networks. We will consider the simple use of terminal emulation on to a mainframe. We also will investigate a sophisticated multilayered network that permits a wide range of information sharing:

Within a department.
Among different departments.

With the mainframe.
With public data networks (PDNs).
With the services that are offered by these PDNs.

One observer estimates that about half of all the processing power in the world is currently housed in personal computers. This may be a year or two premature, but it certainly behooves us to manage this DP resource wisely. We would never willingly tolerate duplication, waste, ineffectiveness, and inaccuracies in our mainframe systems. Is it not just as wise to make sure that we develop networking policies that safeguard against these failings in the other half of our processing resource—our microcomputers?

WHAT TYPES OF ACTIVITIES BENEFIT MOST FROM PC NETWORKING?

The office worker of the future may well snicker at the concept of the written memo and the game of "phone tag"—that phrase may not even have meaning in the dictionaries published in the next century. We can hope!

Let's look in on the capabilities of a modern electronic mail-filing-retrieval system as already practiced by a number of corporations.

A department manager needs to meet with the managers of two other departments. He sits at the PC and enters the attendees, duration, and purpose of the meeting: "Tom Smith, Bill Jones, tab, tab, tab, 2 hours, tab, review February's forecast." Five seconds later, the computer responds that there are four blocks of time in the next two weeks where that much time is available for the three of them. He selects the first block (Tuesday, January 12, from 3 to 5) and sends a message to the other two managers: "I'd like to meet on the subject of the new products coming out for the spring season and their impact on February's forecast." He might include a brief agenda, mention one or two products associated with the agenda, and then sign off. (Note the advantage over phone tag—it is estimated by one researcher that only about one third of all calls actually make contact with the individual desired. The other two thirds fall off the edge of the earth.)

As the other two managers sign on after lunch, they see that a new meeting has been arranged; its recent inclusion is indicated by the * placed after it. They acknowledge the message. They might even send back a response if they have any ideas to be shared. The purchasing manager decides to include two of his staff members. Their calendars are clear; he sends them a note that they have also been scheduled for the meeting.

He also feels it wise to talk over one or two ideas that have been on the back burner as new products. He takes the rough notes now on the screen, copies them into a document for one of his vendors, sends that document into a public mailbox where the vendor will pick it up in the next hour or two. (Remember that a public mailbox is available through a PDN via phone lines. Anyone can transmit a message to your mailbox, but only you can retrieve it on your screen.)

The purchasing manager creates another memo that will be distributed to related committees about the development cycle for the new projects. This done, all of the information relative to this particular product line is then put together in a file where it can be retrieved at any time by the date, by the name of the author, by the names of the products themselves, or by several other generic indexes which are actually developed by the filing system itself.

Our original department manager then turns to a second product idea, one which has just completed development. He sends out a notification of the product along with some product details which he copies over from the original product specification document. Next he creates a memo for distribution to a list titled, "New Product Update." His PC then automatically sends that particular memorandum to the 18 managers (including his own manager), who have asked to be copied in on all new product releases. All these managers now have waiting in their electronic mailboxes this notification of the new item.

This particular specification was actually developed in conjunction with the design engineering team in the engineering part of the plant. That same team operating with PCs not only went through the original product design but also developed a set of specifications on a PC which, through program logic controllers, translated the engineering specifications into detailed machining requirements. This information was then downloaded into an NC lathe and actually drove the process through which the different parts were created to eventually complete this product.

An updated copy of the specifications had also been sent to the loading dock since several new part numbers have been approved and the purchasing department has issued blanket orders for these items. The PC at the loading dock has printed out receipt tickets. As these purchased items are received, the loading dock will be aware of the new purchase numbers preventing any delay to their entry into the plant.

The service organization is also affected by the change in the spare parts needed for the repair of these items as they go out into the market. Therefore, a slightly reformatted version of the specifications has been distributed to a "bulletin board" (an electronic mailbox in the PDN that many users can open), which is accessible by all of the dealers that carry this product line.

The purchasing department, recognizing a need to revise purchasing plans for several of the new parts, has sent a notification to the six vendors involved of the changes in specifications. As the vendors take a look at their individual mailboxes they can discover the new specifications and can actually make their bids through the mailbox of the buyer.

FUTURE IDEAL OR CURRENT REQUIREMENT?

All of the preceding represent technology that is already in place and being practiced by some manufacturers today. Imagine suggesting to the micro users of such a corporation the removal of the PC network in order to return to the use of telephones, memos, blueprints, USPS, and so forth. It would be tantamount to telling the more traditional office workers that the telephones were being replaced by pneumatic tubes and mailboys for distribution of information.

If the benefits are so compelling, why isn't there more of an outcry to implement the systems of PC networks depicted above. Part of the reason is the limited offerings by some system suppliers. More of the reason is the widespread ignorance regarding the systems that are available and the cost associated with them and a bit of incredulity relative to the benefits which may be derived from such a system. The believing, it seems, is in the seeing and not vice versa.

MICROCOMPUTERS AS PRECURSORS, COMPONENTS, AND FACILITATORS OF COMPUTER-INTEGRATED MANUFACTURING

In "Move over Mainframe: Make Way for the Micro," Shindelman and Utzig write:

> Microcomputers will be linked together and with mainframe computers to form integrated information networks. They will serve as the CIM workstation, perform much of the daily processing, and provide users with the abil-

ity to access and analyze information stored in private and corporate databases. Mainframe computers will be limited to processing high-volume transactions, maintaining the corporate database, and monitoring the network.[1]

Shindelman goes on to present a most captivating view of the evolution of the microcomputer as the principal medium, or milieu, through which the realization of computer-integrated manufacturing (CIM) can be accomplished. He says that the networking is simple enough, that the PCs are flexible enough, and that they are really the only devices that can be expected to link all of the different activities of factory automation together.

It is a rather interesting and possibly farsighted hypothesis and one whose resolution will have to remain outside the scope of this particular book. I know of one plant doing nearly all its computer-integrated manufacturing and office automation functions on microcomputers. Certainly, for many smaller manufacturers the micros offer the only affordable road to such functionality.

HOW IS IT DONE?

The intent of the next few pages is to give the esteemed Reader an overview of the techniques behind the already-named possibilities, to introduce him or her to some of the vocabulary involved, and to explain some of the alternatives as they relate to manufacturers.

The medium of exchange in international markets is the dollar or the yen. The medium of exchange in this economy of personal computers is most often the local area network (LAN). The explanation is simple. LANs have the opportunity to connect a variety of different PCs. They can operate at very high speeds relative to many data communication links, and they provide the flexibility necessary for the PCs to communicate to the many different types of information and control devices that arise in the manufacturing arena.

There are essentially four dimensions in which we might analyze the networking of PCs:

Topology—actual physical arrangement of the network.
Access—signaling method.

---

[1] Lester S. Shindelman and Carter C. Utzig, "Move over Mainframe: Make Way for the Micro," *1986 APICS Conference Proceedings*, p. 467.

FIGURE 7-2 Star Topology

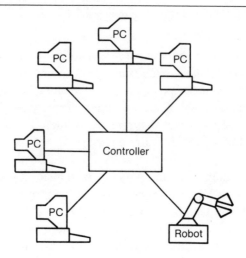

Hardware—cable upon which the transmission occurs.
Degree of integration—functionality offered to network users.

Topology

Essentially three topologies are in widespread use today, according to Shindelman. The star configuration relies on a central processor that routes messages to the outlying nodes. This is depicted in Figure 7–2. The cable to each one of the personal computer stations has to go all the way from the central node to the individual PC. This means that if a large number of PCs existed on a factory floor, cable would have to be run from every single PC all the way to the central controlling node. If a message were to be transferred from one PC to another on the factory floor, it would actually travel from the PC back to the central node and then be sent back out to the next PC.

This can involve a great deal of cable in the plant. The network under this topology is also critically dependent on the central processor. If that goes down, then the entire network is down. While this configuration may be suitable for some office environments, it seems highly unlikely that this is going to prove widely acceptable in the manufacturing arena.

Star networks, by the way, are most frequently used in digital telephone exchange systems, although increasingly the telephone system is going to be the network system. Another point of consideration in the development of PC networks deserves a NOTA BENE:

FIGURE 7–3 Ring Topology

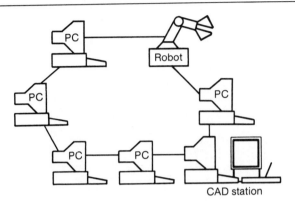

CAD station

NOTA BENE

Be sure that the needs of the micro network are compared to voice/phone requirements. Increasingly, the voice and data will become the same network.

The next configuration is the ring configuration, depicted in Figure 7–3. It offers a good distributed control scheme because the message travels through the ring from one PC to the next. The ring is not dependent on a central processor. However, if one element of the ring fails, then the ring is broken—the circuit is no longer complete. This means that all of the members on the ring are then disabled.

Typically, the ring technology is limited to relatively small clusters of terminals because of the extensive need for wiring. By the way, it should be noted that ring and loop do not mean quite the same thing. The loop technology implies the use of a master controller computer of some sort in the loop which serves all of the devices attached to it. In this way, it is directly akin to the star system in that the failure of the master controller paralyzes the entire loop. The ring topology implies a distributed intelligence with all of the attached devices enjoying equal status. Here again, though, the failure of one device does disable the entire ring.

The third type of network topology is the bus configuration (Figure 7–4). This bus configuration is the most promising for manufacturing environments. Cable can be run throughout the plant with terminal/PC plugs every foot if desired. It allows PCs and other devices to plug in at will. Furthermore, this topology permits distributed control of the network,

FIGURE 7–4   Bus Topology

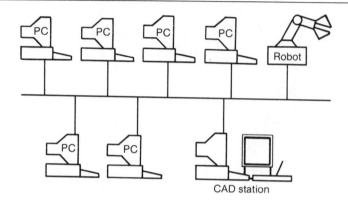

CAD station

meaning the network can actually be controlled by any one of the PCs that is suitably equipped to drive it. It also allows communication from one PC to the next. Expansion is extremely easy—we are not breaking the ring to introduce a new item nor running a lengthy cable to the central node as is the case with the star LANs. Importantly, a single node failure does not disable the entire network. This type of plug-in network has been adopted by many manufacturers.

Access Protocol and Signaling Considerations

An entire terminology has sprung up to describe the different activities necessary to control the readiness of terminals to send a message out, the readiness of others to receive it, and the protocol (detailed procedures and rules of conduct) through which they will talk to each other. We will not get deeply into this area, but will offer a generalized description of the issues.

The International Standards Organization (ISO) has developed what is called the open systems interconnection reference model (OSI). This model has decomposed the task of network control in general—not just in factory situations but in the entire world of data communications—into seven layers of activity. These layers are illustrated in Figure 7–5. The Reader is not required to memorize all of the details of this particular architecture. However, it is important to recognize that for two systems—PCs or robots or coffeemakers—to communicate with each other, they must agree on all seven layers. In effect, they must be mutually compati-

---

FIGURE 7–5   The ISO-OSI Reference Model

Application	"Here's the inventory inquiry!"
Presentation	"What size screen does this message fit?"
Session	"Let's log onto the inventory program."
Transport	"Mainframe message coming at you! Duck!"
Network	"Who's on this line anyway?"
Line	"With this ring, we're going steady."
Physical	"OK, I want five volts, 9600 baud, sync . . ."

---

ble (fluent) at every layer. If any layer is unrecognized by the receiving system, no communication takes place. It is not simply enough, for example, for two systems to have the same physical characteristics in the network or for two systems to share the same data encoding scheme. Total agreement or no talking! This indicates the challenges involved in establishing networks in this arena. In Figure 7–5 the various functions of each layer are lightly suggested by the hypothetical dialog at each level. Every layer in the sending system talks to the same layer in the receiving system. This is analogous to communications between two businesses— I talk to you; my staff talks to your staff; my boss talks to your boss. The dialog between the systems is best understood from the bottom to the top.

IBM has supported the ISO-OSI model. However, because of the large number of IBM products remaining in the field (notably, many of their minicomputers) that are not compatible with this, IBM continues more strongly to support its own SNA, or Systems Network Architecture model. Its six layers are hauntingly reminiscent of ISO-OSI. Nonetheless, IBM's vast preponderance in the field has clouded the issue of standardization. SNA must be reckoned with as a de facto standard in many quarters. This dual standard has caused only a limited resolution of the difficulties of standardization in data communications. Right now dozens of standards exist, and many efforts are being made to settle this down into one clear architecture built around the ISO-OSI model.

General Motors has been making a noteworthy effort in the last two years to develop a standardization of networking protocol that supports the OSI reference model and conforms to a number of standards set by the International Electronic and Electrical Engineering Society (IEEE). It is called the Manufacturing Automation Protocol or MAP for short. Although it has been widely acclaimed and a large number of computer vendors are expending millions to develop a capability in MAP, only a modest number of actual installations have been reported so far.

Rather expensive controlling computers are necessary to operate these networks which engender some of the same limitations as with the Star networks. Indeed, among plant managers (even in GM) there has appeared some resistance to the complexity and systems support required to become genuinely operational in a MAP environment. This resistance notwithstanding, we will see considerable activity in MAP, especially among GM suppliers.

All these efforts toward standardization are aimed in the direction of allowing different types of systems to communicate with each other. It is expected that the MAP systems can accommodate not only personal computers but also mainframes, minicomputers, robots, a wide variety of terminals, and other such devices.

Hardware

The communication link also depends, of course, upon there being a channel through which the information can run from PC to PC. Over and above all the aforementioned issues, there has to be some sort of electrical connection. Essentially three types of hardware are available for this purpose: the twisted wire pair, coaxial cable, and optical fibers.

The *twisted wire pair* was the most common in years past. It is relatively simple to run and very inexpensive. One problem arises, though, in that the signal is actually traveling through a wire that is insulated but unprotected from electrical interference. In one particularly notable case twisted wire pairs had been installed throughout the factory. During an apparent brownout in the installer's head, one twisted pair was installed only inches away from an 18,000 volt AC feed to a substation of the factory. The enormous energy of this electrical field, expanding and contracting 60 times per second, induced an electrical field in the twisted wire pair of more than 600 volts. This violent voltage surge in the communications cables actually fried several PCs before the culprit was detected.

More factories will install *coaxial cable* instead. In a coaxial cable, the signal is actually carried on an internal wire that is completely shielded by a grounded covering. This, to a great degree, protects the transmission signal from the vagaries of electrical noise that is frequent in most factories. In fact, twisted pairs are increasingly being shielded as well.

Optical fibers offer great promise for the more exotic networks of the future. They can transmit large volumes of data at very high speeds and with very low error rates. They are virtually immune to electrical noise since the signal is a beam of light. However, the technology is just awakening and remains very expensive. Therefore, coaxial cable will most likely remain the system of choice for the next several years. The broadest experience has tended to support the suitability of coaxial cable and bus type networks, allowing simple plug-in connections from location to location along the factory floor or in the office.

Another disadvantage of the optical fibers, or fiber optic system, is that currently there are no T-style connectors for branching off into a bus network. They actually have to be received by a device and then retransmitted. There is no simple device that can, in effect, "T" into the beam of light moving through the optical fiber.

Degree of Integration between Mainframe and Micro or Micro to Micro

The fourth dimension in the establishment of PC networks has to do with the degree and flexibility of integration allowed by the software that performs the logical linking of the networks. We will consider three different tiers of current integration strategies (and describe typical sessions at each one of these). I confine these examples to software I have used personally to temper the discussion with the grit of realism. Then I'll speculate a bit and suggest what the future may hold.

Several dozen offerings are currently available for the micro mainframe link, ranging all the way from $195 to $40,000, and some lists of such items may be found among the sources listed in Part Five.

The simplest and typically first type of PC link merely allows the PC to emulate a terminal. The IBM Personal Computer, for example, can be made to emulate a 3270 terminal. DEC micros can emulate VT100 terminals. Unisys B25s can emulate MT985 terminals, and so on. In such a mode, the usual terminal functions can be performed in conjunction with the mainframe.

Consider a mainframe system whose application software includes a stock inquiry. The micro under terminal emulation can then be used as a dumb terminal making the stock inquiry into the mainframe. It is also possible to type in a new inventory part number, to update balances, or to perform any of the other functions that would be provided by a terminal on-line to the mainframe, but no further communication features are provided.

In the second tier of the mainframe integration, other mainframe capabilities are accessible to the terminal. At this level we not only can conduct a typical terminal session with the mainframe, but it is possible to open up several terminal sessions with the mainframe. One product allows four mainframe sessions to be run on the PC, each one of which acts as its own terminal session. For example, we might do a stock inquiry in the top window of the PC screen. In the second window of the PC screen we might be writing a COBOL program to be compiled and run on the mainframe. The third window of the microcomputer might include a report request that we are typing into the mainframe to be printed at another time, and the fourth window on the PC may refer to a local PC program such as a spreadsheet that has nothing to do with the mainframe. The user can move back and forth among these applications continuously.

At this level of integration a bit more sophistication is available. In this particular package it is also possible to use the resources of the mainframe as an extension of the personal computer. This can refer to taking a file from the microcomputer and storing it on the mainframe or vice versa. In effect, the mainframe can be used as a massive extension of the storage capabilities of the micro. In similar fashion the mainframe printers can be enlisted to perform the printing tasks of the micro; files can also be shared from micro to micro by being passed through the mainframe. We might think of this as sharing the resources of the mainframe among the entire micro user community.

The third layer of integration involves the specific development of application tools (in the micros *and* the mainframes of the network) that support this interactive link. Under this type of integration the software resources of the mainframe are made more fully available to the software resources of the microcomputer.

An example of a session might run like this: The microcomputer user starts by opening one of these interactive sessions (in one of the windows) as a terminal. This particular terminal application would call up a database inquiry program in the mainframe. This database inquiry allows freely formatted inquiries performed against, for example, the inventory information. In this case we might say, "Find all the part numbers that have the word *Moped* in them, that are purchased from this particular group of vendors, and that the annual demand for which is greater than $25,000."

Typical mainframe database inquiry tools can quickly interpret this command, scan the entire database, and return a table of this particular information for all of the items that meet these multiple criteria. This table can then be extracted into a spreadsheet such as 1−2−3 from Lotus or

Microsoft Multiplan which could then be analyzed in another window of the micro by flipping to that window. It is now possible to perform the types of flexible inquiries that might be useful to a purchasing manager seeking a discount, to an engineer performing value analysis on particular part numbers, or to an inventory planner considering a better scheme for consolidating orders for the plant.

It is also possible to take the information that has been developed from the mainframe and extract it into databases on the micro, allowing the micro to manipulate it and to develop cost models, projections, and simulations. The micro user could also take an overall look at the business strategic plan, for example, by consolidating data from a number of financial, production, and marketing databases maintained on the mainframe. It is clear from this example that this third level of integration offers great possibilities for organizing the data, verifying data consistency, and eliminating redundancy. Consider just the auditing value of such inquiry tools!

Moreover, consider the need of every manufacturer to develop clear decision-driving analyses that meld the various operational and planning systems of the corporation into a clear, cohesive look at the overall directions, trends, tendencies, balances, and trade-offs among the major operating units of the company. This type of information is enormously useful to senior management and can be a great asset to members of middle management in terms of assessing a clear corporate view of the major impact of different design decisions, of marketing decisions, operational decisions, and so forth.

Some of the examples which will be explored in Chapter 9 ("Strategic Business Planning") will draw upon this fully integrated relationship between the mainframe databases and resources and the microcomputer resources. This link assists the user in developing the clearest picture of what the company is doing, where its strengths are, where its weaknesses are, what is its overall performance, and what are the areas of improvement needed to capitalize on the resources deployed.

IMPLEMENTING NETWORKS

To decide how best to implement networks and to secure the network advantages described here, it is first important to recognize, as mentioned before, that these decisions need to have been made much earlier on. As we are initially getting involved with the business of selecting and implementing our PCs, we need to think through the following: what types of *data*, what types of *applications*, what types of *users* do we have? Where are the great advantages in sharing this data among the different users? Which users do we expect to eventually link together into networks, both departmental and organizationwide? What types of hardware, software, and databases will be needed? What types of support will be needed on the mainframe to integrate all of this?

In many cases the mainframe load has not tended to go down, as might be expected, but rather, the mainframe load has tended to remain about the same or possibly even creep up in supporting the PCs even though much more processing is being done at the point of the PCs themselves. Especially, as fully integrated software is required, the mainframe load shifts from sorting, reporting, and cavorting with the data to maintaining the database, processing transactions, and loading information into the micros. It will be important to select appropriate topologies, hardware, access methods, and protocols. Of course, it will be necessary to organize centralized training and a support facility as is described in the next chapter.

The phases involved in the implementation of networks are generally identical to the phases for the implementation of micros described in Chapter 5. The detail steps are comparable: defining the needs, selecting appropriate hardware, purchasing strategies, putting into place sound policy statements, organizing the support network, coordinating with the MIS group, and then implementing the strategies in a phased approach.

Daryl Lanvater offers some useful advice to the implementors of any system—mainframe or micro.[2] It could be considered the triple-threat approach to success in any implementation.

1. Start small. Start with an application that is easily defined. Electronic mail and/or file transfer among departments may serve this purpose. Start with a small and easily definable task.

2. Stack the deck in your favor. Find an application with a nice payback ratio, that appears very manageable, and has had success in other companies. Choose a pilot project that has the visibility necessary to broadcast the success after you are complete.

3. Next, build on the success of some of the earlier network installations. As you derive some success, publicize it. Put out a newsletter. Let the users know about it. Get some excitement in the group and then start

[2] Daryl Lanvater, presentation with R. Dave Garwood, "How to Gain a Competitive Edge That Is Second to None," APICS Conference, 1986.

developing some of the more sophisticated applications necessary to realize all of the potential of the network.

CASE STUDY—BOEING COMPANY

In times past there had been a well-defined line between office automation and data processing at the Boeing Company. The integration that has come about in recent years has emerged largely through the widespread use of PCs. These micros have received very strong emphasis all the way through senior management. The corporate information retrieval system obviously helps by putting micros on corporate executives' desktops. It provides access to internal as well as external news sources and offers the operational data, status information, manpower information, personnel records, electronic telephone directories, electronic messaging capabilities, and much more.

Currently, Boeing Company has five major data centers all administered by Boeing Computer Services, a company which works both for Boeing and for hundreds of other companies. Their primary client, Boeing itself, has more than 5,400 PCs, hundreds of minicomputers, and approximately 40,000 software packages. As these resources are combined, they can be enormously effective in managing the company.[3]

Boeing's User-Derived Policy Standards

A key to the successful implementation of all of these microcomputers was a corporate information system standard that brought a focused, integrated approach to the computing activities—The Boeing Network Architecture or BNA. One of the key ingredients of the success of this program is that the standard was developed by the users in cooperation with the computer services people. It has limited the number of vendors through tough vendor screening processes and developed a president-to-president line of communication with strategically selected key vendors to assure rapid response to hardware and software problems.

Before doing business with one of these companies, Boeing asks for four basic commitments from the suppliers of hardware and software. They must provide a published network architecture, a briefing on their products and the direction of those products, an implementation of IBM

---

[3] Richard Metz, "Boeing's PC Practices," *Datamation*, January 15, 1986, p. 85ff.

SNA, and a long-term plan to adapt the International Standards Organization OSI Reference Model.

Boeing is using the MAP protocol of General Motors. They have specifically adopted the Technical and Office Protocol (TOP) of MAP for developing the networks. They are also operating at the departmental levels for exchanging information through the TOP protocol and are also operating at the level of organizationwide distribution of information among the many mainframes and minicomputers. The PCs also support the 3270 Terminal emulation with the 3270 Terminal Emulation Board and the standard software package that supports this. They are allowed to get involved in programming in BASIC, COBOL, Pascal, C, and Fortran, with only two or three compilers approved for each language in order to keep the language idiosyncrasies to a minimum.

One of their earliest applications was data entry. A second early application was the development of local databases among the different departments. Data that is needed throughout the organization is retained on the host computers although they are developing links for extracting portions of this information and downloading it into PCs.

Data processing is performed in a highly distributed fashion. Boeing uses the Document Content Architecture (DCA) translator, for the universal communicator of the different documents. This is a standard form of word processed document that can be used by many different word processing packages.

Other important PC applications include project management, mathematical and statistical analysis, and computer-based training (which will be discussed more in the next chapter). The regulated diversity of applications plus the standards that allows them to be supported, maintained, and integrated goes a long way toward explaining the success which Boeing has enjoyed in their operations.

One of the cornerstones of their personal computer program is their personal computer store concept.

> The store provides all of the services that a first-rate computer store would and integrates them into the corporate environment. It is responsible for system installation, maintenance, inventory configuration control. The standard PCs and peripherals are stocked in a central staging area; demonstration centers at each of the major factory sites provide users with hands-on demonstrations of standard hardware and software. Field representatives provide on-site services and consultation.[4]

---

[4] Ibid.

The store has developed a 350-page personal computing catalog that makes it easier for the users to select from the many applications. Printed twice a year, this catalog lists all the recommended hardware and software products and includes available training items. They also developed a 30-page "Getting Started on the PC" manual which covers such topics as PC installation, basic guidelines, how to obtain technical assistance, and how to order supplies.

The PC procurement organization is reviewing the financial health and integrity of the vendors in question, comparing their network standards to the Boeing Network Architecture and evaluating the different areas of data access, data integrity, backup and recovery, vendor copyright protection, and related issues.

CONCLUSION

The number of new PCs at Boeing was doubling every year. The number of software packages was quadrupling! The only solution was a systematic definition of policies and a strong support arm in Boeing Computer Services. This combination led to skillful selection of the PCs involved, clear hardware and software standards, widespread training, and the discipline to wisely manage the use of the network.

Given this combination of management leadership, sound training, and discipline, Boeing illustrates the significant gains in daily efficiency that are available through the networking of micros.

Learning to Use the System

Steve Jobs founded Apple Computer, served as its chief executive officer, made many millions of dollars, and retired at the zenith of his career
in his first third of a century. Now he spends his leisure hours contemplat-
ing an interesting way to spend the next third.

He philosophizes that the microcomputer becomes a "personal computer" to its user. A one-to-one personal relationship seems to emerge
that gives the user a feeling of dominion, mastery, independence, and
power that seems unusual if not mystical, to the nonuser or the infrequent
user. Personal computers, Jobs continues, should be seen as tools which
amplify the natural capabilities of the human mind.[1]

The greatest gains in productivity rarely come from simply mechaniz-
ing the routine tasks of the workplace. The need is to rethink these tasks.
In the illustration about Karl Schmidt, the production planner (in Chapter
1), we discovered that it was not just the automatic tabulation of down totals and cross-footing of columns that allowed Karl to be more productive
in the production planning of the Ford chassis and axle plants. The key
was that he could formulate many plans in a very short time period. He
could also vary the elements of these plans to do the "what if" type of
thinking that enabled him to discover "inspired" solutions among the
many possibilities for scheduling these plants. It is precisely this increase
in flexibility and this change in orientation that achieve the great benefits
in microcomputers.

NOTA BENE

Real training is not just the impartation of operational skill. It allows and impels
the learner to see his task and himself in a new light. Unless this root change in
thinking occurs, old thought patterns reassert themselves, and the great benefit
of training is forfeited.

---

[1] Dimitris N. Chorafas, *Office Automation, The Productivity Challenge* (Englewood
Cliffs, N.J.: Prentice-Hall, 1982), p. 86.

As we review the training needs, it is important to recognize the several dimensions of training—the who, the what, and the how.

WHO NEEDS TO BE TRAINED?

First, there are the *executives* of the company who will need some training in the new corporate involvement with microcomputers. This is critical for two reasons. First, they need to support and manage the selection and implementation of the systems; and second, they can use the micros for themselves for a number of purposes.

The next tier of the *who* in training are the *managers of the individual departments*. They need to be aware of the details arising from acquisition, implementing, planning, and scheduling training for their people. Of course, they need the same user training themselves in order to make use of these systems.

The *departmental coordinators* will have somewhat more in-depth training on the system's capability, function, and problem solving and become familiar with the support structure of the organization. In most cases they will need the most extensive training (other than the support team itself) in order to answer many of the questions that will arise in the department. The level of the training necessary for most of the departmental users can be shallower if a good departmental coordinator is at hand to get the user over the occasional hurdles.

The early use of microcomputers is especially fraught with the obstacles that completely block the user from taking the next step. For example, the user may know how to summon up the help screen but not how to return to the previous screen. The instructions may say, "Type in the command LOTUS, press RETURN." The PC responds with "No such file." Now what? Actually, the directory was wrong, but how would the novice know that? He assumes that it's broken and that he's out of luck.

The department coordinator can give great assistance in clearing those hurdles. He can go far toward making the user feel comfortable with the system. Also, he is the point man (as always, both men and women are assumed) to inculcate the *change in thinking* about the activities and the tools necessary to get the best use out of the systems.

The *support team* itself is going to need considerable training. In many cases this will be outside the firm in order to bring this training knowledge to the appropriate depth and at the appropriate time to the various members of the organization. Often, if only one individual from the firm is sent to a specialized course on a new software package, it will be someone from the support team. Thus, it behooves these team members to have at least some instructional experience in order to teach this knowledge upon their return.

Last, and most important, the *users of the microcomputers* themselves will need to be trained. This most often will filter down from the support team and the micro coordinators. Also, as will be mentioned later, much self-instruction is available for these systems.

WHAT KIND OF TRAINING IS NECESSARY?

There are really three different types of training. The first might be considered *conceptual*. It does not relate so much to the microcomputers themselves but more to the way we approach our tasks and to the business value of those tasks as weighed in the scales of organizational objectives.

For example, it is not enough just to teach the purchasing manager that if he follows a particular sequence he can analyze the discount values and compare these to the detailed material plans for a particular part. The knowledge of this specific technique is necessary but far from sufficient. It is much more important that he understand the relative trade-offs involved if he exercises these discounts. He needs to question the value of these trade-offs to the organization. He must consider the effects of changes to the buying schedule to other departments, such as production and master scheduling.

This more conceptual training is necessary in all organizations to make people more effective and, certainly, to take the largest advantage of the new capabilities and flexibility offered by microcomputer systems. This training investment may well be the most beneficial of all.

The second type of training might be considered *motivational*—an unstated element of all education. In training adults it is not sufficient to tell them to do X or to memorize Y. Adults need to know *why* they should learn the topic at hand. They want to understand the relationship to their particular task of the knowledge they are going to receive and the operational skills they are going to gain.

Some people learn to use the micros quickly and naturally. It is all the more important for such "PC naturals" to be sensitive to the needs of those who do not. They must imagine how nerve-racking typing on a keyboard can be if one fears that the next keystroke may obliterate the whole day's work—or the whole database.

The author has overheard the following actual comments from good, faithful workers upon their introduction to such new systems. "I got so nervous when they brought these new things in." "I couldn't even sleep at night just for worrying about the new system." "Those young girls picked it up so fast; I felt like I was just not cut out for computers." "I thought about just quitting or retiring." "The instructor knows it so well, but he just doesn't explain it to us simple folks."

By the way, every person quoted above eventually learned the systems and felt comfortable with them in time. In fact, they would never go back to the former methods. But this change of thought does not appear automatically. It requires time, patience, gentleness, and good instruction to nurture this budding confidence.

As we are asking them to change some of their working practices and to adopt new styles and skills in their daily work activities, it is very important to maintain a strong motivational thrust. For example, if they see that their peers have accepted these new systems and are quite enthusiastic about them, this is strongly encouraging. It can go a great way toward removing the fears and anxieties that most adults face when they are dealing with new ways of performing their daily tasks.

The training includes a recognition of the structure and accessibility of the support team. It may include meeting a member or two of the support team (the instructor, for example). This also dissolves much of the fear that blocks the implementation and utilization of new systems. The failure to adequately address these concerns is seen as the principal reason why many personal computers end up being abandoned after very brief usage. The users are simply not comfortable enough with the systems to perform their tasks on them, and failing in that, they are not comfortable enough with the support organization to take the next step toward using these systems more effectively.

The third dimension of the kind of training is *operational skills*. What particular steps need be performed to do a particular task, what programs are necessary, how can changes be made, what type of backup procedures are appropriate, what security measures are in place, what policies and practices relate to the individual user in his daily tasks?

HOW IS THE TRAINING TO BE DONE?

A wide variety of mechanisms are available for training at each of these different organizational levels and in each of the three dimensions named above. These include: courses offered by colleges and universities (credit or noncredit), outside seminars and classes offered by vendors of systems and software, internally conducted seminars by outside training vendors, classes conducted within the company by members of the company, individual one-on-one hand-holding sessions as users are developing new applications, and a wide variety of self-study materials. The latter category includes user guides, reference manuals, computer-based training, video tapes, audio tapes, and interactive video disk materials. Later, more will be said about some elements of this wide spectrum of possibilities in the delivery of the training.

WHO MANAGES THE TRAINING?

Despite the wide variety of training material available, training management is actually one of the most vital assignments. As mentioned earlier, most micro systems fail by not providing the early training and the managerial direction necessary to make best use of the systems.

NOTA BENE

Training can easily fall between the cracks. To prevent this, it is very important that a single individual be assigned the complete responsibility for coordinating the training effort for an organizational unit.

In many cases the manager responsible for the micro investigation gradually assumes responsibility for implementation, then responsibility for the support team which assignment would naturally include training for his plant or division. Although these tasks need not coincide in responsibility, it seems to be a natural pattern for many manufacturers. In so doing this individual will have the responsibility for developing the three dimensions of the training strategy identified earlier. As users first experience "close encounters of the micro kind," it may seem quite "alien" to them. Thus, these early encounters should be managed gently.

This gentleness includes the time and expense of providing other human beings to conduct the initial training. Few users can be expected to begin to learn a microcomputer by computer-based training, by the use of manuals, or by the use of video tapes. The author has seen efforts in all of these directions, and I have never seen genuine, broadly based success without that first contact coming through another human being! This first contact need not be more than an hour or two. It may just include the rudiments of operating the system, getting comfortable with the keyboard, recognizing the PC's application to the task at hand, and learning the first tier of help and recovery steps.

Once this is established, in many cases, the learner can then go on with these other media and learn a great deal on his own. Still, help should be within shouting distance—in the form of a hot line, a departmental coordinator, or a support person known to the individual.

Classes (perhaps as short as a couple of hours) that include hands-on use with the system can accomplish this first introduction. This may also be done in a one-on-one fashion between departmental coordinators and individuals within the department. This need not be a terribly time-consuming task; it may only involve a few hours when a new employee enters the department or as employees are newly gaining access to microcomputer systems. As new applications are implemented some further personalized instruction may be required to get the users comfortable with the new systems. Often, new operational skills are learned through self-instruction once that early familiarity and comfort level is established for the micro user.

HOW ARE THE INSTRUCTORS CHOSEN?

Volunteers among the departments or among the MIS group often will reveal themselves in casual conversation. Champions of the microcomputers are regularly quite willing to take responsibilities in this area. They might be individuals who have a microcomputer at home already or a personally owned micro at work. They may be involved in local user groups. In some cases, these individuals may have been campaigning for the use of microcomputers even prior to their implementation in the company. These sorts of individuals, *provided* they have the instructional skills necessary, may prove important in developing the network of support for the organization.

The instructors who are going to be involved in conducting the classes and introducing the multitudes to new micro applications need experience in instruction. It has been proven time and again that those who are very capable *doers* of particular tasks are often not acceptable as *instructors* of that task. The *transfer* of knowledge requires a different set of skills than the *acquisition* of knowledge.

For larger organizations it is quite natural to have a full-time training staff available for the development of these courses, for working with the departmental coordinators, and for implementing the detailed support that will be necessary over the long term.

A somewhat predictable pattern emerges in observing these (successful) first encounters with micros:

2– 4 hours—Training by a knowledgeable user or instructor.

8–20 hours—Experimentation (within "shouting distance" of helpers).

2–10 days— Reasonable confidence to continue on one's own.

In all cases the largest part of the learning took place individually, not in the presence of others. But the very early hour or couple of hours of personal contact seem most important to overcome the immediate mental obstacles and to gain the confident relationship with the system that is necessary to use it with competence that can grow to mastery.

In a handful of rather exceptional cases the author has known "hard chargers" (with engineering or strong accounting and systems backgrounds) who have brought computers up, out of a box, on their own. Without benefit of counsel they have followed instruction guides, reference manuals, or computer-based training and have become relatively successful and skillful in the use of microcomputers without any apparent long-term psychological scars. Again, I think these individuals are somewhat unique and that the largest class of users tends to fall into the earlier category.

As the circle of those individuals who are comfortable with the microcomputers expands, the training tends to feed on itself. There is then often a helping hand only a desk or two away as the users are getting up to speed. In time it becomes a part of the corporate culture and tends to be taken for granted. But even then an ongoing effort needs to be made to develop the training, especially in the directions of the concepts involved and the new operational skills necessary as new applications are being developed and shared.

It will probably become appropriate in medium to larger companies to form some sort of internal user group which will enable the users to get in contact with other departments. It also fertilizes the micro garden by disseminating others' solutions using computers and uncovering the wide variety of new materials, devices, and techniques that are always becoming apparent as this evolution develops.

Many users join external user organizations such as the Microcomputer Application Special Interest Group of the American Production and Inventory Control Society, local PC user groups, or the users groups of the various vendors represented in the corporation. At these exchanges a great deal of useful information changes hands. It is very worthwhile for some, who feel the call, to get involved in working with these organizations, perhaps taking leadership rolls, giving addresses to these various meetings, and so forth. It is a broadening activity that is of value to the individual, to the company he represents, and to the larger user community that is outside the walls of that company.

HOW DO WE MEASURE THE SUCCESS OF THE TRAINING EFFORT?

One slim measurement is provided by the responses of those who have participated specifically in the training. It is more readily assessed, though, by the quality of the work produced by the microcomputer users. If they are doing the types of analyses, generating the types of reports, creating the types of graphic outputs, making the types of decisions that are most desirable for the operational groups involved, then it goes without saying that they have successfully learned how to use the microcomputer. Also, through the subjective evaluation of the general morale in the use of the computer, the "management by wandering around" approach, we can get a sense of the relative effectiveness of the training and support systems.

CASE STUDY: A TRAINING, SCHEDULING, AND REPORTING SYSTEM THAT RUNS ON MICROCOMPUTERS — UNISYS CORPORATION

The Unisys Corporation (formerly Burroughs) developed a package for scheduling all training for one division on a Unisys B20 microcomputer using the Unisys database manager. This database handled not just microcomputer training but all training (systems, manufacturing, marketing, distribution, and so forth) in this division. This system involved a network of four microcomputers at one training center and a network of two microcomputers at the other training center with diskettes being exchanged on a regular basis between the training centers.

The total population of students numbered more than 5,000; the total number of course offerings was well over 100; and the courses ran from two days to as long as four weeks. The database included all of the students, their titles, addresses, and job assignments. The system maintained a history of all of the training taken by any particular employee, all of the courses scheduled for a particular employee, all of the students who had taken a particular course, and all of the students planned for upcoming courses. Reporting systems were designed to provide information for locally contracted lodging arrangements and in-house accommodations for lodging and meals. Also, the system projected future training costs and graphed trends and summary data for divisionwide training.

Data entry (for example, a new course, a new employee, or the scheduling of a course for an employee) was laid out in simple screens. The fill-in-the-blank screens were undergirded by strong editing and checks. In fact, temporary workers, with less than an hour's training, could enter this information into the system.

The system was developed with indexes for both social security numbers and names as well as course numbers and instructors. In this way it was possible to report information for particular instructors, for particular courses, for particular students, or for particular branches, districts, or regions or divisionwide. The system was actually developed by one of the instructors in a training center. It was also maintained by that same individual throughout its use.

LEARNING ABOUT THE MICROCOMPUTER FROM THE MICROCOMPUTER

A variety of mechanisms are now available through which the microcomputer can take on much of the task of training the user in the use of itself. Through clever instructional screens and carefully scripted questions, the learner is guided down the path of knowledge. This is called computer-based training. The computer can lead the user through a series of explanations, test his understanding at each point, allow him to jump over segments of the instruction, reexamine difficult segments of instruction, or take alternate routes to learning. Much environmental software (spreadsheets, databases, and so forth) and many application programs at this time include some measure of computer-based training as a part of the package.

A variety of "authoring" systems are available for the company willing to develop its own internal computer-based training. This can be rather expensive, though, because it requires from 50 to 150 hours of developmental effort for each hour of computer-based training produced. There may be advantages, though, in developing such customized computer-based training. It can specifically highlight the operational issues, details, questions, and concepts of the individual corporation.

Certain graphics interface cards adapt the microcomputer to television output and video disk player input. The learner can now receive video sequences as well as computer-based branching, testing, evaluation, and logic. This is usually called interactive video disk. (To be perfectly technical, it is Level Three Interactive Video Disk.)

A number of companies have found this a very successful way to conduct training on many topics beyond just learning how to use micros. Ford uses IVD to train mechanics how to repair a five-speed manual transaxle (transmission). Other manufacturers train sales people in this way about the features and benefits of upcoming new products. Robot and computer repairmen learn from IVD how to actually conduct a variety of tests, perform diagnostic analyses, and make a number of repairs.

CASE STUDY: ROBOT MAINTENANCE TRAINING AT THE FORD MOTOR COMPANY—COMPUTER SIMULATION PROVIDES THE TRAINING

Bill Mallory, one of the robotics trainers at the Ford Motor Company in Dearborn, Michigan, believes that trainees "are more motivated than you'd think, *if* you give them training relevant to the job. That kind of training is more useful than theory."[2]

This job-related training takes place in a special learning lab. There the trainees practice manipulating a computer-controlled electric robot. This simulation of shop activities is valuable and much less expensive than using a real robot. Mallory states, "A real robot—at least the large ones used in the auto industry—is expensive and dangerous. The lab gives the trainee the first cut at programming—an opportunity to build finesse."[3]

With this simulated on-the-job training (OJT), the employee can become acquainted with the strange new world of robotics at his own pace. The program is self-instructional and self-paced. This type of training also is very important from a safety standpoint. If a trainee disables the hydraulics on a real robot, the arm can fall off, seriously injuring someone. Thus, simulated OJT via computers is safe and nonthreatening since it is self-paced.

After the skill and finesse in operating the robot are acquired on the

[2] Quoted in Carol Fey, "Working with Robots: The Real Story," *Training,* March 1986, p. 49ff.

3 Ibid.

computer, trainees get true OJT on the plant floor. Here they perform a "criterion performance demonstration" supervised by a trainer who watches closely to ensure safety.

BENEFITS OF COMPUTER-BASED TRAINING

There are several. For one, the training proceeds at precisely the pace of the individual involved. It has often been estimated that much classroom training operates too fast for a third of the class, too slow (to the point of boredom, disinterest, and loss of information) for a third of the class, and at the right speed only for a third of the class. It has also been estimated that learners recall perhaps 15 to 20 percent of what they have heard in a classroom setting.

The learner sitting at the microcomputer is constantly being challenged to answer questions, try out the applications, or make choices along the path. The training, therefore, moves at a pace with which he is perfectly comfortable. This assures constant reception at least, if not comprehension, of the learning. The slow learner can go more slowly. There are many opportunities for review. The quick learner can move quickly, jumping over unneeded sections.

This sort of learning has proven effective for those for whom English is a second language or for those who may have lower levels of literacy. Inasmuch as the training can be done in largely a pictorial way, many opportunities for easier comprehension are afforded. Also, it is possible for the foreign-language speaker to look up the words in an English/(native language) dictionary before proceeding on to the next screen. Again, because the pacing is completely user-directed, it tends to be a most efficient way of teaching new tasks.

A wide variety of studies (by manufacturers, governmental organizations, and academic institutions) have compared the relative effectiveness of computer-based training and classroom-oriented training. Study after study reports that computer-based training can compress the learning time by about one third with no loss in comprehension. Again, remember that the learner may need a bit of encouragement, the human touch, to jump over the first hurdles toward getting comfortable with such a system. But once that has been traversed there are great opportunities for self-directed learning thereafter.

As a final note about training materials, it should be mentioned that bookstores abound in titles to assist the newfound PC user. I noticed about 200 different books on micros in the Boston Logan Airport book-

FIGURE 8–1   Scene from a Tokyo Bookstore

store and an equivalent number in a bookstore in downtown Tokyo—
nearly the same titles (see Figure 8–1).

HURRAY! COMPUTERS ARE LEARNING ENGLISH, TOO—SORT OF

Lotus Development Corporation, publisher of personal computer software, introduced in 1986, software which allows micros to understand plain English. The HAL program, a $150 add-on to 1-2-3 from Lotus, now permits the user to access the computer in plain English instead of computer language. Less technical users can now type on the computer, "Graph column 3 as a pie chart" and they see a pie chart on the screen.[4]

---

[4] Mark Lewyn, "1-2-3 gets 1 step easier," *USA Today*, October 6, 1986, p. 1.

CONCLUSION

In Chapter 1, we noted that two elements dominate in separating the successes from the failures in microcomputer implementations—management leadership and training. Management issues have been presented in much of the first three parts of this book. This chapter rounds out the success pie with the element of training. With these elements correctly deployed any firm has gone far toward assuring its productivity with micros. It should now be ready to exploit the many departmental benefits offered in Part Four.

Departmental Applications

Departmental Applications

CHAPTER NINE

Strategic Business Planning

What is your company's most critical resource—materials, processes, market share?

It's probably not the raw materials you buy. Your competitor could buy those as well as you could. It's probably not just the particular processes, although these may be patented. It is still likely that there are other effective processes available to your competitors as well. It may not even be your market, because there are—in all likelihood—competitors who operate in that market and can certainly develop the same avenues and accesses your company has.

No, the most critical resource of your manufacturing operation is the *skill, vision,* and *leadership* embodied in your people. This—far more than the externals named above—really differentiates your operation from your competitor's. It is the basis of your firm's value among its peers.

Such valued leadership skills are neither introduced nor guaranteed by computer technology. But microcomputers can play a catalytic role in facilitating these leadership and planning skills within your operation.

This chapter addresses two facets of the *simulative planning tools* available for the strategic business planner. The strategic modeling or simulative tools are valuable (1) in the actual conduct of business planning within a company (at the executive level, typically) and (2) in teaching this same type of broadly based critical thinking at various levels within the company.

These broadly based insightful views tend to breed more cohesive extensions of the corporate strategy (for example, divisional-level plans). These views are also needed to communicate that cohesive strategy to the various operational disciplines that must combine to execute that strategy. Therefore, microcomputers will be considered both as tools for the actual business planning and as educational simulative devices to communicate these broadly based strategic viewpoints to other levels.

WHO DOES STRATEGIC BUSINESS PLANNING?

All companies engage in this type of strategic business planning. Some companies just do it unconsciously—more or less by default—merely continuing down the path. Others plan by more conscious decisions—exercising the particular disciplines necessary to weigh the business in the strategic scales of manufacturing advantage, market position, leveraging of financial strengths, and so on. It takes time, vision, and foresight to take a longer term look at the directions the business is headed—the particular manufacturing, marketing, financial, and operational strengths of a firm, the corresponding weaknesses, and the strategic directions that best exploit the strengths and minimize the weaknesses.

The microcomputer lets the planner (or learner) visualize the business in a comprehensible size and shape. It allows him or her to interact with this conception testing simulated effects of a variety of different plans. It is easy to develop graphic vehicles for both communicating and teaching the strategic plans to the other decision makers or the execution team.

A business plan could be developed on a sheet of paper. I have seen at least one on a cocktail napkin! The PC adds to this single-sheet simplicity the capability of reassessing changes to the plan, considering more variables, extending the planning horizon, and addressing more detail. It also offers an immediacy of response, graphic manipulation, and an accessibility that (in most cases) greatly eclipses that afforded by mainframe systems or napkins.

Subordinate elements of strategic business plans such as forecasting and production planning will be addressed in later chapters.

A Word from the Real World

Kirk Woodruff is the president and CEO of Allied Marine Industries, a $60 million per year company engaged in manufacturing, distributing, and shipping in Norfolk, Virginia. Kirk has a PC on his desk at work and one in his den at home. He takes a handful of diskettes back and forth regularly and finds the PC indispensable for developing and refining financial and operational plans.

He observes that this type of planning is equally indispensable to management thinking and decision making among his team. He says, "I don't see how any manager can get along without this type of assistance (PCs and electronic spreadsheets)."

VARIOUS STRATEGIC BUSINESS PLANNING TOOLS

We will review three categories of strategic business planning tools. First is a simple financially based modeling tool—the Du Pont Model. Second, we consider more sophisticated planning models that have been developed through spreadsheets and modeling software. Finally, we consider sophisticated business simulators—modeling tools available for both instructional and business planning purposes.

Du Pont Modeling—Financially Based Simulations

The Du Pont Model has been in practice at business schools for years as a mechanism for introducing the students to the various elements of financial reporting. It also serves to cultivate a keen eye for the relationships and ratios among these different financial elements. We see in Figure 9–1 a portrayal of an abbreviated Du Pont Model.

The top half of the chart depicts the elements of financial reporting drawn from the balance sheet at the close of a fiscal period. The bottom part of the model indicates the operational reporting elements drawn from the profit and loss statement of the company, summarizing the results of the past period—a year in this case. The model operates at increasing levels of consolidation from the left to the right. Notice the plus signs and lines of inclusion indicating the summarization.

The cells in the left column correspond to actual lines on a typical balance sheet report. In an example of consolidation, the various fixed assets, including LAND, BUILDINGS, MACHINES, CONSTRUC'N (buildings under construction), and DEPREC'N (accumulated depreciation), are consolidated into the cell labeled FIXED ASSETS. Then at the next level of consolidation, we observe that FIXED ASSETS is combined with CURRENT ASSETS, INVESTMENTS, and OTHER ASSETS to equal TOTAL ASSETS.

In the next column SALES is divided by TOTAL ASSETS to give ASSET TURNS. If a company with $1 million of assets sold $2 million worth of goods, this represents an asset turnover of two per year. In the particular case of the company shown above the assets have turned over 1.97 times per year.

The lower third of Figure 9–1 portrays the profit and loss statement. The various elements of the cost of goods sold have already been consolidated into COGS (cost of goods sold). The elements of COGS (materials,

FIGURE 9–1 Du Pont Model for ABC Company

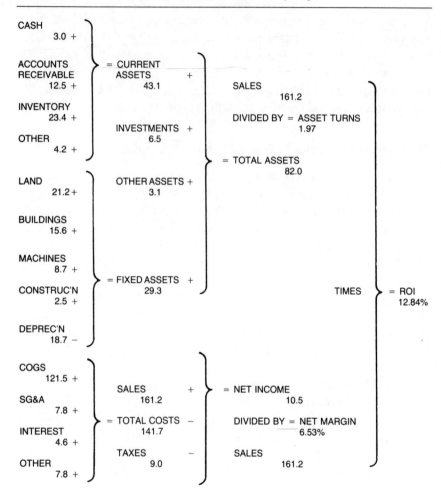

labor, overhead, or others) could be part of this spreadsheet but not currently visible on the screen. In fact, this spreadsheet is usually used with the schedules of greater detail preceding the one screen summarization given here. COGS, SG&A (selling, general, and administrative), INTEREST, and OTHER combine to give TOTAL COSTS. The TAX cell contains the formula (SALES − TOTAL COSTS) ∗ .46. Note that sales is only entered once (at the top of the figure). The other cells containing SALES copy this automatically. SALES − TOTAL COSTS − TAXES gives NET INCOME. NET INCOME/ (note that / means divided by two spreadsheets) SALES calculates NET MARGIN which is 6.53 percent in this example. The highest level of consolidation involves multiplying AS-SET TURNS by NET MARGIN to give ROI (return on investment)— 12.84 percent here.

The great advantage of this type of modeling is flexibility. The effects of certain financial decisions could be tested by substituting the effects on the model. Jim Clark has a nice discussion of this approach entitled "Selling Top Management—Understanding the Financial Impact of Manufacturing Systems" in the *1982 APICS Conference Proceedings*. This article was reprinted in the new *APICS Material Requirements Planning Reprints*.

By manipulating some of the detailed elements, such as engineering costs, break-even points, acquisitions of new capital equipment, and so on, these many subordinate plans can be consolidated together into electronic pro forma balance sheets and financial statements. These, in turn, can be consolidated into the Du Pont Model, giving senior management a quick look at the financial outcomes and key financial ratios of different proposed actions.

Other meaningful ratios can be added to this type of a spreadsheet. Many companies (especially in Japan) would include a cell labeled EM-PLOYEES. Then other cells could be used to calculate the assets per employee and the sales per employee. These two ratios, combined with asset turnover and ROI, give a thorough look at the relative effectiveness of a firm in turning resources into dollars. Other financial ratios can easily be included, such as acid test, leverage, and return on equity.

These types of models have also proven very effective for presenting to senior management the potential outcomes of proposed financial and operational decisions. As well, these models graphically illustrate top management's concerns (couched in the phraseology of the key ratios) to the various members of middle management who must transform plans into "products out the door."

NOTA BENE

Successful managers must gain a working knowledge of the critical financial and operational measurements by which senior management judges itself. This working knowledge is demonstrated by clearly portraying the economic effects of the decisions that are sought of senior management.

As Oliver Wight said: If you know how a man is measured, you know how to make a presentation to him that will get his attention. For example, consider the different manner in which the following two pitches fall on the executive ear:

"This proposed automated transfer line will increase our production from 430 to 520 trucks per month, and it only costs $8.6 million!"

"This proposed automated transfer line will increase revenue by $5.5 million, increase the asset turnover from 1.97 to 2.11, and move the ROI from 10.75 to 11.25."

The first line sounds great to the operational gang, but it loses its punch in the walnut-paneled offices. The second—if accurately developed—carries more weight with the CEO and CFO. Add a few well thought out graphs and a Du Pont Model of before and after, and you're on your way. A word to the wise: Be sure you have lined up the bean-counters on your side before presenting to the chief. To paraphrase Davy Crockett, "Make sure your assumptions are right, then go ahead!"

Extensions of the Du Pont Modeling Technique

The primitive concept of the pro forma Du Pont Model can be extended beyond sums and ratios. Most spreadsheets also support such financial wizardry as net present value, amortizations, and internal rate of return analyses. This enables the deft planner to develop a series of Du Pont Models based on the net present value of different streams of cash flow, revenue, asset turnover, profit ratios, and so forth. It brings a high degree of financial sensitivity to the activity of strategic business planning in the deceptively simple clothing of the humble spreadsheet. It allows the planner or the executive to refine intuitive hunches about future directions with a hard, clear look at the financial impact of the various actions.

Other Financial Modeling Techniques

The Du Pont Model, just presented in spreadsheet form, offers but one example of financial modeling with spreadsheets. These financial models run the gamut from the simplicity illustrated above to highly sophisticated models involving thousands of cost elements and hundreds of relationships among the variables. Increasingly popular are spreadsheet templates. A template is a skeleton spreadsheet with prefabricated logic and formulas into which one inserts his own figures.

We observed a model that estimates the impact of key competitors. It portrays assumptions about the activity of these competitors, the relative market share of each player, expenditures for advertising, and so forth. Some micro models even include Monte Carlo simulations of random surprises to better imitate corporate life.

Exotic examples include specific programs that operate on the assumptions that are entered and that present information graphically or in tabular fashion. This may include such techniques as linear programming or goal-seeking programs to search for optimal balances among conflicting constraints.

Although the author has observed a few rather heady examples of the programmer's art for business planning in languages such as Pascal, BASIC, C, and so on, rarely do such silicon sculptures significantly surpass the benefits available through the clever and informed use of the standard spreadsheets. These standard spreadsheets offer the additional benefit of greater flexibility in terms of designing new models and new relationships and in terms of modifying the models and relationships to perform simulations of different courses of action. So, with few exceptions, the companies willing to take the time to develop their own models and to gain the expertise in-house to maintain and manipulate these models can probably achieve the results comparable to any of those that could be purchased off the shelf.

EXPERT MANAGEMENT SYSTEMS

One possible exception to the preceding generalization is in the area of the so-called expert systems for strategic business planning and tactical management. These expert systems grow wise by accumulating databases of the sales force, the market, capital sources, and operational constraints. Expert systems are programmed to adopt a growing system of rules for making patterns of the complex arrays so acquired.

The author has talked with the developers of the Thoughtware® expert system for senior marketing management. The system, in attempting to simulate the activity of the business, asks a large number of questions to build a quantitative reference model of the different operational, personnel, and financial constraints of the corporation it is modeling.

It tracks exception conditions to draw the manager's attention to particular actions that need correction (as far as the system judges). In many cases, it suggests particular corrective actions. As these prove successful or unsuccessful or acceptable or unacceptable to the manager, the expert system modifies its decision rules. Over a period of months it should make better modeling assumptions. Consequently, it would make better suggestions for the correction of undesired conditions. Presently such systems function as useful nags and reminders, but rarely offer startling insights. Presumably, given enough time, a large enough memory, and better systems of adaptive rule formation, the system could assimilate much of the management expertise to which it is exposed. Conversely such a system, in the hands of a poor manager, might become a *very* poor manager.

BUSINESS SIMULATORS—FOR PLANNING AND EDUCATION

Wickham Skinner comments on the need for strategic thinking and planning for the manufacturing activity as well as the marketing and financial dimensions of the enterprise:

> A company's manufacturing function typically is either a competitive weapon or a corporate millstone. It is seldom neutral. Yet, the connection between manufacturing and corporate success is rarely seen as more than the achievement of high efficiency and low costs. What appear to be routine manufacturing decisions frequently come to limit the corporation's strategic options, binding it with facilities, equipment, personnel and basic controls and policies to a noncompetitive posture which may take years to turn around.[1]

A number of simulators have been developed by large corporations, and by the academic community, that attempt to address the issues of strategic relationships between manufacturing capabilities and financial necessities. These simulators can serve as both planning and educational tools. They can serve to test and illustrate the effects of various types of strategic manufacturing decisions such as just-in-time reforms, computer-integrated manufacturing, changes in equipment, and changes in the vertical and horizontal relationships between different plants.

Stephen A. De Lurgio and Jiguang Zhao describe such a simulator developed to teach manufacturing concepts in college classes.[2] It in-

---

[1] Wickham Skinner, *Manufacturing: The Formidable, Competitive Weapon* (New York: John Wiley & Sons, 1985).

[2] Stephen A. De Lurgio and Jiguang Zhao, "A Manufacturing Planning and Control System Simulator, Using Spreadsheet Programs," *1986 APICS Conference Proceedings*, p. 53ff.

cludes all of the modules typically associated with a closed-loop (MRP II) system—production planning, master production scheduling, material requirements planning, lead time offset, bills of material, detailed routing, shop scheduling, cost accounting systems, and financial planning systems. Its design permits very easy modification for considering different types of industries and products.

The system was developed to use 1-2-3 from Lotus, Supercalc 3, or PC Calc. Its flexibility and transparency enable students to grasp the principles of production and inventory management much more readily than would a live MRP software system. The forest is less obscured by the trees. It allows hands-on interactive experience with a plantwide system. It also integrates accounting and engineering information into this manufacturing system. It allows the student more immediate control, feedback, and motivation than directly working with a MRP system, and it reinforces the discovery of new relationships because of the "what if" capability. The flexibility in modifying the software allows the discovery of more effective choices and trade-offs.

A similar concept had been developed earlier by visiting professors Bob Ballard and Bill Berry at the London Business School. This seminar is directed at the general manager in manufacturing. The course centers around a complex decision exercise in building a business plan for the Gulfways Equipment Company, Inc. The key lies in integrating the marketing, production, and financial elements of the company at the operational level. Solutions include the development of plans for cash flow, manpower, information systems, inventory policies, forecasts, pro forma financial reports, marketing, and others. These plans are given credible testing via an elaborate series of linked Microsoft Multiplan spreadsheets. Multiple periods can be simulated, and plans must be developed right in the thick of the unfolding scenarios.

These types of simulation systems are also used by manufacturers for internal training—including Unisys and IBM. Newly hired individuals and senior managers of these firms are expected to work with the simulators to gain a sensitivity to the interplay of decisions made in the engineering, financial, and manufacturing arenas. The students learn to view the effects of these decisions on the overall effectiveness and competitiveness of the corporation.

The author has seen similar systems developed for the testing of distribution requirements planning systems where a number of plants and distribution centers can be modeled. The relationship between the plants, transportation issues, and the relative effectiveness of locating new warehousing or stocking points can be tested. This raises the "what if" questions that enable companies to develop better distribution networks.

CONCLUSION

Simulators and models offer significant benefits both to strategic planners and to learners at all levels who would better grasp the strategic issues that drive corporate decision making. They also allow the presentation of information in highly graphic fashion, making it easier to *visualize* the trade-offs, links, benefits, and opportunities. This more visual presentation also is an aid to communicating the issues and balances to those who will be affected by the decisions, including those who must make the corporate decisions of tomorrow.

Forecasting

Tom Brown, a serious forecaster of considerable experience—and a veteran APICS wit—offered the following definition of forecast (amplified from Ernie Theisen).[1]

> We can analyze the term by considering its components.
>
> "Fore!" is an ancient sporting term of warning, bearing the threat of harm at worst and uncertainty at best, to those within the potential range of a golfer's drive.
>
> "Cast" is similarly drawn from the world of sports—fishing in this case—but refers to the act of serving up a projectile to the unseen, and usually unknown, finned client lurking beneath the deceptive surface of the fluid medium.
>
> We conclude then that a forecast is a *warning* to those who use it, a confession of *uncertainty* if not *deception* by those who create it, and a *threat* of considerable harm to those who stand directly in its path.

In the late 1960s, I spent a summer working as a statistician for the Naval Air Systems Command Representative, Atlantic Fleet. My particular charter was to develop improved forecasting systems in order to better predict manpower requirements for the Naval Air Rework Facilities (NARF) on the East Coast. Each NARF boasts mammoth hangars for the repair and rebuilding of Naval aircraft, and each one needs thousands of skilled workers. The NARF in Norfolk, Virginia, employed about 6,000 industrial workers.

I worked in the Management Information Systems department. Interestingly, there existed another department with the name of Data Processing. For all its infatuation with computers in the 60s, even the Navy

---

[1] George W. Plossl, "Getting the Most from Forecasts," in *Forecasting*, 2nd ed. (APICS, 1979), pp. 28–29.

recognized the distinction between data processing and management information.

Our department's charter was to boil down the daily boxes of data into information that could be used for the many decisions made by senior officers. Being the eager young forecaster that I was, I immediately plunged into the murky catacombs of linear regression to subdue the forecasting challenge. I was completely overwhelmed by the tons of paperbound data provided faithfully every day. So was everyone else in the department. The old pros assured me that I needn't concern myself with the reports. They were neatly stored against the partition like empty egg crates and just as neatly discarded a few days later.

Nonetheless, I set about the task of building the better forecast with determination and matrix determinants. Essentially, the task could be reduced to choosing the most significant variables from the 20 or so that were faithfully recorded for every aircraft that flew into our facility. After a few weeks, I admitted I was not making the needed progress. Inconsistent results erupted from the tidy mathematics. For example, the greater the number of carrier landings, the more extensive the repair needed. That made sense. An aircraft landing on an aircraft carrier goes from 175 miles per hour to a dead stop in about two seconds. Pilots call it a controlled crash.

But other results were inexplicable. The mathematics suggested there was a negative correlation between the number of months of deployment and the extent of repair when the aircraft was finally returned to the NARF for overhaul. In layman's terms, this meant that the aircraft that had been in use the longest required the least repair. I would have expected the opposite—that those planes that had the most usage would require the most repair.

At this point, a thoughtful veteran of the forecasting game taught me a lesson in this arcane art that has stayed with me ever since. Seeing my earnest labors over the numbers, he suggested one day that we break out of the cold fluorescent caves of the MIS section and visit the shop. I had only seen the actual planes from a distance, and I had no real idea of what happened to them in the shop. For a few hours we walked among the disassembled A-6 Intruders in the hangar. I asked dozens of questions of the shop people.

I discovered a very simple answer to the puzzling negative correlation between months of deployment and repair needs. Pilots had considerable influence over the selection of aircraft for the repair and rework program. The pilots were sending the jets with the poorest repair records (the "dogs") back first. The best planes were held as long as possible. Only when they were finally forced to give them up did they send them in for the rework program. Since the dogs came in early (and tended to be neglected in the field) they naturally tended to require more repair. The favored jets came in late and received favored treatment during their service life; hence, they required less repair.

That day several other mysteries were solved by the simple process of questioning the shop folks. The lesson was simple but profoundly important.

NOTA BENE

Don't forecast what you do not understand. Even then, test each forecast for reasonableness.

By understanding the issues that were creating demand on the NARF, I was eventually able to discard most of the variables and to arrive at a fairly good forecasting method for manpower and shop loading requirements.

This simple principle found application almost two decades later while I was attempting to improve the forecasting of mainframe computers at several Unisys plants. After spending considerable effort in developing clever forecasting techniques on microcomputers, I remembered the lessons of the NARF. I chatted with the plant manager of the mainframe plant most affected by these forecasts.

After firing a broadside blast at marketing, he explained what numbers were most important to his plant and how best to state the expected demand and the risks associated with the predictions of demand. Once again the solution was not particularly complicated. It just demanded thinking about the issues from the side of those most affected by the forecasts. It reinforced the rule of two decades earlier.

NOTA BENE

The more you know about the markets and manufacturing needs of a product, the more likely that you will select sound methods to forecast its demand.

This caveat founded, we can safely proceed to examine a few examples of effective forecasting techniques on microcomputers. As is always the case, the techniques need to be made appropriate to the intended user. In the case of forecasting there are actually two users. The first is the *individual* who will be performing the analysis, sifting the numbers, and pronouncing the forecast. The other user is the *plant* that will be required to gear production to this forecast. In both cases clarity and understandability do much to ensure that the forecasts will be of real value.

CASE STUDY: FORECASTING AT
THE UNISYS CORPORATION

While the author was an employee at Unisys Corporation the forecasting was performed by district sales managers in the marketing organization. This was a savvy group with typically a decade or two of marketing experience and very modest statistical training. The forecasts were to be used by the corporate schedulers for building annual, quarterly, and, eventually, monthly production plans for the plants. We decided upon a method that used a series of simple spreadsheets.

The most controversial part of the process was to get everyone to agree on what should be forecast. This is where the above-mentioned research with the plant managers helped. This allowed us to boil down thousands of potential computer configurations to about 40 key items for the forecasting system.

We next had to decide upon the key variables. Again, by staying close to our users (in this case, the district sales managers) we were able to isolate the four key factors—namely, manpower (including training), user base, market niches, and historical sales. From these we developed a simple spreadsheet for each of these facets that allowed the managers to manipulate the assumptions and observe the results. In some cases the first assumptions were faulty, but the wide disparity in the results brought this clearly to light.

For example, the forecast based on the manpower spreadsheet might lead to an annual forecast of 12 units of Model B per trained salesman. If a branch has 10 salesmen trained on Model B, this suggests a forecast of 120 per year. However, a survey of the users and potential users revealed only 20 real sales opportunities for Model B. The best forecast is probably much closer to 20 than 120.

Since the spreadsheets could easily be changed, the managers could try various combinations until they developed numbers that made good business sense.

Occasionally an intuitive link developed between the numbers floating about the screen and the business of running a district. A few managers discovered that hiring plans, territory assignments, or market niches would have to be adjusted to fulfill the demands of the plan. Even so, this methodology would have failed in all likelihood if it had not gone one step further.

Every district manager in the United States was required to attend training for a long day (10 hours). At this session they got a chance to understand more about the system itself; but more important, they saw it used by their peers and their management. They heard from the plants about how the system would affect their ability to service the needs of the markets. They received the advice and encouragement of very experienced managers.

Conclusions from the Unisys Case

Once again the people side of the equation—training, communication, and support—made the difference. The resulting forecasts reflected much more thought. They were measured against actual performance (bonuses were paid based on forecast accuracy). Better forecasting was the inevitable result. A nice extra was that the forecasts could be mailed or transmitted from districts to regions to corporate planners—easily consolidated on the micros at each tier. This greatly speeded the accuracy and timeliness of the consolidated forecasts at world headquarters.

This Unisys case also provides a nice illustration of the *pyramid principle* of forecasting. The pyramid principle conceives forecasting as a series of hierarchical layers as in Figure 10–1. The layer principle can apply to (1) organizational layers, (2) regional grouping, (3) product grouping, (4) time buckets, or (5) planning horizons.

The key point is that the different layers of forecasting structure can improve the balance and breadth of viewpoint of the eventual forecast. The highest level of management (in this particular case, corporate vice president) has a very broad view of the developments of the market, the activities of competitors, and so on. In Figure 10–1 only three dimensions of the possible pyramids are shown: organization, product grouping, customer grouping.

Regional vice presidents, operating in eight regions in the United States, were somewhat closer to the actual activity of major customers and were regularly receiving the input of their district sales managers. In many cases they had had corporate experience and could often temper

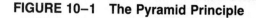

FIGURE 10–1   The Pyramid Principle

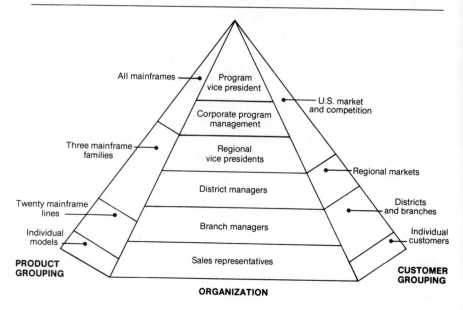

some of the wild-eyed plans of the corporate program managers with some of the hard lessons of reality learned in field experience.

The district sales managers were often very close to a number of the customers and were in regular contact with the branch managers. At the lowest level of the pyramid the sales reps had a very clear knowledge of particular deals that were working and of the time frames for those deals. They knew the specific activity of competitors in their marketplace, and they were actively encountering all of this information on a first-hand basis.

The essence of the forecasting technique was to build on the information at all of these levels, to consolidate it meaningfully across the product lines, and to develop overall corporate forecasting models that could actually be used to serve several of the forecasting objectives for the corporation. The focal point of the forecasting process was a series of microcomputer spreadsheets.

The four dimensions of the forecasting were *manpower* (including training), *user base*, *market niches*, and *historical sales*. In each dimension the forecasting moves through layers of consolidation from the highest level to the lowest and then back up again. At each layer the responsible managers assign risks and opportunity assessments to their numbers and build marketing plans to meet these assessments. Each forecast not only gets stronger at every turn but gains the various commitments necessary to grow beyond a forecast to a marketing plan: specific unit and dollar goals, manpower and training objectives, timetables, quarterly goals, monthly goals, and so forth.

The microcomputer system wrought benefits both obvious and subtle: it strengthened the managers' ability to deal with the multifarious dimensions of good forecasting; it certainly improved the speed, ease, and accuracy of consolidation; and it allowed much more trial fitting of the various elements of forecasting before satisfaction was reached at each level. It also furnished management (both field and staff) a useful follow-up tool for monitoring and adjusting the activity of marketing, planning, and follow-through in the field.

The program was well received by many disciplines of the company. The financial group reported that it gave them the best basis they had ever had for developing their revenue and other financial forecasts. The field management also applauded its practical discipline and has, in fact, improved the quality of its forecasting and sales planning through its use.

ANOTHER VIEW OF FORECASTING FROM ZILOG INCORPORATED

Terence E. Barton is sales operations manager for Zilog Incorporated, a microcomputer processor in Campbell, California. His experience spans both production control and marketing. He brings a rather unique perspective to the following comments. He represents a company that makes microprocessors, and he is responsible for forecasting.

With tongue firmly in cheek, he compares the art of forecasting with a video arcade game in terms of engaging the user, being highly visual, and giving constant feedback to assure that the user is on the right track.

> Clever engineers have found a way to get people to put coins into the sides of computers. Over 5 billion quarters have been plunked into Space Invaders games alone. That's more than one game per earthling. Even more amazing is that people are paying solely for the challenge of operating a computer without even receiving any productive output. Centipedes, tooth decay, ditch digging, and making hamburgers have suddenly become interesting subjects since being glorified by computer games.
>
> The enthusiasm about video games, which has inspired songs and movies, contrasts sharply with the resistance, anxiety, and frustration often encountered by users of computers in business. Forecasting and production

planning are certainly no worse than ditch digging and tooth decay. If computers can make dreaded subjects challenging and interesting, perhaps the same enthusiasm can be generated about business problems by using the same techniques. . . .

Despite all of its importance only one thing is certain about forecasting—it will be wrong. The size of the errors [indicated by percent or by a range], how fast we react to them, and the effectiveness of the corrections will determine how successful our business is.

Given the lack of data and market research in most businesses, we must not promise accurate forecasts or act as if we had them. Our best hope is for a forecast that keeps us going long enough to find its errors and prepares us to make the corrections. . . .

The large number of diverse items for which forecasts must be done and the amount of data involved require that each individual forecast be done quickly, inexpensively, and easily. Thus, the job is often turned over to a computer.

Some *interactive* computer systems [for forecasting through visual depictions of the results] generate glowing enthusiasm among users, while reactions to others are openly hostile. Pleased users frequently mention positive feelings concerning

- Mastery of the system.
- Competence in performing their task.
- Ease in learning the system.
- Confidence in retaining knowledge.
- Enjoyment in using the system.
- Eagerness to show it off.
- Desire to explore more powerful aspects.

Systems designed using the principle of direct [eye to hand] manipulation can produce these benefits:

1. Novices learn quickly, usually by demonstration.
2. Experts can work rapidly.
3. Users retain concepts.
4. Users can immediately see if their action is accomplishing their goal.
5. Errors are usually self-evident.
6. Users feel confident.

Through direct manipulation the user is able to apply his judgment and intelligence directly to the problem at hand rather than on the system being used. This greatly simplifies the task because thinking is more concrete and results are instantly visible.[2]

A THIRD CASE—SMALL VOLUMES, MANY ITEMS, SEASONAL VARIATIONS

Harvard Business School conducted a study several years ago on the forecasting practices of small and middle-size companies. The study determined that executive opinion was by far the most prevalent method of forecasting. Beyond that, judgments of staffers and simple historical repetition were widely used. The study's most significant conclusion was that the vast majority of forecasting done by small and middle-size companies could be greatly improved by the simple adoption of two techniques—*exponential smoothing* and *seasonal decomposition*.

These techniques have not always enjoyed good public relations. They suffer the stigma of appearing somewhat statistical, if not downright subversive. In truth, they are certainly not beyond the grasp of any of the inventory practitioners and sales managers that have responsibilities in the forecasting arena. Exponential smoothing merely clarifies the trend factor. Seasonal decomposition isolates the seasonal cycles. The following spreadsheet (Figure 10–2) illustrates these two techniques applied to the forecasting of a product group with significant seasonal variations.

In the actual case this product group included about 150 particular items that were grouped together because of like seasonality. By this is meant that the sales tended to peak in the same months of the year for all of these products and tended to fall off in the same months. This seasonality depended largely on weather, since this equipment was usually installed out-of-doors.

Several things should be observed about the products in the spreadsheet that made this approach particularly valuable. First, the sales of individual items were not large enough for any meaningful seasonality to appear. Imagine trying to develop a seasonality based on the sales of Item 1—they are so erratic that no clear pattern emerges. By consolidating all of the items (in this example 4 items but in the actual case 150

---

[2] Terence E. Barton, "Is Your Forecasting System as Much Fun or as High Scoring as Pac-Man?" *APICS Microprocessor Seminar Proceedings*, January/February 1984, pp. 68–72.

FIGURE 10–2 Forecasting Using Exponential Smoothing and Seasonal Decomposition

Groups/Products	Months Jan	Feb	Mar	Apr	May	Jun	Jul	Aug	Sep	Oct	Nov	Dec
***** Group A *****												
Item 1	10	12	20	17	15	13	14	16	9	16	14	17
Item 2	30	26	32	25	20	18	20	24	18	16	23	26
Item 3	42	45	39	51	22	31	30	21	48	38	34	31
Item 4	12	10	18	11	8	9	15	20	11	14	12	15
Total Group Sales	94	93	109	104	65	71	79	81	86	84	83	89
Monthly average	86.5	86.5	86.5	86.5	86.5	86.5	86.5	86.5	86.5	86.5	86.5	86.5
Seasonal Index calc	1.09	1.08	1.26	1.20	0.75	0.82	0.91	0.94	0.99	0.97	0.96	1.03
Seasonal Index judg	1.08	1.12	1.20	1.20	0.80	0.80	0.90	0.95	0.95	0.95	1.00	1.05
De-seasonalized Group Totals:	87.0	83.0	90.8	86.7	81.3	88.8	87.8	85.3	90.5	88.4	83.0	84.8
Smoothed De-seasonalized Group Totals:	87.0	87.0	86.4	87.1	87.0	86.1	86.5	86.7	86.5	87.1	87.3	86.7
Seasonal Group Forecast calc:	94.0	97.4	103.7	104.5	69.6	68.9	77.9	82.4	82.2	82.8	87.3	91.0

Seasonal Group

Forecast judgm:	96	98	107	107	75	75	80	84	85	86	91	94
Ratio to Group:												
Item 1	0.11	0.13	0.18	0.16	0.23	0.18	0.18	0.20	0.10	0.19	0.17	0.19
Item 2	0.32	0.28	0.29	0.24	0.31	0.25	0.25	0.30	0.21	0.19	0.28	0.29
Item 3	0.45	0.48	0.36	0.49	0.34	0.44	0.38	0.26	0.56	0.45	0.41	0.35
Item 4	0.13	0.11	0.17	0.11	0.12	0.13	0.19	0.25	0.13	0.17	0.14	0.17
Forecasted ratios:												
Item 1	0.11	0.11	0.11	0.13	0.14	0.16	0.17	0.17	0.18	0.16	0.17	0.17
Item 2	0.32	0.32	0.31	0.31	0.29	0.29	0.28	0.28	0.28	0.26	0.25	0.25
Item 3	0.45	0.45	0.46	0.43	0.45	0.42	0.42	0.41	0.37	0.42	0.43	0.42
Item 4	0.13	0.13	0.12	0.13	0.13	0.13	0.13	0.14	0.17	0.16	0.16	0.16
Forecasted items:												
Item 1	11	11	12	14	10	12	13	14	15	14	15	16
Item 2	31	31	33	33	22	22	23	23	24	23	22	24
Item 3	43	44	49	46	34	32	34	35	32	36	39	40
Item 4	12	13	13	14	10	9	10	12	14	14	15	15

FIGURE 10–3A   Unsmoothed Item Data

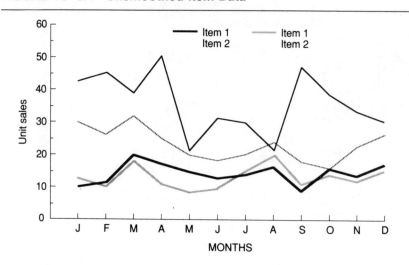

items), it is possible to get a sense of the actual seasonality for this entire group of like products.

By adopting the reasonable assumption that the same seasonal pattern must apply to the individual items, we have sharpened the sensitivity of our forecasting to the seasonality of our market. Figures 10–3A and 10–3B illustrate the erratic bouncing of the sales of the four individual items and the somewhat smoother line generated by the sum of their sales. The tendency toward meaningful curves is even more pronounced when larger numbers of items with like seasonality are summed. This seasonality is expressed by seasonal indexes.

In Figure 10–2 the "Seasonal Index calc" is simply the ratio of the "Total Group Sales" to the "Monthly Average". In months where sales are high (like January) the index is greater than 1; in months where sales are low (like May) the index is less than 1. If there were no seasonality, every month would equal the average, so the index for each month would be 1. In all cases, the indexes must add up to 12.

A variant approach to seasonal indexes is based on the annual sales instead of the monthly averages. Under this approach, the indexes are fractions of the whole year such as .0675 and .0912. The 12 indexes would then add up to 1. Both systems give the exact same answers (they are equivalent mathematically). I mention this variant approach merely to avoid confusion in the minds of those who have seen the variant. I find

FIGURE 10–3B   Total of All Four Items

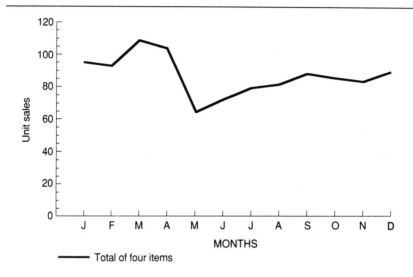

— Total of four items

the indexes described in this spreadsheet to be more meaningful, since each index obviously compares each month's sales to an average sales rate.

NOTA BENE

Remember that the most important element of any micro forecasting scheme is between the keyboard and the chair!

Take a minute to think about that. That's right—the most important element is the forecaster—in particular, the judgment, wisdom, insight, and fortitude of the forecaster. This model includes three specific lines that are completely manual—the forecaster can take or leave the calculations as his conscience dictates. After all, his name, not the micro's, is on the eventual forecast. The first of these is the very next line, "Seasonal Index judg[ment]."

The "Total Group Sales" are divided by these judgment-based indexes to give "De-seasonalized Group Totals." Now we have a flat line of data to work with. Applying exponential smoothing to these numbers, we calculate "Smoothed De-seasonalized Group Totals." This information could be used to hunt for trends from year to year, trends that could never be seen among the erratic patterns of the raw sales figures at the top.

If we add a trend rate, it could easily be inserted at this point. For the sake of simplicity, it is omitted here. Next, the spreadsheet uses the judgmental seasonal indexes from above to reseasonalize the trend line into the "Forecast calc[ulated]." This is the computer's guess at next year's total group sales by month. Again, the forecaster is invited to take or leave them on the next line, "Seasonal Group Forecast judgm[ent]."

By then taking the ratio of each one of the products to the total sales for all of the group, we can then take the group forecast and extend it to each individual line item—shown in the lowest section of the spreadsheet. Finally, the forecaster may either leave the numbers as they fall or change them on the basis of his knowledge of future promotions and changes in the market.

This technique is very powerful where there are a number of items in a group that have kindred seasonality and where it would be very tedious to develop seasonal indexes for each one of the items. It would also be very tedious to make individual forecasts for the individual items. Through the mechanism of the spreadsheet it is possible to generate a seasonal forecast for each month for 150 items in a matter of a few minutes. Also this type of spreadsheet can be extended to actually compare the forecasts of the items with actual results through the use of tracking signals.

Tracking Signals—Keeping the Forecast Unbiased

Tracking signals offer a mathematical means of detecting bias (consistently high or low tendencies) in a forecast. It is easy to compute the *mean absolute deviations* (MADs) of each month's forecast of each of the 150 items (or whatever). These mean absolute deviations can be compared to a running sum of forecast errors, also calculated directly by the spreadsheet. In this way a tracking signal is developed which is the ratio of the running sum of the forecast errors to the mean absolute deviation.

The spreadsheet can be designed to highlight visually the tracking signal above a preset level—often a level of six to eight can be used. If the tracking signal is larger than six, for example, a verbal message can be displayed to the forecaster indicating that the forecast for this particular item has gotten offtrack. With the watchful help of the micro, he is free to handle the routine items routinely. He can generate a spreadsheet forecast for a large number of items. If the forecast proves to be biased his attention is drawn to the items where he needs to reevaluate his assumptions—and perhaps to do a bit of manual forecasting.

Conclusions from This Example

This example illustrates several useful aspects of micro forecasting: (1) a two-tier pyramid approach is used to forecast both group and individual items, allowing each to force the other into a better approximation, (2) it forecasts routine items routinely saving the scarce resource of time for those items that actually need that attention, (3) it allows for the judgment of those responsible for the forecast, and (4) the spreadsheet automatically calculates seasonal decomposition and exponential smoothing.

FOCUS FORECASTING ON MICROS

As one final note on micro forecasting, Bernard T. Smith and others (in his wake) have written extensively about a clever technique called focus forecasting. This also applies some of the simple principles which have been mentioned so far, taking such things as seasonal comparisons, quarter-by-quarter history, basic trend information, and so forth.

The microcomputer is programmed to take a variety of techniques (from as few as 7 to 20 or more) and determine which one of the forecasting techniques would have been most successful in predicting last month's actual sales. The winning technique is awarded the opportunity to predict this month's sales. This deceptively simple technique has actually proven very successful in generating reliable forecasts, especially in an environment where there are a very large number of items to forecast (hardware parts, for example). Facing so many part numbers, it is simply not reasonable to expect the forecaster to intervene manually at every level of the forecasting.

The microcomputer lends itself very naturally to this activity by using interactive graphics, displaying the techniques involved, and feeding this information into simple screen formats where the forecaster can interact with the data.

CONCLUSION

Forecasting with micros, as all forecasting, must grow beyond simply trying to predict the future. It must enter the arena of coherent, explainable, and communicable sales plans. The explanation of these plans must include a statistical communication of the uncertainty associated with those sales plans. Finally, those who form the plans must accept accountability for monitoring the results in order to make the plans happen and to develop better plans for driving production planning.

This, in fact, is the title of the next chapter. In Chapter 11, "Production Planning," we take a look at some methods for folding the forecast information we have derived so far into sound production plans to drive the manufacturing process.

CHAPTER ELEVEN

Production Planning

When Lee Iacocca took over the Chrysler Corporation he encountered a host of challenges, not the least of which was the utter absence of any meaningful communication between the various departments. He writes:

> There was no real committee setup, no cement in the organizational chart, no system of meetings to get people talking to each other. I couldn't believe, for example, that the guy running the engineering department wasn't in constant touch with his counterpart in manufacturing. . . .

> Nobody at Chrysler seemed to understand that interaction among the different functions in a company is absolutely critical. . . .

> The manufacturing guys would build cars without ever checking with the sales guys. They just built them, stuck them in a yard, and then hoped that somebody would take them out of there. . . .

> Nobody at Chrysler seemed to realize that you just can't run a big corporation without calling some pregame sessions to do blackboard work.[1]

Production planning is a vital element of this blackboard work. The production plan is both the instrument and the result of hammering out the tough decisions between the various functional elements named above.

Production planning can be considered a planning buffer between the heady world of strategic business planning, the arcane art of forecasting, and the gritty reality of the plant. It deals with major product groups of a manufacturer—typically five to a dozen product families—grouped by commonality of marketing and manufacturing responsibility. The production plan that emerges from this phase of planning typically stretches over a horizon of one to three years. It is usually stated in time increments of

---

[1] Lee Iacocca, *Iacocca: An Autobiography* (New York: Bantam Books, 1984), pp. 152–53.

months. For some firms the first year may be broken into months with the remaining increments (often called time buckets) in quarters.

WHO DOES PRODUCTION PLANNING?

Production planning is a level of planning above the master production schedule—both in level of detail and in managerial responsibility. It is usually conducted in monthly meetings with senior managers of accounting, production, marketing, and sometimes engineering present. This may include the controller, the chief financial officer, the plant supervisor, the vice presidents of manufacturing, marketing, and engineering, and the general manager.

The titles are not as important as the balance between the countervailing objectives of marketing (maximizing service, minimizing lead time, high product diversity), finance (high revenue, low cost, stable monetary performance, minimum investment in raw material, work in process, finished goods, and capital equipment), and production (long runs, low product diversity, abundant raw materials, stable schedules, and constant demands on plant resources). Although these demands may occasionally seem at opposite poles of any conceivable production plan, they must be brought together.

With dedicated efforts in streamlining the flow of value through the plant and a will to strip all wasteful expenditure of resources (inventory, manpower, equipment, time, or money) out of the process, increasingly stronger manufacturing muscle can be developed. As discussed in Chapter 9, the manufacturing arm of the firm can become the strategic competitive weapon that it must become in order to venture into world markets. In this setting ever stronger plans can be developed and executed.

The production plan represents a contract among the members of the management team. It may be modified monthly at the blackboard sessions as market demands require, but stability should be its baseline. For many manufacturers the microcomputer furnishes a powerful and visible mechanism for gaining the balance among key goals of these players. First we consider a typical batch-oriented manufacturer. Its production plan might be framed along the lines of the spreadsheet in Figure 11–1.

PRODUCTION PLANNING ELEMENTS

The example is a slight simplification of techniques in actual use. It has been reduced to one year—12 months—and includes only three product

---

FIGURE 11–1   Production Plan

Families:	Jan	Feb	Mar	Apr	May
Bicycles	1400	1400	1500	1550	1750
Wagons	750	800	850	900	900
Tricycles	400	475	500	600	600
Monthly Totals	2550	2675	2850	3050	3250

Bill of Resources

Resources: Units:	Steel (tons)	All Labor (std hr)	Assembly (std hr)	Revenue ($)	Gross Margin ($)
Bicycles	0.0049	0.84	0.187	41	16
Wagons	0.0056	0.35	0.068	15	7
Tricycles	0.0029	0.41	0.098	18	9

Resource Requirements Plan

Resources: Units:	Steel (tons)	All Labor (std hr)	Assembly (std hr)	Revenue ($)	Gross Margin ($)
Jan	12.2	1603	352	75850	31250
Feb	12.7	1651	363	77950	32275
Mar	13.6	1763	387	83250	34450
Apr	14.4	1863	410	87850	36500
May	15.4	2031	447	96050	39700
June	15.6	2073	457	98100	40500
July	16.1	2157	475	102200	42100
Aug	16.1	2157	475	102200	42100
Sep	16.1	2157	475	102200	42100
Oct	16.1	2157	475	102200	42100
Nov	16.1	2157	475	102200	42100
Dec	16.1	2157	475	102200	42100
Annual Totals	180.4	23925	5268	1132250	467275

---

groups. The anticipated production for each group for each month is entered in the top section. The totals for the groups and months are then calculated by the spreadsheet. These numbers are the basis for discovering agreement during the process of production planning.

To measure the approximate impact of these numbers on the critical resources of the plant a *bill of resources* is developed for each product group. For this plant the critical resources are steel, labor (in total), assembly labor (requires the longest lead time to recruit and train), potential revenue, and gross margin. The bill of resources for the bicycles group can be interpreted to mean the following: the average member of this group—the average bicycle—requires .0049 tons of steel, .84 standard hours of all types of labor, .187 standard hours of assembly labor in particular; this average bicycle will sell to the dealer network for $41 and will generate a gross margin of $16.

In nearly all plants the major materials and manpower are critical. Product design engineers and purchasing managers can identify the vital material needs and their contribution to the product group. The manufacturing engineers or industrial engineers will be able to identify the key manpower and machine capacity resources and their impact on the model. Other items become critical as circumstances dictate. In steel plants with electric furnaces kilowatt hours may be critical. In the Southwest water (gallons of river water per day) may be a critical variable. In the manufacture of microcomputers certain integrated circuits (Intel 80286, Motorola MC68010, and so forth) are critical due to high demand and long lead times.

Notice the inclusion of financial variables in the model. In car manufacturing key variables in production planning include the capital to be tied up in production, tooling, and finished goods inventory. Any of the variables could be "dollarized" by adding a column that extends the resource by its dollar value. The marketing and accounting departments can furnish the data necessary to develop the monetary elements of the model.

THE RESOURCE REQUIREMENTS PLAN

Once the projected quantities are entered into the production plan and the bills of resources are developed for each group the spreadsheet can automatically extend and summarize the resources into the *resource requirements plan*, shown at the bottom of Figure 11–1. As changes are made in the production qualities or in the bills of resources these changes are immediately reflected in the needed resources.

Suppose, for example, that marketing seeks to increase the production of bicycles in January. The effects of this increase are immediately visible. If this produces an overload in a resource it may be necessary to reduce production in the other categories or to arrange for increasing these resources through special steel purchases, overtime, subcontracting, or other measures. At some plants these spreadsheets are actually projected on the wall (via video interfaces connected to projecting TV sets) for all responsible managers to see. As the compromise is shaped and consensus is reached all can see both the *process* and the *outcome* of the agreement. As one general manager is fond of reminding them, "All of you built the plan, you had your chance to buy into it or to object, and now the plan is *your* plan. Make it happen!"

A PRODUCTION PLAN FROM A REPETITIVE MANUFACTURER

The repetitive manufacturer is less interested in the particular items or part numbers to be run and more interested in the rate of production. Many of the subordinate plans, including capacity and material plans, are

---

FIGURE 11–2   Production and Inventory Plan

FAMILY: Bicycles
Beginning Inventory: 20

	Jan	Feb	Mar	*QTR*	Apr	May
WORK DAYS/MO.	22	20	21	63	21	22
PRODUCTION RATE	60	60	60		64	64
SALES PLAN	1200	1200	1300	3700	1400	1400
PRODUCTION PLAN	1320	1200	1260	3780	1344	1408
INVENTORY PLAN	140	140	100		44	52

MPS Calendar

MONTH-WEEK NO.	JAN-1	JAN-2	JAN-3	JAN-4	JAN-5	FEB-6
WORK DAYS/WEEK	2	5	5	5	5	5

Weekly Production Schedule

Bicycles MPS Item:	Mix Forecast	1	2	3	4	5
B77 26 in	0.20	24	60	60	60	50
G77 26 in	0.25	30	75	75	75	75
B79 20 in racer	0.20	24	60	60	60	60
T14/6 bicycle	0.30	36	90	90	90	90
B145 banana bike	0.05	6	15	15	15	15

oriented to this rate. As manufacturers shift their philosophy of production from discrete batches to constant flow of repetitive parts, a production plan similar to the one shown in Figure 11–2 may prove useful.

For simplicity's sake this plan just considers one product group or family: bicycles. As was the case in the earlier example the numbers are smaller than the actual case. The actual spreadsheet extends out for a year or more. Note also that this example displays production, sales, and inventory objectives. The relation is obvious: for each month Ending inventory = Beginning inventory + Production − Sales.

The sales plan began as a forecast but achieved the status of plan through the processes discussed in Chapter 10. The production plan is calculated by multiplying production rate by work days/mo. Even though the number of work days varies from month to month, the rate of 60 bicycles per day is constant during the first three months; then it changes to 64 per day. The 22 work days of January times the production rate of 60 gives the production plan for January of 1,320.

The 22 work days of January are broken down into a weekly work calendar in the next section. The first week of January (JAN-1) only has two days, the second week of January (JAN-2) has five days, and so on for the weeks of the year.

In the Weekly Production Schedule we are expanding the production plan into a master production schedule. The two are similar in concept, the difference being in the refinement of the time buckets from months to weeks and the expansion of item detail from product families to actual part numbers (salable end items).

Since this schedule is oriented to the production rate, the calculation of individual items is obvious. The mix forecast gives the expected breakdown of demand by model type. For example, it is expected that 20 percent of the sales for the bicycle family will be the B77 (boy's) 26-inch bike. Therefore, the schedule of item B77 for the first week of January is the production rate (60) times two days times .20 which equals 24 units. The mix forecast is here shown to be constant through all the weeks. Some manufacturers who use this approach have seasonal variations in the mix ratios. This is accommodated by introducing different mix forecasts as necessary throughout the year.

CONCLUSION

This chapter has explored two particular methods of developing production plans on microcomputer spreadsheets. There are many other methods. Some companies face limits on use of material or processes that are best modeled by systems of constraining equations. For example, total output of all processes in a refinery cannot exceed the storage tank capacity; total output cannot give rise to pollutants in excess of EPA allowances.

Faced with such constraints, production planners use spreadsheets for examining various alternatives, but they apply specialized application programs to calculate linear algebraic solutions. Although this may yield the mathematically optimal solution, the spreadsheet flexibility permits manual tinkering with the optimum to explore more intuitive alternatives. Other specialized applications are available for the myriad of production situations.

However, for a very large number of manufacturers the flexibility of the spreadsheet serves the production planning process very well. It serves as a transparent medium for exploring possibilities. It allows the dynamic definition and modification of the bills of resources. It illustrates the resource requirements plan that translates the production numbers into their impact on manpower, equipment, and finances.

In the next chapter we follow production planning to the level of master production scheduling—refining from months to weeks and from product families to specific end items.

CHAPTER TWELVE

Master Production Scheduling

George Plossl, the patriarch of manufacturing consultants and one of the most respected practitioners of the art of management, constantly underscores the importance of master production scheduling. He describes this phase of planning as management's handle on the business and also as the steering wheel by which the direction of senior management is transferred to the plant.[1]

WHO DOES MASTER SCHEDULING?

Most companies have an individual in the Production and Inventory Control Department with the title of master production scheduler. In one typical small plant that manufactured architectural components for the building trade the 460 end items (salable products as opposed to the components that constitute them) were master scheduled by this one individual.

By way of contrast the master scheduler in a large computer plant has a staff of a dozen planners, analysts, and clerks. The products are significantly more sophisticated. The master production schedule (MPS) in this case reflects not the actual items sold to customers (large computers) but the major components of these end-items, processors, controllers, disk drives, and so forth. In this case it is also necessary to develop the final assembly schedule (FAS) that governs the activity of assembling these major components into actual configurations as ordered by the customers.

As in the case of production planning discussed in the last chapter, the master production schedule reflects the consensus of financial, engineering, production, and marketing interests of the firm. Typically, the process is conducted at a managerial level one notch lower than the pro-

---

[1] George W. Plossl, *Manufacturing Control: The Last Frontier for Profits* (Reston, Va.: Reston Publishing, 1973), Chap. 2.

duction plan. Furthermore, the production plan constitutes the limiting shell within which the MPS is formed. The total units planned by the MPS for a month should agree with the units planned for that month by the production plan within some specified percentage.

If *no* master schedule that is feasible by marketing and production standards can be made to fit the production plan, this indicates larger problems. It may be necessary to rethink the earlier commitments of manpower, materials, and money that are represented in the production plan. The MPS can thus serve as a warning of the risks of misallocating resources.

NOTA BENE

The master production schedule should be the barometer of the effectiveness of the planning and control function at the plant.

The MPS offers a degree of specificity that makes it a valuable baseline for measuring many aspects of plant performance. It plans actual part numbers (that is, the part numbers that are either end items or significant spare parts salable as end items). Furthermore, it plans quantities for these parts week by week. (About 70 percent of North American manufacturers conduct master scheduling in weekly increments.) Therefore, we either make the plan each week or we don't—the results are painfully clear to all concerned. A simple spreadsheet of weekly results and line graphs summarizing the performance—posted in prominent places—speak eloquently of a plant's real performance.

A SAMPLE MPS CONSTRUCTED AS A SPREADSHEET

A firm with only a few hundred items to schedule and only a handful of critical work centers to contend with can actually perform master scheduling with spreadsheets. Some firms engaged in the manufacturing of textiles, bicycles and tires (for three examples) do just this. An example is shown in Figure 12–1.

The method used in this example is very similar to that of the first example in the last chapter. The resources in this case are the critical or bottleneck work centers. In this example only two work centers are felt to qualify for this attention, the welding operation and the final assembly operation. The load profile relates each product to these two work centers.

FIGURE 12–1 A Simple Master Production Schedule with Rough-Cut Capacity Planning

Model:	Jan	Feb	Mar	Quarterly Totals
B77 26 in	2500	2300	2400	7200
G77 26 in	1250	1350	1450	4050
B79 20 in racer	250	200	150	600
T14/6 bicycle	2500	2300	2400	7200
B145 banana bike	1250	1350	1450	4050
Monthly Totals	7750	7500	7850	23100

Load Profile per Unit
for Critical Work Centers (Standard Hours)

	Welding Shop	Final Assembly
B77 26 in	0.0750	0.1000
G77 26 in	0.0842	0.1000
B79 20 in racer	0.0500	0.0800
T14/6 bicycle	0.0328	0.0650
B145 banana bike	0.2000	0.3200

Projected Load by Month
(Standard Hours)

Welding Shop	637	642	678	1957
Final Assembly	958	963	1017	2937

For example, consider the load profile for the B77 26-inch bike. The total welding for such a bike (including the frame, crankshaft, front fork, and so forth) adds up to .0750 standard hours. The final assembly of such a bike requires .1000 standard hours—this may encompass assembly, inspection, packing, and hiding the parts necessary for the parents of the world to panic over on Christmas Eve.

What load does the planned schedule place on the welding shop? The calculation is hidden in the load summary line: 2,500 B77s are planned for January. This will require 2,500 times .0750 standard hours of welding or 187.50 hours. This is shown in tabular form below.

	January Schedule	×	Standard Hours Welding	=	Projected Load
B77 26 inch	2,500	×	.0750		187.50
G77 26 inch	1,250	×	.0842		105.25

B79 20-inch racer	250 × .0500	12.50
T14/6 bicycle	2,500 × 0.328	82.00
B145 banana bike	1,250 × .2000	250.00
Total		637.25

Summarizing the load generated by each product line, we arrive at the total load on the welding shop, 637.25, which was rounded to 637 in the bottom section of Figure 12–1 mentioned previously.

Although this gives us a rudimentary look at the total load on the two critical work centers, it doesn't really tell us how this load compares to the plant's ability to meet this demand. Figure 12–2 seeks to address this shortcoming.

This MPS is essentially identical to the one above except that it is defined by weeks instead of months. The capacity element is more thoroughly developed. For each week "Scheduled Hr" is noted on the top line (for example, for the welding shop, two workers are scheduled for 40 hours = 80 hours). However, the plant supervisor will be the first to point out that scheduling 80 hours in a work center does not mean that 80 standard hours of work will be produced there. Some of the time will be dissipated in equipment maintenance, waiting for parts, breaks, cleanup, and so forth.

The ratio of hours actually worked on products to the scheduled hours is called utilization. On the next line the "Utilization" of 91 percent is shown. On the next line a further concession to realism appears, the "Efficiency" of 84 percent. Efficiency is defined as the ratio of standard hours of operations performed compared to hours actually expended on those operations. For example, the final assembly of a B77 bike has a standard of .1 hours per bike. If two workers assemble bikes for 30 minutes, they have expended one hour on that operation. If they produce nine complete bikes during that time, their efficiency is .9 (.1 times 9 bikes) divided by 1 hour, or 90 percent.

The "Net Capacity" of the Welding Shop is 80 hours times 91 percent utilization times 84 percent efficiency, or 61 standard hours per week. The net capacity is shown every week. In this example it is assumed that these three factors are constant over the first seven weeks. In actual practice these vary, and the spreadsheet can be used to reflect the variances. The next line is the "Load (Std Hrs)" which is calculated from the load profiles (not shown) and planned quantities of each product. This calculation is identical to that of the first example. Finally, the "Load (Std Hrs)"

FIGURE 12–2 Master Production Schedule with Capacity Detail

Week No:	1	2	3	4	5	6	7	8	9	10	11	12	13	Totals
Model:														
B77 26 in	48	58	56	55	57	48	58	59	58	61	60	60	46	724
G77 26 in	40	50	52	62	52	53	51	52	50	50	51	52	55	670
B79 20 in racer	52	54	58	59	42	45	58	54	55	58	54	57	54	700
T14/6 bicycle	82	84	85	110	90	88	84	90	72	84	85	84	82	1120
B145 banana bike	35	40	40	34	40	46	40	44	42	37	38	38	40	514
Weekly Totals:	257	286	291	320	281	280	291	299	277	290	288	291	277	3728
					Projected Load by Week									
Welding Shop:														
Scheduled Hr	80	80	80	80	80	80	80	80	80	80	80	80	80	
Utilization	0.91													
Efficiency	0.84													
Net Capacity	61	61	61	61	61	61	61	61	61	61	61	61	61	
Load (Std Hrs)	52	58	59	62	58	59	59	62	57	58	58	59	57	
Load Percent	85	96	97	102	94	96	97	101	94	95	95	96	93	
Final Assembly:														
Scheduled Hr	120	120	120	120	120	120	120	120	120	120	120	120	120	
Utilization	0.89													
Efficiency	0.81													
Net Capacity	87	87	87	87	87	87	87	87	87	87	87	87	87	
Load (Std Hrs)	75	85	86	89	84	86	86	89	84	84	85	85	82	
Load Percent	86	97	99	103	96	98	99	103	97	97	97	98	95	

FIGURE 12–3   Excello Machining Center Load Report

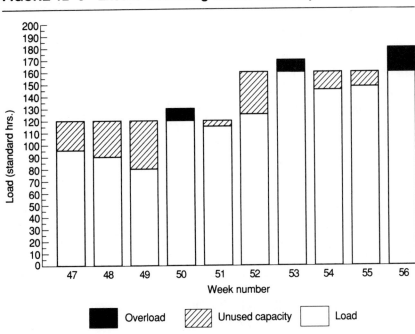

is divided by the "Net Capacity" to give the "Load Percent" displayed on the bottom line.

COMMUNICATING THE LOAD GRAPHICALLY

It has become increasingly popular in many plants to graph the results of this load analysis in a manner similar to Figure 12–3. These graphs can be displayed in the production area to let the work force be aware of constancy of workload even if that workload is no longer as visible in stacks of work in process as it has been in the profligate times of yesteryear. This is a nice way to improve the level of trust between management and the work force.

The author knows one plant where the production manager actually treats the Master Production Schedule as a contract with the foremen of the various departments. They sign off on the capacity promised to meet the plan. If marketing demands a change in the first four weeks of the MPS the production manager will not authorize it until these foremen sign off on it. The effectiveness of this respect between the departments as enforced and communicated by the MPS procedure has caused the on-time shipments to rise from 50 percent to 95 percent in two years and they are now holding this level.

This is literally the bottom line of this exercise in that it compares the desired production with the plant's rough-cut capacity. If discrepancies are observed at this point, it may be necessary to adjust capacity through the addition of workers, overtime, equipment changes, subcontracting, or other measures. Failing to achieve the needed capacity, it may be necessary to reduce the planned production. The methods of dollarizing the economics of these trade-offs that were discussed in the last chapter are just as appropriate here.

NOTA BENE

The final decisions in master production scheduling are never merely computational but economic and judgmental, reflecting the informed assessment of marketing, finance, and manufacturing management.

AVAILABLE TO PROMISE LOGIC— MARKETING THE ATTAINABLE

The stories of the over-promising sales rep are legendary. But he is not entirely to blame. Remember the sales cards that we placed in the pocket of every rep on the force? It listed the key products on the right, the price in the middle, and the factory lead time on the left. If you wanted to buy a B77 bike from him, a glance at the card confirms that you can take delivery in three weeks—that's the lead time on the card. If you want to buy 6,500 of these bikes for your chain of department stores, the lead time is still three weeks—it's still on the card! The obvious problem is that we have not consulted the planned production of these bikes nor the existing orders that have already been placed against this production.

Figure 12–4 illustrates the logic of *available to promise*—a method to combat the spurious logic of the lead time card and give honest answers to the question, "When can I have it?"

Although this technique can be performed on standalone microcomputers, it is almost never done in such splendid isolation. As can be seen from Figure 12–4 the calculation depends on the sum of orders that have already been placed for a particular item. This information is almost always kept on the mainframe. The high volume of order transactions and the extensive interrelatedness of the order-entry database virtually de-

---

FIGURE 12–4   Available to Promise Report

MPS item: B77
    26′ Boy's Bicycle
    Current on Hand: 25

	Jan	Feb	Mar	Apr
Actual Demand				
Customer Orders	125	85	60	25
Warehouse Orders	80	155	30	95
Inter-plant Orders	0	0	10	0
Total Actual Dmd	205	240	100	120
MPS Orders	250	240	260	0
Avail to Promise	70	0	40	0

---

mand this. Therefore, such logic is best performed either on the main-frame or (increasingly) on a microcomputer that is on speaking terms with the mainframe (see Chapter 7 for methods and examples of this).

One very sophisticated (Phase 4) system of networked micros (sans mainframe) includes all the functions of order entry, inventory, available to promise, and accounting. This case is considered in the next chapter.

The logic of the calculation is relatively straightforward. Consider the January column. The total of all existing orders is 205. Production for January is 250. This means that 45 more will be built than are spoken for. Add to these the 25 in inventory currently, and this leaves 70 that can be delivered in January to meet yet-untaken orders. This means that 70 are available to promise.

Note that February's production is completely sold out. Since no B77s are scheduled for April, the production order of 260 in March will have to address demand in both March and April. Since orders for these two months total 220, this leaves only 40 available to promise in March and none in April.

Suppose that our hypothetical bike magnate now approaches our earnest sales rep with an order for 6,500 bikes. Only 70 can be promised in January, another 40 in March, and so on. "Of course, for such a sizable order, we could always bump a few."

Alas, this technique does not guarantee the integrity of every sales-man's promise, but it does furnish an honest assessment of the plant's ability to meet these promises. It closes the feedback loop between the marketing arm and the productive capacity of the company.

**FIGURE 12–5 Master Production Schedule—
Two Level**

Planning Bill for MP65
   3 HP engine - 60%   On hand -   4
   5 HP engine - 40%   On hand -   5

	Jan	Feb	Mar	Apr
MP65 MPS Orders	150	165	200	200
MP65 Avl to Prom	40	100	160	200
Firm Orders 3 HP	50	20	13	0
Prod Frcst 3 HP	24	60	96	120
Tot Exp Dmd 3 HP	74	80	109	120
3 HP MPS Orders	75	80	110	120
3 HP Prj Avl Bal	5	5	6	6
Firm Orders 5 HP	60	45	27	0
Prod Frcst 5 HP	16	40	64	80
Tot Exp Dmd 5 HP	76	85	91	80
5 HP MPS Orders	75	85	90	80
5 HP Prj Avl Bal	4	4	3	3

TWO-LEVEL MASTER SCHEDULING—FOR
MODULAR OR HIGHLY-OPTIONED PRODUCTS

This final micro MPS example addresses the needs of the master scheduler who must schedule at more than one level. (See Figure 12–5.) The products of his firm are offered with a number of options or can be sold in a modular configuration. Computers are one example, as are cars, tractors, mopeds, and some electronic testing equipment.

The key to scheduling these products is an estimate of the distribution of the options. In this case consider a moped (MP65) that is offered with a choice of two engines (3 HP and 5 HP). The estimate of the relative popularity of the engines is called the planning bill for MP65. It is represented here as 60 percent for the 3 HP engine and 40 percent for the 5 HP. In this example we have four mopeds on hand that already include the 3 HP engine and five on hand that have 5 HP engines.

A total of 150 mopeds are scheduled ("MP65 MPS Orders") for production in January. The model uses the available to promise logic of the former example to determine that 40 mopeds are yet unsold in January. Using the planning bill the model estimates that 24 of these (40 times 60 percent) will use 3 HP engines, and the remaining 16 will use 5 HP engines. This leads to an expected demand of 74 3 HP engines and 76 5 HP engines in January. On this basis production for engines ("3 HP MPS Orders" and "5 HP MPS Orders") is fixed by the master scheduler at 75 each. Subsequent months follow the same logic.

CONCLUSION

Microcomputers serve much the same role in master production scheduling that they serve in production planning. The transparency of the logic, its flexibility, and the ease with which many iterations of a plan can be considered support the master scheduler in several ways. It obviously simplifies the routine calculations of his work while eliminating mistakes and documenting his assumptions and footsteps. The micro serves as a fine visualizing vehicle for communicating the plan, or for negotiating the plan, among the managers affected by it. Its obvious logic and transparent presentation of results encourages the serendipity solutions that often represent the best compromise amidst imperfect conditions.

CHAPTER THIRTEEN

Inventory Management

Bruce Chartier made an observation in 1984 about the emerging interest in microcomputers for production and inventory management that is still apropos:

> If productivity can be equated with getting the "biggest bang for the buck," then microcomputers may be the answer to productivity problems for manufacturing firms of all sizes. . . . Although this atmosphere of constant change [referring to the stirs in the market] can be disconcerting to potential users, it should not be allowed to discourage them. Making the move to PCs may be a bit like trying to jump onto a moving train, but the alternative could well mean being left behind.[1]

Productivity is the heart and soul of better inventory management. No black magic is involved. If we only had to manage one item, any of us could keep the book count exactly equal to actual count, order the right quantities at the right times, store it carefully, and account for its every move. The techniques are almost always well known but less frequently applied simply because of the grand diversity, proliferation, and interrelatedness of manufacturing inventories. If managers are not extraordinarily productive in their use of time and effort, the volume and complexity of decisions overwhelm them, and stopgap solutions step into the breach. These include safety stock, safety lead time, staging parts early for production orders, and so forth.

Microcomputers offer a variety of techniques for helping the frenetic inventory manager corral these wild horses. This chapter offers several such ideas in the hope of sparking many others in the Reader.

---

[1] Bruce A. Chartier, "Microcomputers = Productivity Power," *P&IM Review and APICS News,* January 1984, pp. 32–37.

GET THE BIG PICTURE—BEFORE GETTING FLOODED BY THE DETAILS

I've known inventory managers who are bears on the detail line items while letting millions of dollars accumulate in unneeded stock. This is like combing the tassels on one corn stalk while letting the raccoons have the rest of the field. One way to keep the raccoons out is to build a fence around the crop. *Aggregate inventory performance measures* are designed to build just such fences—to keep the long and high view clearly in front of the decision makers and policy setters.

There are two dimensions to the measurement of aggregate inventory goals. One is the measurement of the inventory itself; the other is measurement of the formal systems designed to control it.

Mike Hunter offers an example of the former dimension. He suggests the development of simple models based on the functions that inventory serves in manufacturing—safety stock, lot size, hedge, anticipation, and transportation.[2] Although the allocation of stock to these categories is often not perfectly precise, such a model enables the planner to compare planned levels of these functional areas to actual results. Because of the difficulty of this allocation, more inventory managers summarize stock by segment: raw materials, work in process, stocked components/subassemblies, finished goods, and maintenance/repair/operations (MRO). In either case, if the micro is connected to the mainframe, these aggregate figures can be downloaded into spreadsheets for summary, comparison to plan (probably in a micro spreadsheet), and graph building.

The second aspect of aggregate measures concerns the soundness of the control systems. Here again, a spreadsheet is well suited to monitor such key success criteria as reduction of inventory levels, ratio of on-time orders to all orders, accuracy of inventory records, comparison of scheduled production with actual production, purchasing performance (in price, delivery, and quality), stockouts, and stock turnover. An example of one such application is offered in Figure 13–1. Formal system performance measures can be extended far beyond inventory-specific questions to all of the key performance measures. That subject was covered in Chapter 2.

Richard P. Artes and John N. Petroff of Comserv Corporation describe an approach that is similar in its macro outlook but novel in its ac-

---

[2] Mike Hunter, "Inventory: Asset or Liability?" *1986 APICS Conference Proceedings,* p. 261ff.

FIGURE 13–1 Tracking MRP II Key Performance Indicators

CLOSED LOOP AREA	RESPONSIBILITY	MEASUREMENT	CALCULATION	1987 Jan	Feb	Mar	Apr	May
INVENTORY MANAGEMENT	VP Mfg. Mtls. Mgr. Inven. Mgr.	Inventory Investment v. Plan	Inventory $000 Actual Inventory $000 Planned	2015 2042	2041 2035	2087 2040	2104 2050	2064 2035
		Inventory Record Accuracy	Correct Cycle Counts/ Cycle Counts Taken %	87.4%	87.9%	88.1%	87.8%	89.6%
		Open Order Accuracy	Correct Open Orders/ Open Orders Sampled %	91.2%	93.5%	92.5%	96.1%	94.3%
		Transaction Accuracy	Trans. Processed/ Trans. submitted %	83.4%	86.4%	89.7%	91.5%	92.3%
		Inventory Turnover	Inventory $/ Cost of Goods Sold	4.356	4.410	4.568	4.239	4.651
		Stockouts	Line Items picked/ Line Items %	86.5%	85.9%	87.4%	90.2%	88.6%

SOURCE: Jeffrey H. Cooper, "The Microcomputer—a Multipurpose P&IC Tool," *1984 APICS Conference Proceedings (Computers and Software)*, p. 4ff.

FIGURE 13–2 Projected Inventory

Beginning Inventory: $ 83533

MODEL	JAN	FEB	MAR	APR	MAY	JUN
			UNITS			
Hydro II	10	15	20	30	35	40
Flow Master	30	30	30	30	40	40
Mister Miser	100	120	110	140	150	170
			DOLLARS			
Standard Cost:						
25.00	250	375	500	750	875	1000
100.00	3000	3000	3000	3000	4000	4000
225.00	22500	27000	24750	31500	33750	38250
Total Shipng Plan	25750	30375	28250	35250	38625	43250
Labor & O/H offset	5205	4890	6010	6695	7430	0
Material offset	23360	29240	31930	35820	0	0
Cost accumulated	28565	34130	37940	42515	0	0
Inventory change	2815	3755	9690	7265	0	0
Projected inventry	86348	90103	99793	107058	0	0

SOURCE: Richard P. Artes and John N. Petroff, "Solving Manufacturing Problems with a Personal Computer," *APICS Microprocessor Seminar Proceedings*, January/February 1984, pp. 211–18.

counting for work in process and material ordering. It is shown in Figure 13-2.

This model was used by a small manufacturer to project inventory investments. This spreadsheet formed the basis of inventory investment plans for the primary product line which included about 10 items. It was of particular value in drawing the master production scheduler into meaningful conversations with finance. It got both of them talking the same language. In actual practice it proved about 95 percent accurate in predicting investment levels over a 12-month horizon.

The products are listed under MODEL with production units in the top section and with dollarized costs in the lower section. The "Labor & O/H offset" line assumes that labor is added the month before shipping. The "Material offset" line assumes that material is brought in-house two months before shipping. Thus, the "Material offset" for January plus the "Labor & O/H offset" for February adds up to the "Total Shipng Plan" for March, which, in turn, is the unit plan times the standard cost. The model is simple but 95 percent effective for them. I wish all (or even most) of my predictions were as good!

ANALYZING WORK IN PROCESS AT WESTINGHOUSE ELECTRIC

The simple model in the preceding example does account for raw materials and work in process in the straightforward circumstances of that firm. Most manufacturers face a more complicated and difficult accumulation of costs as work progresses from raw material to salable end item. Figures 13–3 and 13–4 illustrate a clever scheme for quantifying the addition of value (material, labor, and overhead) to work in process. This is a variation on a theme by Victor W. Emmelkamp of Westinghouse Electric Corporation (specifically, the Power Generation division in Orlando, Florida). He writes,

> The general manager . . . asked me to calculate the right amount of inventory to support the 1985 production plan for [the] plant. Furthermore, he wanted to know what impact several new product lines being readied for production would have on inventory.
>
> These are the perfect questions to be answered using engineered inventory standards. And just to give us a challenge, he wanted the answer in 10 days! Twice before we generated standards for his plant, and it took eight industrial engineers about four weeks of full-time effort to develop the answer using a totally manual method. This time only two engineers were available. But by utilizing an IBM XT and the 1-2-3 from Lotus spreadsheet the task was accomplished in just eight days.[3]

Two examples have been created here to illustrate this technique in two environments. Item 1 is typical of a job shop. Most of the material is issued to the first operation. The operations take one to three days each. Consider the first day: Material worth $275 was issued to the order. Twelve hours of labor (at $12.45 per hour) was added for "Labor cost" of $149. The "Overhead rate" of 40 percent is multiplied by the "Labor cost" to give "Overhead cost$" of $60. The total cost added to the order on Day 1 is $275 + $149 + $60 = $484. During the second day the job is still in operation 10. "Labor cost $" of $75 and "Overhead cost$" of $30 are added for an accumulated cost of $589. In this manner we build a profile of cost buildup for the work order. The sum of scheduled work orders can be used to model the flow of accounting cost into the shop. The second item (assembly area) illustrates the flow of accounting cost in a more repetitive environment with more operations, lower labor cost, and

---

[3] Victor W. Emmelkamp, "Engineered Inventory Standards the Easy Way—Using Lotus 1-2-3." Unpublished.

FIGURE 13–3   Work in Process Cost Build-Up

Item 1 - Job shop: batch of 100

Day number	1	2	3	4	5	6	7	8	9
Operation	10		20			30	40	50	
Added matl	$ 275					28			
Labor hours	12	6	12	0	0	5.5	6.5	3	2
Labor rate	12.45	12.45	11.65			15.85	16.5	12.5	12.5
Labor cost	$ 149	75	140	0	0	87	107	38	25
Overhead rate	40%	40%	40%	40%	40%	40%	40%	40%	40%
Overhead cost	$ 60	30	56	0	0	35	43	15	10
Accum. cost:	484	589	785	785	785	935	1085	1138	1173

Item 2 - Assembly area: batch of 100

Day number	1	2	3	4	5	6	7	8	9
Operation	10	20	30	40-60	70	80-110	120-180	190	200
Added matl	$ 115	15	20	72	65	80	88	65	6
Labor hours	3.5	1.5	0.5	1.6	4.6	2.9	1.5	7.5	7.4
Labor rate	9.45	8.50	7.85	6.85	5.90	9.50	8.75	9.50	5.65
Labor cost	$ 33	13	4	11	27	28	13	71	42
Overhead rate	40%	40%	40%	40%	40%	40%	40%	40%	40%
Overhead cost	13	5	2	4	11	11	5	28	17
Accum. cost:	161	194	220	307	410	529	635	799	864

FIGURE 13–4   Work in Process Cost Build-Up

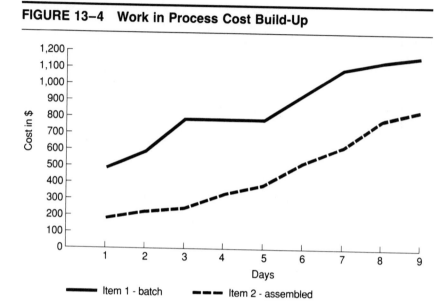

constant addition of material. Figure 13-4 illustrates the accounting cost buildup for both items in graphic form.

I say accounting cost because it must be remembered that we will probably pay the force to work on something tomorrow anyway. We can't eliminate this expense by canceling the work orders. Second, many plants are making strong efforts to evolve in the direction of just-in-time manufacturing. As the schedule is leveled, the costs become daily constants, and accounting for work in process becomes transparently simple.

PHYSICAL CONTROL OF INVENTORY AND CYCLE COUNTING

The next case concerns a vertically integrated textile and apparel mill that incorporates four separate businesses in one location: yarn manufacturing, knitting, dyeing/bleaching, and cutting/sewing. The first three are highly capital-intensive and very repetitive processes. The last is labor-intensive and somewhat less repetitive. The company has selected micro-computers — networked together — to address inventory control, storage, production planning, ordering, and shop floor feedback.

In the textile business, lot control is vital. The micros support a random access locator system through a system of bar-coded labels which are printed by printers and read by scanners all attached to the micros. This gives the benefit of up-to-the-minute information on every dye lot during three shifts. Training was critical in inculcating the attitude that the PCs were as vital to the work as the manufacturing equipment. The whole shop was well rehearsed in the care necessary to make the system work. In turn, the use of bar codes and regular cycle counting minimizes opportunities for errors.

Roy Piciacchia comments: "It is important that employees and management have active participation in the design and execution of the cycle count program. By allowing employees to participate in the design, the system [supported] the bottom-up management style of developing daily, weekly, and monthly procedures which would be adhered to by the working group."[4]

Cycle count lists—organized by location—were available to the users of PCs. The users selected the order in which to carry out the counts. The system generated pre- and post-count documentation to guarantee that all counts had been made and monitored the resulting level of inventory accuracy (see examples in Figure 13–5).

DISTRIBUTION MODELS

Alan Dunn observes that it is virtually impossible to consider all the contingencies of physical distribution—truck loads, carloads, weight, volume, transportation strategies, carrying costs, customer service, and so on—without PCs.[5] One such schematic for analyzing the total raw material-to-customer cost is offered by VanDeMark.[6] He develops spreadsheets for calculating the five elements of this total cost: unit cost, set-up cost, carrying cost, freight cost (public carriers), and transfer cost (company conveyances). These costs are evaluated in the context of seven flow strategies—from purchase for immediate shipment to branches at one end of the spectrum all the way to purchase centrally, process, store centrally, and then transfer to branches. For a given product line, the

---

[4] Roy Piciacchia, "Microcomputer Applications in a Vertically Integrated Textile and Apparel Manufacturing Environment," *1985 APICS Conference Proceedings,* pp. 140–45.

[5] Alan Dunn, "Distribution Management in the 1980s," *1986 APICS Conference Proceedings,* pp. 394–98.

[6] Robert L. VanDeMark, "The Path of Flow Dynamics of Network Distribution," *1986 APICS Conference Proceedings,* pp. 412–15.

FIGURE 13–5 Three Steps to Cycle Counting

CYCLE COUNT LOG

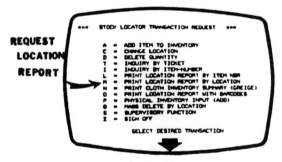

CYCLE COUNTING – DAILY PROCEDURE

CYCLE COUNT REPORT

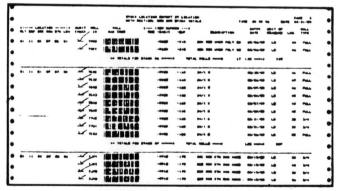

SOURCE: Roy Piciacchia, "Microcomputer Applications in a Vertically Integrated Textile and Apparel Manufacturing Environment," *1985 APICS Conference Proceedings*, p. 143.

seven strategies are evaluated as shown in Figure 13–6. In this simulation the lowest-cost strategy is the sixth one (note that strategies 1, 3, 5 did not pertain for logistical reasons).

A DISTRIBUTION NETWORK BUILT ENTIRELY AROUND MICROCOMPUTERS

The success and growth of this diverse manufacturer caused them to reexamine their computer system. The production director explained: "The way it was developed in the early days left production with one set of programs, sales another, costing yet another. It came to a point 18 months ago when we had to decide whether to stay with the investment and information already available to us or completely change the philosophy of the way we were doing it."

The firm required cost-effective computer power in four locations: a head office and two factories in England and a European depot in Holland.

"As we are a sales organization, we cannot afford a single moment when we cannot translate an order into a picking document, into a dispatch, into an invoice. So we need a network, capable of going around a breakdown or going to a second machine in order to keep our sales moving."

A cluster of Unisys micros and related software handles every order from each of the 200 sales representatives. Orders are received at the head office, input directly into an order evaluation system, and printed out in the warehouse 120 miles away. Once the order has been picked, confirmed as picked, and is on the road to the customer, the computer is informed, and that night the invoice is prepared to follow the goods.

The larger configuration at the head office contains the company's sales histories, customer archives, and more. The European depot's micro controls stock in that location. The redundant links in the network allow work to proceed in the event of the failure of any single system or communications link.

CONCLUSION

This chapter has only opened the window on a wide world of micro solutions in inventory management and control. The classical system functions of inventory database maintenance, transaction processing, order processing, and such can also be done with micros if volumes are modest.

FIGURE 13–6   Calculating Optimum Flow through a Distribution Network

---

The first example is a manufactured item in a company which now has 1 factory, 3 central warehouses, and 15 sales branches. The data for this simulation are as follows:

Unit cost - $4.600 each for 2000 quantity (#2, #4)
            5.220 each for 800 quantity   (#6)
            6.360 each for 200 quantity   (#7)
"K" cost - Factory is 24% or .24
        Warehouse is 24% or .24
        Branches use 30% or .30
Monthly usage - Factory 1200
              Warehouse 340
              Branch 80
Freight cost - Factory, included in the unit cost
Transfer cost - Truck $30 per hour
            Labor $18 per hour
            Round trip, M to W - 6 hours
                      W to B - 2-½ hours
                      M to B - 9 hours
            Weight: 9000# to warehouse
                     3200# to branch
                     1.5# per item
Set-up cost - Factory $12 (paperwork only)
           Warehouse $18
           Branch $9
Order quantity - Factory 2000
             Warehouse 800
              Branch 200

For this example, the simulation includes only options numbered 2, 4, 6, and 7. The options #1, #3 and #5 do not pertain. The analysis is as follows:

		2	4	6	7
Unit cost	UM	4.600	4.600	5.220	6.360
Set-up cost	SM	.006	.006		
Carrying cost	KM	.767	.767		
Unit cost	UC		5.373	5.220	
Transfer cost	TC		.046	.046	
Set-up cost	SC		.022	.022	
Carrying cost	KC		.123	.123	
Unit cost	UB	5.373	5.564	5.411	6.360
Transfer cost	TB	.203	.056	.056	.203
Set-up cost	SB	.045	.045	.045	.045
Carrying cost	KB	.168	.174	.169	.199
Outgoing cost		5.789	5.839	<u>5.681</u>	6.807

SOURCE: Robert L. VanDeMark, "The Path of Flow Dynamics of Network Distribution," *1986 APICS Conference Proceedings*, pp.412–15.

We have assayed to highlight only those micro applications whose originality and utility commend them to the preferred Reader.

It is not the particular applications themselves that will eventually bring the greatest value. It is the methodology of detecting problem areas, modeling the relevant trade-offs and relationships, solving the problems, and executing the new vision in the workplace. This problem-solving cycle is as personally satisfying as it is corporately profitable. The micro can serve as a tireless clerical catalyst toward this noble goal.

CHAPTER FOURTEEN

Production Activity (Shop Floor) Control

So far, most of the applications considered in this part of the book have addressed planning—strategic planning, forecasting, production planning, master production scheduling, and so on. Now the discussion advances to production activity control where, finally, something gets built!

There are dozens of applications for microcomputers on the shop floor. These range from work performance monitoring to robotic control. The major case study in Chapter 3 illustrated the use of micros in planning and measuring utilization, efficiency, and actual production by work center. This chapter offers a few more examples of successful use of micros on the shop floor, from the straightforward measurement of work content at Optical Engineering to the very sophisticated robotic adjustments and line balancing at Nippon Electric Company. The conclusion of the chapter lists diverse applications of micros to kindle the imagination of the Reader.

A word of caution is in order prior to taking up the case studies. For all their convenience and portability, microcomputers are still sensitive electronic devices highly susceptible to the intrusion of dust, strong magnetic fields, voltage spikes, and factory fluids. I have observed many varying provisions for the health of micros in the shop. Some micros get special cases and positive air pressure systems with good filters to protect them. Some are enclosed in small booths and desktop covers to shelter them from the fluids. Some are guarded by surge protectors purchased from local computer stores. Some merely have dust covers (usually jammed between the steel table and the steam pipe) which afford little real protection. Many are brazenly abused—covered with dust, metal filings, and grease. Although they seem to display a certain stoic reliability under such duress, sooner or later this causes a failure—usually of the disk drive, sometimes the keyboard. In some environments, such as electronic assembly areas, the factory ambiance is as perfectly suited to micros as would be the cushy office. In rougher areas some measure of protection such as clean voltage and dust covers will pay more than commensurate dividends.

SHOP FLOOR PERFORMANCE MEASUREMENT
AT OPTICAL ENGINEERING

The Woodworking Division of Optical Engineering, Inc., makes about 100 different laser-engraved walnut specialty items. The division used an IBM mainframe to generate the master schedule and capacity plan.[1] Originally, this system also generated reports on plant performance and wood yield, but these reports lacked timeliness and specificity. Paul Scott writes:

> A chart that graphed plant performance showed variations of up to 45 percent over two-week increments. Even though the overall trend of the graph was upward, the jagged saw tooths were of concern because there was no way of knowing what had happened to cause a drop or a rise in the graph. . . . Perhaps these oscillations were caused by a low quality shipment of lumber, or by a machine that was malfunctioning, or by the shipping schedule itself.[2]

Gathering the needed information into a spreadsheet brought a clearer view of the causes and effects on the shop floor. It also saved two hours a day of manual effort. Figures 14–1 through 14–4 illustrate the techniques used. The spreadsheet in Figure 14–1 calculates the material needed on the basis of scheduled orders, material standards, and year-to-date yield percentages for that particular grade. The bottom window (beginning at R40) is a permanently stored list of all grades with the associated standards and YTD yields; these are then copied up to the actual report in the top window as needed.

Figure 14–2 presents an updated priority list of current work orders. This tells the shop what order to work on next. Figure 14–3 calculates the work center loads and pieces per hour standards for the workers. Figure 14–4 calculates plant performance based on earned hours and direct labor hours. Scott notes, "By producing the report 'on site' and in a timely manner, we now have the ability to respond to any significant changes in performance and immediately analyze any contributing factors." He also

---

[1] John Paul Scott, "Micros and Manufacturing," *APICS Microprocessor Seminar Proceedings,* January/February 1984, pp. 252–58.

[2] Ibid.

FIGURE 14-1

SOURCE: John Paul Scott, "Micros and Manufacturing," *APICS Microprocessor Seminar Proceedings*, January/February 1984, p. 254.

	C1	C2	C3	C4	C5	C6	C7
R1							
R2			MATERIAL RELEASE WORKSHEET		Date: _____		
R3			***********************************				
R4						B/B: .65	<<<<<<<<
R5						4/4: .75	LUMBER
R6						5/4: .72	YTD YIELD
R7						6/4: .81	<<<<<<<<
R8							
R9	WORK		SCHED	TYPE	MATERIAL	YTD	MATERIAL
R10	ORDER #	ITEM #	QUANTITY	STOCK	STANDARD	YIELD%	RELEASE
R11	***********************************						
R12	1295	16-00029	3000	3/4	1.55	.65	7154 BD'
R13	1296	16-00018	2500	4/4	4.33	.75	14433 BD'
R14	1297	16-00035	5500	5/4	7.45	.72	56910 BD'
R15	1298	16-00021	1200	6/4	3.25	.81	4815 BD'
	(FORMULA FOR MATERIAL RELEASE =				SCHED/QTY*MTL.STD./YTD YIELD%)		
					= COL.#4 * COL.#6 / COL.#7		
R40	......	16-00000	......	3/4	1.85	.65	......
R41	......	16-00001	......	4/4	5.75	.75	......
R42	......	16-00002	......	5/4	3.25	.72	......
R42	......	16-00003	......	6/4	6.55	.81	......
R43	......	16-00004	......	3/4	8.33	.65	......
R44	......	16-00005	......	4/4	2.5	.75	......

FIGURE 14-2

	C1	C2	C3	C4
R1				
R2		PRODUCTION ACTIVITY WORKSHEET		
R3		**		
R4		DATE: _____		
R5	**			
R6	WORK/ORDER #	ITEM NUMBER	DESCRIPTION	SCHEDULED/QTY
R7	**			
R8	1340	16-2900-442	JEWELRY BOX #5	9600
R9	1373	16-2900-452	PLAQUE #7	3356
R10	1376	16-2900-445	JEWELRY BOX #1	2750
R11	1375	16-2900-476	PLAQUE #3	2750
R12	1360	16-2900-432	PLAQUE #5	6000
R..	**			
R50	. . . .	16-2900-400	PLAQUE #1	. . . . .
R51	. . . .	16-2900-401	PLAQUE #2	. . . . .
R52	. . . .	16-2900-402	PLAQUE #3	. . . . .
R53	. . . .	16-2900-403	PLAQUE #4	. . . . .
R54	. . . .	16-2900-404	PLAQUE #5	. . . . .
R55	. . . .	16-2900-405	PLAQUE #6	. . . . .
R..	. . . .	. . . .	. . . .	. . . . .
R100	. . . .	16-2900-500	JEWELRY BOX #2	. . . . .

SOURCE: John Paul Scott, "Micros and Manufacturing," *APICS Microprocessor Seminar Proceedings*, January/February 1984, p. 255.

developed spreadsheets to analyze the relative performances of various products.

The average yearly improvement in plant performance ranged from 6 to 8 percent. During the first six months of use of the microcomputer tracking, performance increased 23.5 percent. Scott notes:

Was this dramatic increase in productivity generated by the microcomputer? I think not. It was the entire work force who had the benefit of more accurate routings and time standards, more believable and up-to-date schedules. Also each employee was aware that management was asking them for something extra and involving them in a project that required their input (daily tally cards) and their cooperation (accurate production data). Furthermore, when very definite production goals were communicated to them they were oftentimes exceeded.[3]

MICRO KANBAN[4]

This case presumes some familiarity with the kanban system of production control as practiced by Toyota, several other Japanese manufactur-

---

[3] Ibid., p. 257.

[4] Bernard J. Schroer, J. T. Black, and Shou Xiang Zhang, "Microcomputer Analyzes 2-card Kanban System for 'Just-in-Time' Small Batch Production," *IE (Industrial Engineer) Magazine*, June 1984, 54–65.

FIGURE 14–3

	C1	C2	C3	C4	C5
R1					
R2			PRODUCT ROUTE WORKSHEET		
R3			**		
R4		DATE: _____			
R5		PROD./SHAPE: 16-000-543			
R6		DESCRIPTION: PLAQUE #8			
R7					
R9	**				
R10	SEQ/OP#	MACHINE	MFG/PRINT	TIME/STAND	PARTS/HOUR
R11	**				
R12	1/430	PLANER	MFG-1987A	.0004	2500.00
R13	2/447	RIP SAW	MFG-1987A	.0008	1250.00
R14	3/432	CHOP SAW	MFG-1986A	.0012	833.33
R15	4/433	LAMINATION	MFG-1986A	.0075	133.33
R16	5/440	ABRASIVE SND	MFG-1986A	.0034	294.12
R17	6/453	PANEL SAW	MFG-1985C	.0065	153.85
R18	7/456	SHAPER	MFG-1985C	.0053	188.68
R19	8/451	FORM SANDER	MFG-1985C	.0044	227.27
R20	9/477	FINISH	MFG-1984B	.0073	136.99
				.0368	27.17

SOURCE: John Paul Scott, "Micros and Manufacturing," *APICS Microprocessor Seminar Proceedings*, January/February 1984, p. 255.

ers, and a number of firms in other lands. It is of note that a number of kanban users are migrating to direct computer-to-computer links for the communication of production signals from workstation to workstation, and from buying plant to supplying plant. This trend notwithstanding, there continues to be interest and value in the use of the two-card kanban system.

The two cards are the move kanban (authorizing the material movement) and the production kanban (authorizing production). The question naturally arises: How can one best balance the plant, minimize inventory, and not pay an undue penalty in underused workcells? The answer requires years of experience, engineering savvy, and sound planning. The control points include the assignment of personnel and machines and the deployment of kanbans.

Schroer, Black, and Shou have addressed this difficulty by "building" simulated assembly plants in the microcomputer using the SIMAN simulation language on an IBM Personal Computer. This enables them to simulate workcells, stockpoints, delivery carts, and production demands. Then they test the value of additional kanbans (or delivery carts) and alternate flow schemes in relation to production. Although simulation is always less than an exact duplicate of reality, it can successfully predict

FIGURE 14–4

	C1	C2	C3	C4	C5
R1		PLANT PERFORMANCE WORKSHEET			
R2		**			
R3	FILE: PLANT/PERF			DIRECT LABOR/HRS:	929.25
R4	MFG/WKS: 46 & 47			EARNED/HRS:	968.83
R5	DATE: _____			PLANT PERFORMANCE:	104.26
R6	************	******************	******************	******************	**********
R7	ITEM/NUMBER	DESCRIPTION	SHP/QUANTITY	EARNED/HRS	TIME/STAND.
R8	************	******************	******************	******************	**********
R9	16-000-338	PLAQUE # 4	2305	39.185	.017
R10	16-000-641	PLAQUE # 6	3359	80.616	.024
R11	16-000-782	PLAQUE # 3	1566	377.406	.241
R12	16-000-905	PLAQUE # 8	2339	144.5502	.0618
R13	16-000-422	PLAQUE # 1	5591	327.0735	.0585
R14					
R15				968.8307	
	***********	******************	******************	******************	**********
R50	16-000-541	PEN SET #1	. . . . .		.017
R51	16-000-542	PEN SET #2	. . . . .		.0693
R52	16-000-543	PEN SET #3	. . . . .		.094
R53	16-000-544	PEN SET #4	. . . . .		.0367
R54	16-000-545	PEN SET #5	. . . . .		.0603
R55	16-000-546	PEN SET #6	. . . . .		.0082

SOURCE: John Paul Scott, "Micros and Manufacturing," *APICS Microprocessor Seminar Proceedings*, January/February 1984, p. 256.

certain problem areas, and it offers valuable insight into the trade-offs involved. It is far less expensive to discover the problems in the PC than in the plant after it is laid out.

FED UP WITH ONE-WAY FEEDBACK?

There are as many variations on shop floor feedback as there are shop floors. We will briefly consider three quite different approaches among many to acquaint the Reader with this fertile field for efficiencies.

The vertically integrated textile and apparel mill described in the last chapter also employs a microcomputer to print out bar code knit/dye tickets (see Figure 14–5). These are then read by bar code readers throughout the production process, which performs the needed tracking of particular fabric and dye lots with unblinking consistency. If the bar code image is wrinkled, soiled, spindled, or mutilated, the part number can be keyed in manually. This system successfully manages an average of 7,000 to 9,000 rolls of cloth in various states of process.

In Liege, Belgium, overlooking the ancient churches and orchards of the Meuse River valley, is a thoroughly modern facility for the produc-

---

FIGURE 14–5   Knit/Dye Ticket

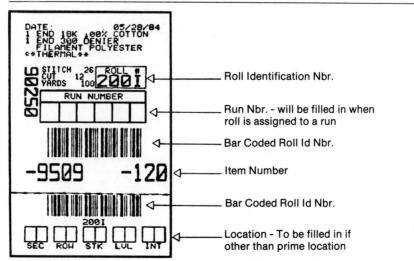

SOURCE: Roy Piciacchia, "Microcomputer Applications in a Vertically Integrated Textile and Apparel Manufacturing Environment," *1985 APICS Conference Proceedings*, p. 141.

tion of microcomputers and terminals. This facility extends the concept of shop floor data collection (also via bar code) to shop floor feedback. Those in the plant who need to know the location of particular orders, purchased parts, and workers can secure this information from the mainframe systems to which all the data collection devices are connected. As with Optical Engineering, timely information in the plant—right at the point where decisions and improvements can be made—fully justifies the cost of providing it.

A sister terminal plant in New Jersey adds a twist of its own. Much of the information is gained via "free reads"—that is, a scan of the bar code that does not involve the worker. Each circuit board has a unique bar code label affixed to it at a cost of about five cents (one cent for the label and four cents for the labor of attaching it). As these boards are transported through wave solder machines or into the oven for drying, embedded bar code readers automatically scan the code and feed the information into program controllers which, in turn, pass it along to microcomputers. Each micro can control 16 program controllers. Each program controller can manage 16 bar code readers. Before some eager young analyst suggests that we only need one micro to run 256 bar code readers, let me point out that the micro would never keep up.

The micros constantly generate multicolor bar graphs displaying the quantities and "ages" of the work in process. The work that has been in the circuit board shop less than three days is shown in green; the work that has been in the shop between three and five days is shown in yellow; the boards languishing in the shop for more than five days are depicted in telltale red. This provides constant visual feedback to the workers on the line (and to their supervisors and management) of the relative effectiveness of their work. It also highlights quality problems (that keep circuit boards from leaving on time) to expedite the resolution of these problems before they multiply the bad parts.

MICROS AND COMPUTER-INTEGRATED MANUFACTURING (CIM)

The acronym CIM verges on the tragic loss of meaning associated with such lamented, great monikers of the past as MRP, "easy to use," and "state of the art." Rare is the computer vendor who does not offer CIM, but rarer is the one who can define it meaningfully. Without trying to fix the spectrum of meanings of CIM, we confine ourselves to a discussion of the linking of intelligent programmable devices such as distributed numeric control machine tools (DNC), robots, computer-aided design workstations, planning and control systems, and automated material handlers.[5]

Although several valiant attempts have been made to develop completely integrated manufacturing systems, only a handful have succeeded. Many of these noble efforts founder on the shoals of incompatible network protocol (discussed in Chapter 7). Shindelman and Utzig boldly suggest that PCs may prove to be the glue that binds islands of information into cohesive CIM networks. Their hypothesis is that the simpler protocols of PCs lend themselves to simple networks among themselves, while their flexibility enables them to communicate to a wide variety of CIM components such as CAD workstations, robots, mainframe planning and control systems, and DNC tools.[6]

While this is feasible so far as creating intelligible links, it minimizes the towering issue of what these devices say to each other once they can

---

[5] Wayne L. Rhodes, Jr., "Pulling It All Together," *Manufacturing Systems,* Summer 1984, pp. 14–18.

[6] Lester S. Shindelman and Carter C. Utzig, "Move over Mainframe: Make Way for the Micro," *1986 APICS Conference Proceedings,* p. 468.

talk. Suppose that a conference call could be arranged between 30 diplomatic representatives, each speaking but one of 30 different languages. Who speaks first, and who understands him? The CAD station stores diameters, cartesian coordinates, and FORTRAN data arrays. Without a great deal of help, it cannot relate to the item file, product structure, and open orders of an MRP system. PCs may be the links, but great translator programs must be written first.

These difficulties notwithstanding, the author has secondhand knowledge of at least two highly integrated manufacturing systems that are based on microcomputer links, but this must await the discussion of engineering systems and micro MRP in later chapters. Although it does not qualify as full CIM, the next case study does give a firsthand account of rather clever integration of microcomputers into the repetitive manufacturing of consumer electronic goods.

CASE STUDY—NIPPON ELECTRIC COMPANY

Nippon Electric Company (NEC) has dozens of plants throughout Japan, South America, and Georgia. Last fall I visited their new state-of-the-art facility in Gotemba, Japan. Here, in the very shadow of Mount Fuji, they manufacture video tape recorders (what we call VCRs). They are only running two of the three lines designed, and each line has a capacity of 1,000 to 1,200 VTRs per day. Quality is critically important. The plant is pervaded by the philosophy that poor quality leads to lower sales and higher costs hence making them twice noncompetitive. The spirit of Shigeo Shingo (Japan's quality guru) palpably haunts the halls.

Coincidentally, the first name of the plant manager is Takumi—the Japanese word for the continual quest for excellence. Now that gives the American visitor pause!

There are about 700 workers in the plant, but nearly 200 of those are subcontracted workers who are laid off when volume requirements go down. About 280 are women who are also laid off—the lifetime employment (of song and legend) only applies to 220 of the 700 workers in the plant. There are about 60 microcomputers throughout the plant, all of which seem to be operated by the "lifetime" employees.

Microprocessors abound in the robotic and autonomation devices (over and above the 60 PCs).[7] For example, the actual VHS drum heads (which have the most critical tolerances of the VTR) are made in essen-

---

[7] Autonomation means autonomous, self-correcting automation.

FIGURE 14–6A The Stages in Manufacturing VTR Drum Heads at NEC (from Right to Left)

FIGURE 14–6B The Automated Line That Does This Manufacturing

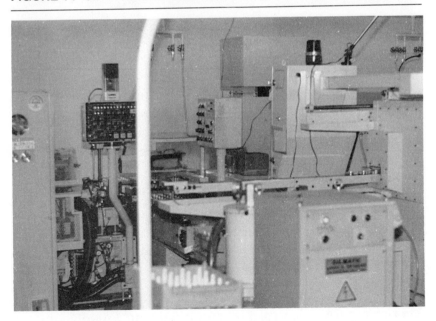

tially an autonomated process (see Figures 14–6A and 14–6B). The aluminum castings go through all milling, grinding, drilling, deburring, polishing, and so forth without being touched by humans.

The first several stations (see Figure 14–7) along the assembly line

FIGURE 14–7 Microprocessor-Controlled Stations at NEC Testing the Completed VTR Drum Heads Prior to Assembly

test for flatness of the planar surfaces, roundness of the drum surface it-self, static testing, and so on. If a drum head fails for any of these items, it is automatically kicked off the line. It isn't a true poka-yoke (Japanese for mistake proof) system in that it does not actually stop the process that is producing the heads, but it is a very quality conscious process and one that uses rather sophisticated robotics and microprocessor electronics.

It is interesting to note that this entire plant was designed in about six months, largely by a group of 20 engineers in the plant, one of which was the plant manager, a very experienced engineer. They also worked with their suppliers, to some degree, to develop these poka-yoke devices. The expertise, concepts, programming, testing, and training seems to have come largely from the internal plant engineers (average age—barely out of college) and the suppliers themselves.

Microcomputers Control Test and Alignment Equipment

The head and video signal alignment involves 11 microcomputers driving half a dozen screwdrivers each (see Figure 14–8). These actually lower into the potentiometers and variable resistors on the printed circuit boards and perform very sophisticated alignment and adjustment. When the unit

FIGURE 14–8 NEC PC Controlling the Calibration and Alignment of VTRs

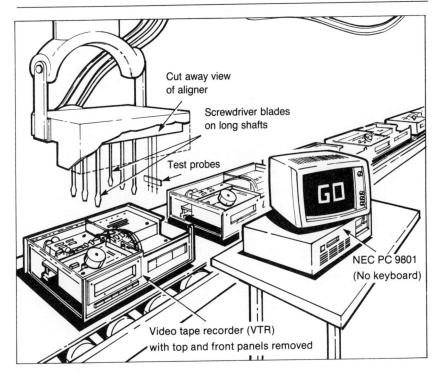

Cut away view of aligner

Screwdriver blades on long shafts

Test probes

NEC PC 9801 (No keyboard)

Video tape recorder (VTR) with top and front panels removed

is correctly aligned at each station, the PC screen displays GO in large letters and sends the VTR to the next station.

New employees get about 10 days of training. This includes several days in the classroom, the biggest part of which is devoted to the corporate philosophy—quality and excellence. They then get some practice in unit testing, quality control methods, and the rudiments of one job. They continually learn new jobs. This is considered a natural part of their growth.

The mainframe manufacturing planning and control system (running on a NEC system in Tokyo via a NEC S/150 concentrator in Gotemba) resembles—as nearly as I can tell—classic MRP II. It includes the inventory files, bills of materials, order processing, purchasing records, offsets for lead time, production rates for capacity planning, and so forth. The 60 microcomputers are all NEC PC9801s (see Figure 14–9). They run MS-DOS (level 3.01), and commands are in English and Japanese.

FIGURE 14–9 **The Corner of the Assembly Floor Where the Production Control Staff Constantly Monitors the Assembly Process**

[As an aside, I noticed many familiar names in Japanese software distributors—MS-DOS, Microsoft Multiplan, 1-2-3 from Lotus, BASIC, and so forth.]

Interestingly, the PCs are not connected to the mainframe. Rather, they are directly connected to the equipment in the assembly lines. In Figure 14–10 we see a representation of the assembly line itself at the top of the screen with a graphic depict of each of the different stations along the line. Any problem or stoppage shows up in red on this visual "instrument panel" of the assembly line.

Pacing the Assembly Line

Every assembly line has several key processes that pace the rest of the line. That is just as true here. The cycle times of these processes are continuously sampled by the PC. The average cycle time for the last five minutes is portrayed by the bars in the lower half of the screen. In a perfectly balanced line, the cycle times would all be the same, hence the bars

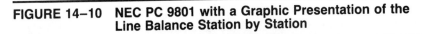

FIGURE 14–10 NEC PC 9801 with a Graphic Presentation of the Line Balance Station by Station

would all remain the same length. In practice this allows the production control staff (a combination of programmers, engineers, and planners) to constantly balance the processes—experimenting with the lines while interactively monitoring the actual equipment and operators. As they observe one operation to continually have a different cycle time, they will analyze the reasons and make appropriate adjustments to the operation in order to maintain the line balance.

CONCLUSIONS

Interestingly, this production control department—micros and all—is actually on the plant floor. There is not even a partition between them and the actual plant floor. They can actually see the stations that are being monitored by the microcomputer. This proximity hints at the cleanliness, freedom from dust, and quietness of the assembly plant, but there is a much more important lesson to be learned in this.

The real action in engineering is not behind the video screens but on the shop floor. Shigeo Shingo observed that American engineers in the

1960s spent much of their time solving real problems on the shop floor. By the 1980s they had turned in the hard hats for hookups to CAD/CAM screens. And he found this very encouraging for Japanese manufacturers! Microcomputers should instead support the relentless thirst for problem solving that fuels continual improvement in manufacturing muscle. They should never substitute for excellence in execution on the line.

This system enables NEC, Gotemba, to achieve a remarkably high quality rate and maintain better than 60 inventory turns per year (although this is difficult to calculate directly because of aberrations in Japanese accounting). Nonetheless, this compares favorably with the other high-volume, repetitive plants which were visited in Japan. Certainly it lays down a challenge for those of us who would like to compete in this electronic market. It also serves to illustrate a number of the uses to which microcomputers can be put in production activity control:

1. Numeric control of automated equipment.
2. Testing, quality control, and rejection of substandard parts.
3. Alignment and adjustment control.
4. Monitoring of operations, operator rates, machine rates, and output counting.
5. "Instrument-panel" feedback of line problems.
6. Line balancing through constant cycle-time sampling.

To the specific techniques observed at NEC, we would add several other applications for PCs in production activity control such as:

7. Calculation and performance modeling of kanban quantities.
8. Monitoring shop orders (material allocation, priorities, balance due on the orders).
9. Establishment and measurement of piece rates for production workers (pieces per hour standard and comparisons to standard).
10. Calculation of piece-work payroll and productivity reporting.
11. In the repetitive environment, micros are used for recording production runs. The spreadsheet includes elapsed times, production quantities, downtime (listed by cause and time in minutes). The spreadsheet can automatically calculate aggregate production and uptime rates for the shift or for the line. Summaries can be figured by the day, week, month, or year to date.
12. WIP record storage in "smart cards" that resemble the microprocessors on credit cards in Europe (introduced in France in

1976). The cards accompany the order and accumulate data on hours worked, pieces made, and so forth. In theory such smart cards could be used as the "pull" signal in an electronic kanban system.

13. Input/output control records for each workcenter are maintained in electronic spreadsheets. The planned and actual inputs (variance figured automatically) are entered. The planned and actual outputs are entered. The cumulative variance is reported to assist capacity planning and control.

14. Calculation of critical ratios or other sequencing ratios in order to assign priorities to individual shop orders.

15. Simulation of plant layouts to balance the flow (as in NEC) or to search out bottlenecks in job shops under various mixes of products.

CHAPTER FIFTEEN

Accounting

It may be a bit embarrassing to the guys and gals on the shop floor or to the engineering gang, but in many firms the charge to micros was led by the accountants. Long accustomed to the rigors of the murky green columnar pad and faced with limitless opportunities to compare volumes of numbers in the quest for managerial meaning, they seized micros—especially spreadsheets—with missionary zeal.

This chapter seeks not to inform the accounting professional of the merits or peculiar applications of spreadsheets. Although he or she may find some useful ideas in the chapter, this would usually be preaching to the converted. The chapter more properly serves to acquaint the manufacturing professional with examples of the use of micros by their accounting brethren.

A REAL-LIFE DIALOGUE

ABBY SALE: Don't you just love these budget meetings?

TOM PRODUCT: Like a kick in the shins. For the next two hours we get to hear why inventory is too high, margins too low, and why we need to reduce the number of items in stock.

ABBY SALE: If we reduce our line any further, we'll have to sell the office partitions to make our numbers.

TOM PRODUCT: Why not sell the accounting department instead? Speaking of accounting, here comes Beth Behenkaughnter.

BETH BEHENKAUGHNTER: Do you guys know what the inventory is right now? I'll tell you what it is.

ABBY SALE: We know what it is, and it's not high enough. Finished goods are going to have to increase if we're going to compete in service and product diversity with the national chains.

BETH BEHENKAUGHNTER: What! Higher! Do you have any idea what it costs to have that kind of money tied up in inventory?

And so it goes.

The author has listened to the foregoing scenario in more than one plant. The debate rages on, and each side views its position as righteous and intractable. Often the sides are much closer to an agreement than may appear from the decibel measurement. The need is to reduce the emotional issues of "too high," "no diversity," and "too much" to the common denominator of economic trade-offs. The following spreadsheet (see Figure 15–1) was developed by one small manufacturer to do just this —to move the debate from charge and countercharge to the common ground of financial analysis.

This spreadsheet is actually a summary of a detailed spreadsheet that analyzed the pattern of reorders of existing items and the development and production costs of new items (total of about 500 end items). The financial impacts of the current product replenishment and new item development and production are summarized into a total of 10 categories. There are actually about 30 categories for accounting purposes, but many of these are not greatly meaningful and are grouped together as "Other Products"—the 10th category. For simplicity's sake, only 2 of the 10 categories are shown here.

The logic of the spreadsheet is simple. All figures represent inventory at cost in $1,000s. Marketing and product managers fill in the top rows for each quarter's sales. The next two rows are summaries of the master production schedule (extended by average cost). The bottom row calculates closing inventory by subtracting sales and adding orders to the last period's closing inventory. This gives the accounting management a longer term prediction of cash needs and inventory balances.

All involved recognize the uncertainties of long-term forecasts (both of sales and of production costs). But it gives a better planning perspective than was available before and allows all the managers to test various editions of the production plan. It furnishes a launch point from which to compare alternative proposals and so promotes reasoned agreements (or at least the agreement to disagree) among the team. It also translates the various tongues spoken by the various departments into a common financial language to facilitate senior management's assessment of the issues.

BUDGETING

The departmental manager from information systems to maintenance to personnel has no better friend during the budgeting season than a microcomputer spreadsheet. We do not include an example of a departmental

FIGURE 15–1 Product and Inventory Plan for 1987 and 1988 (dollars in thousands)

	Product Category	Dec 1986	1987 (quarters)				1988 (quarters)			
			1st	2nd	3rd	4th	1st	2nd	3rd	4th
Housewares										
WIP & RM	Sales of current items	45	100	95	90	80	75	70	65	60
	Sales of new items		40	50	55	55	55	55	55	55
FGI	Orders for current items	325	80	90	90	80	85	90	85	86
	Orders for new items		125	75	60	30	50	60	80	50
	Closing inventory	370	435	455	460	435	440	465	510	531
Garden and farm items										
WIP & RM	Sales of current items	35	85	84	84	84	84	84	65	60
	Sales of new items		40	40	40	40	40	40	40	40
FGI	Orders for current items	450	80	85	80	75	75	75	75	86
	Orders for new items		25	30	40	30	30	30	30	50
	Closing inventory	485	465	456	452	433	414	395	395	431
	Totals for all categories	855	900	911	912	868	854	860	905	962

RM = raw materials
WIP = work in process
FGI = finished goods inventory

budget here, for each is individual and most are transparently simple. They include a list of relevant account names, perhaps account numbers, this year's budget, this year's actual, and next year's wish list. If your system accommodates it, this may be loaded from the mainframe on which the budgets and actual year-to-date expenditures reside.

The beauty of spreadsheet budgeting is, of course, the flexibility with which it can be modified and the ease with which contingencies are factored in. For example, the budget for the marketing department may be influenced by total revenue (for bonuses and sales commissions, for example). The expected revenue can be included in the budget model, and the other figures can be calculated from this estimate. If the revenue estimate is revised, all affected line items and all totals are immediately revised as well.

FIXED ASSETS AND DEPRECIATION

Figure 15–2 illustrates another typical use of spreadsheets in accounting: to maintain a register of fixed assets and to calculate depreciation entries at the close of each month. Although there are application programs to perform this task (on mainframes and on micros), accounting pros have found that the meek spreadsheet may offer as much as is needed at a fraction of the cost!

In this example the assets are listed by name and serial number in the lefthand column. The next five columns record the information necessary to calculate the depreciation entries. The next columns calculate depreciation entries by month. Note that the depreciation at 100 percent is constant, but the depreciation at 125 percent and 150 percent decreases each month. It is also possible to add the logic to the cells to test the point at which the 150 percent (or other) depreciation should be converted to straight line.

ALLOCATION OF FRINGE BENEFITS

Figure 15–3 shows a spreadsheet used to allocated fringe benefits across various departments. This manufacturer allocates the fringes by payroll dollars which are displayed in the second column. The next column calculates the allocation ratios (dividing each payroll amount by the total payroll for the week). These allocation percentages are then multiplied by the total amounts of each of the fringe benefits to give the dollar allocations for journal entries to each department's expenses.

FIGURE 15–2   Fixed Asset Register and Depreciation

Asset	Original Value	Resid Value	Deprec to dt	Deprec Factor	Useful Life	Deprec. by month . . .			
						Jan	Feb	Mar	. . .
BDB Machng Ctr s/n 23498	156,250	15,625	55,450	100%	7	1674	1674	1674	1674
Bliss 600T Prs s/n 1705	178,210	17,821	47,200	125%	5	2358	2309	2261	. . .
PDQ Rvlvng Rck s/n 44014	88,255	0	0	150%	5	2206	2151	2097	. . .

FIGURE 15–3 Allocation of Overhead and Fringe Benefits

Department	Payroll	Ratio	Life Insur	Grp Health	Hth2
			$1,540.00	$5,410.24	$2,142.50
Press Shop	$4,050	4.7%	$72.14	$253.45	$100.37
Welding	$2,510	2.9%	$44.71	$157.08	$62.20
Assembly	$12,541	14.5%	$223.40	$784.83	$310.80
Paint	$1,654	1.9%	$29.46	$103.51	$40.99
. . . .					
Accounting	$2,154	2.5%	$38.37	$134.80	$53.38
MIS	$2,350	2.7%	$41.86	$147.07	$58.24
Total	$86,452	100.0%			

PRODUCT COSTING

In Chapter 13 we discussed several methods to calculate the costs of inventory. In the section on calculating work in process we discussed the method of building cost into the product as labor, overhead, and materials are added from operation to operation. This same method can be used to develop standard costs for every part in the plant. These standard costs can be used in conjunction with the product structure files to develop "costed bills of material" for higher level parts. In effect, the individual component costs "tree up" to form the cost of the parent item.

Not only can the costs be so figured for every part in stock, but these costs can be used for value analysis among accounting, purchasing, and engineering. It is possible to look long and hard at all the costs in a part and ask questions about which of the operations and materials are really necessary—which really add value to the product as far as the customer is concerned. Counting parts, inspecting parts, and protecting them from rough handling in the plant do not really add value in the customer's eyes. There may be substitute parts or procedures that can reduce the cost without sacrificing quality.

It is also possible to take the costing developed even further into potential future costs. "What if" scenarios can be developed for such possibilities as increased labor costs (if the contract is coming up for renegotiation), changes in energy costs, or fluctuation in raw material costs. Microcomputers lend themselves to the quick assessment of shifting variables.

FINANCIAL/SALES/PROFIT REPORTING

One medium-size manufacturer owned a minicomputer and associated general ledger applications but was acquired by a corporation that used significantly different reporting structures. The subsidiary was required to submit financial reports covering sales, margins, and operational data by several product lines. The micro quickly handled the reformatting and refiguring of the data necessary to prepare reports in the form desired by the parent corporation.

COST JUSTIFICATION

A micro spreadsheet is a natural for analyzing the cash flows associated with alternative investments. As such it can be a very useful tool for cost justification. Chapter 9 explores several possibilities in constructing less naive cost justifications—analyses that take into account a wide range of financial implications of potential investments. An example is not included here but can be easily gained from nearly any computer or software vendor for the price of a sales pitch.

ACCOUNTING FOR LABOR EFFECTIVENESS IN A JUST-IN-TIME ENVIRONMENT

Many of the traditional measurements of labor effectiveness—utilization, efficiency, and so forth—fall on hard times amidst the radical changes necessary to advance toward just-in-time manufacturing. They just don't measure the key areas of improvement. Several solutions are practiced in industry.[1]

1. Eliminate direct labor costs. Hewlett-Packard just eliminated the direct labor category altogether. It only represented 3–5 percent of the cost of goods sold. It also saved them 100,000 journal entries per month at the Disc Memory Division alone.

2. Treat manufacturing overhead as an expense. If the firm is approaching the very short cycle times associated with JIT, the materials (and labor, naturally) are being turned over several times per month. No useful purpose is served by merely creating bookkeeping to track the month-end spillover.

---

[1] Ken Wantuck, "Measuring Labor Effectiveness in a Just-in-Time Environment," *1986 APICS Conference Proceedings*, pp. 310–11.

3. Reduce accounting for scrap and rework. These should be greatly reduced anyway—hopefully to the point where accounting systems to record and monitor them are no longer justifiable.

For more conservative companies than HP, Wantuck has proposed the concept of *labor effectiveness*. This measurement modifies the traditional definition of efficiency from hours earned/direct hours worked to

$$\frac{\text{Standard hours earned}}{\text{Direct and indirect hours worked}}$$

This tracks output against all labor costs. It captures the hidden costs of material handling, storage, clerical operations, and supervision. By eliminating much of the traditional allocation of overhead, it simplifies accounting—paving the way for the use of simpler systems (such as microcomputers) to manage the simpler databases. Such a calculation is readily performed by a spreadsheet. To paraphrase Vice President Taiichi Ohno, just divide Toyotas per day by people plus purchases. In a study of Ferro Linden Products while undergoing a JIT implementation, the measurement of labor effectiveness proved a far better predictor of variable margin than did traditional measures of labor efficiency.[2] The Reader is referred to the reference for the details of the study.

CONCLUSION

Microcomputers offer as great a productivity increase in the accounting function as in any function in the plant. Besides improving the accuracy and speed of the many accounting analyses, micros permit the consideration of alternative courses of action to facilitate better thinking about these alternatives. They allow the combination of operational and financial information to yield succinct and meaningful reporting between functional areas, and to senior management.

---

[2] Ibid.

Purchasing

When a salesman sells a dollar's worth of product, the company is fortunate if 15 to 20 cents comes back as pretax profit. Every dollar saved in purchasing returns 100 cents on the dollar to pretax profit. That doesn't mean that the salesman shouldn't be out there selling. Without him there would be no need for purchasing or anybody else. But it does mean that the purchasing person has a great deal of leverage.[1]

PURCHASING TO SUPPORT MANUFACTURING, OR WHERE'S THE REQ?[2]

Several years ago Joe Aiello gathered together the mission statements of purchasing and production and inventory control:[3]

Production and Inventory Control

It is our responsibility to see that the finished product is made to the right quality and quantity and at the right time to satisfy the needs of our company at a cost which will allow our company to earn a reasonable profit.

Purchasing

It is our responsibility to purchase materials to the right quality and quantity and at the right time to satisfy the needs of our company at a cost which will allow our company to earn a reasonable profit.

---

[1] Oliver W. Wight, *MRP II: Unlocking America's Productivity Potential* (Boston, Mass.: CBI Publishing, 1981), p. 237.

[2] Much of the material in the first half of this chapter was developed by the author and John P. Flavin—veteran purchasing manager and production control manager—for "PDQ: Purchasing to Support Manufacturing, or Where's the Req?" *1986 APICS Conference Proceedings*, pp. 490–94.

[3] Joseph L. Aiello, "Successful Interaction between Purchasing and Production and Inventory Control," *1979 APICS Conference Proceedings*, pp. 234–35.

On the face of it these two departments of the company do not appear to be in opposite businesses. Ideally, they are in the same business supporting the same objectives with many of the same methods. Cooperating, these two groups have great potential to contribute to the smooth flow of material through the plant, reduced lead times, and productivity that contribute to the profitability and competitiveness of the company. Again, to restate this point negatively, if these two functions are allowed to engage in finger pointing and assignment of blame, they have the potential to drain away a company's opportunity to excel or even survive in today's demanding markets.

THE BUYER'S DAY

From the time he hangs his coat on the nail, the buyer is expediting production parts, newly introduced parts, substituted parts, tooling, maintenance items, and general supplies. In front of this continuous background tapestry is each day's parade of shortages, salesmen, quality defects, price increase announcements, and new order placements. One frustrated buyer actually offered his suppliers numbered excuse lists to speed up the process of apologizing! In such an environment many very worthwhile things (value analysis, sourcing, negotiation, supplier training, and development) are more easily put off than the emergencies *du jour*.

What causes the many little emergencies and the ensuing panic of expediting? The trigger events run the gamut of poor planning and poor control—untimely engineering changes, missed communications, erratic market demands from the plant's own customers, vendor shortfalls, inaccurate inventory records, failure to include purchasing constraints in the master production scheduling process, paperwork errors, and so on. Many of these could be summarized as a failure to, in Plossl's words, "handle the *routine* elements of the job *routinely*."

The microcomputer can do much to smooth the flow of information that swirls about his office. For example, James J. Leahy, corporate purchasing manager at Echlin, Inc., finds the PC indispensable to managing the buying activity of the 100 or so buyers and field purchasing managers.[4] Echlin is a $700 million manufacturer and distributor of auto and truck replacement parts. Leahy uses his PC to:

---

[4] Somerby Dowst, "A Small Purchasing Operation Gets the Big Picture," *Purchasing*, March 14, 1985, pp. 65–67.

1. Prepare requests for quotations (RFQs) and analyze the resultant bids on contracts.
2. Keep track of field purchasing's productivity and standards compliance.
3. Draw graphs and charts on everything from inventory levels to cost reduction to report performance to divisional and senior management.

A typical current project involves 20 of the 31 divisions and about 70 part numbers on which a broad array of vendors compete. It took a while to train vendors to respond in the requested formats. Now the responses can be quickly entered into 1-2-3 from Lotus spreadsheets. It's then easy to spot the most economical allocation of the business. The divisional managers participate in the decision since firm commitments are needed to "maximize our buying power, and shrink our vendor base," as Leahy notes.

Leahy audits the performance of the field purchasing managers and buyers constantly and largely firsthand. Using spreadsheets he tracks the percent of orders placed against competitive bids, the percent placed with sole sources, the percent with more than five days' processing time, the percent received early or late, and the percent overshipped ("a big problem on castings"). Furthermore, the microcomputer can present these results in chart and graph form adding punch to the reports. Although the micro has not replaced the constant face-to-face management that is Leahy's hallmark, it remains a handy aid at the manager's elbow. And most of his future plans for improvement are somehow connected to the PC.

The next step beyond entering information from vendors into a spreadsheet is to actually have the information transferred in PC-readable form. This could be done by having the suppliers send floppy diskettes with the spreadsheets that define the quotation. This would allow the purchasers to manipulate the quote within the parameters of the quotation. These parameters may actually be coded into the spreadsheet. For example, the spreadsheet could include a logical statement like: "If the quantity of part X is greater than 10,000, then price Y applies; if the price is between 5,000 and 9,999, then price Z applies." In Chapter 4 several microcomputer database systems were introduced, among which was dBASE by Ashton-Tate. The National Aeronautics and Space Administration (NASA) now requires all contract proposals to be submitted in dBASE.[5]

---

[5] Sharon Rae, "Micro DBMSs in Mainframe Shops," *Business Software Review*, December 1985, p. 42.

This allows NASA personnel to work through many "what ifs" and iterations without rekeying the data. That's a lift to any buyer!

Already several major firms (such as Ford Tractor Division) are using on-line release programs to transmit weekly releases to first-tier suppliers. It is estimated by the Automotive Industry Action Group (AIAG) that the widespread introduction of on-line order releasing would cut order errors from 5 percent to 1 percent by eliminating manual rekeying of data.[6] This would also begin to recover the estimated $2 billion per year spent shuffling this paper (which works out to an extra $200 per car and truck).

Several software firms offer PC programs to receive these order transmissions and to subsequently develop plant schedules, material orders, and so forth. It is likely that the next few years will witness a tremendous upsurge in on-line transmission of engineering specifications, bids, machining specs, quality parameters, quality reports, and invoices. It is also likely that many of the links in these networks will be micros.

PDQ PURCHASING

Many purchasing pros will continue to operate purchasing systems used with a mainframe-based manufacturing control system. A number of the elements of a successful purchasing support system are intertwined with the elements of the manufacturing control system. This includes but is not limited to valid priority management, inclusion of critical supplier constraints in the scheduling process, engineering data control, sound inventory management, and the management of the enormous volume of daily transactions these require.

In addition to these basic planning and control features, a good purchasing support system should include:

- Quotation processing (RFQs, price, quantity, effectivity).
- Purchase order and requisition processing.
- Buyer data (commodity codes, parts, and so forth).
- Transportation, receipt, inspection processing.
- Vendor relationship management (vendor information maintenance, price, delivery, and quality performance, problem identification and resolution, purchase order management—with or without paper P.O.).
- Value analysis support.
- Purchased component cost forecasting and analysis.

---

[6] Russel Mitchell and Peter J. Heywood, "Detroit Tries to Level a Mountain of Paperwork," *Business Week*, August 26, 1985, 94f.

- Decision support (flexible inquiry, "what if" modeling, summarized and exception reporting).

Very few mainframe purchasing systems actually offer the entire list. They tend to offer the items closer to the top of the list. Note, however, how naturally the micro can fill in the features from the bottom of the list upward. PDQ stands for the three keys of successful purchasing management: price, delivery, and quality. Figures 16–1 through 16–3 suggest one way in which a micro could be integrated with a mainframe purchasing support system.

Several such systems offer performance tracking of PDQ (for example, Unisys and Software International both offer this). These data can be downloaded into a micro spreadsheet for a typical class of vendors as shown in Figure 16–1. In this example, 1.000 represents perfect performance in a category (lowest possible price, perfect delivery, or zero defects). Lower ratings represent the comparison to that standard based on actual history.

Given the considerable disparity between the vendors, which would you select for the next order? As is usually the case, none is the leader in every category. The right answer depends on what is most important.

NOTA BENE

The time has passed when strong purchasing means clubbing the vendor down to his rock-bottom price then extorting another 3 percent. Today the successful purchasing professional needs to balance price with the equally important issues of delivery and quality.

At the bottom of Figure 16–1 we have assigned numeric values to the relative importance of the three PDQ ratings. These weights must add up to 1.000.[7]

In our example we suggest a rather traditional attitude by assigning 70 percent to price, 10 percent to delivery, and 20 percent to quality. The numbers in the right column give the combined evaluation based on these weights. In Figure 16–2 we have asked the micro to sort the vendors by the evaluation column. Thus, the highest rated vendor, Bell Brass, is at the top.

---

[7] An alternate explanation and formulation of these issues of quantifying purchasing performance is presented in Henry M. Jordan, "Just-in-Time Performance Measurement," *First World Congress of Production and Inventory Control*, May 1985, pp. 43–45.

FIGURE 16–1   PDQ Analysis of Vendors

Product group: brass fittings   Buyer: J. Flavin

Vendor Name	Price Ratio	Delivery Ratio	Quality Ratio	Combined Evaluation*
Amark Fittings	0.850	1.000	0.854	0.866
Bell Brass	0.970	0.965	0.905	0.957
Clare Closures	0.775	0.940	0.955	0.828
D. Stephens & Co.	0.840	0.880	0.925	0.861
Biezemeier, Ltd.	0.854	0.945	0.997	0.892
Fuller Fittings	0.945	0.950	0.987	0.954
Greshurizer Company	0.875	0.985	0.991	0.909
Lester Hess Press Co.	0.811	0.950	0.958	0.854
Rioux Metal Works	0.698	0.970	0.998	0.785
Weights of factors:	0.700	0.100	0.200	

*Combined evaluation = (price ratio) * (price factor) + (delivery ratio) * (delivery factor) + (quality ratio) * (quality factor)

Suppose, however, that the plant is aggressively adopting JIT methods. As purchasing is rethinking its role, it may well revise the weights of the PDQ factors to something like those in Figure 16–3—15 percent price, 45 percent delivery, and 40 percent quality. If we now resort the

FIGURE 16–2   PDQ Analysis of Vendors

Product group: brass fittings   Buyer: J. Flavin

Vendor Name	Price Ratio	Delivery Ratio	Quality Ratio	Combined Evaluation*
Bell Brass	0.970	0.965	0.905	0.957
Fuller Fittings	0.945	0.950	0.987	0.954
Greshurizer Company	0.875	0.985	0.991	0.909
Biezemeier, Ltd.	0.854	0.945	0.997	0.892
Amark Fittings	0.850	1.000	0.854	0.866
D. Stephens & Co.	0.840	0.880	0.925	0.861
Lester Hess Press Co.	0.811	0.950	0.958	0.854
Clare Closures	0.775	0.940	0.955	0.828
Rioux Metal Works	0.698	0.970	0.998	0.785
Weights of factors:	0.700	0.100	0.200	

*Combined evaluation = (price ratio) * (price factor) + (delivery ratio) * (delivery factor) + (quality ratio) * (quality factor)

FIGURE 16–3   PDQ Analysis of Vendors

Product group: brass fittings		Buyer: J. Flavin		
Vendor Name	Price Ratio	Delivery Ratio	Quality Ratio	Combined Evaluation*
Greshurizer Company	0.875	0.985	0.991	0.971
Fuller Fittings	0.945	0.950	0.987	0.964
Biezemeier, Ltd.	0.854	0.945	0.997	0.952
Bell Brass	0.970	0.965	0.905	0.942
Rioux Metal Works	0.698	0.970	0.998	0.940
Lester Hess Press Co.	0.811	0.950	0.958	0.932
Clare Closures	0.775	0.940	0.955	0.921
Amark Fittings	0.850	1.000	0.854	0.919
D. Stephens & Co.	0.840	0.880	0.925	0.892
Weights of factors:	0.150	0.450	0.400	

*Combined evaluation = (price ratio) * (price factor) + (delivery ratio) * (delivery factor) + (quality ratio) * (quality factor)

vendors by the newly recalculated combined evaluation, we get the ordering shown in Figure 16–3, bringing the Greshurizer Company to the top because of its excellent record in quality and delivery consistency. The calculation of combined evaluations and subsequent sorting make this superiority immediately apparent, and suggest several strong alternate vendors should capacity limits force the business to secondary suppliers.

DISCOUNT, DISCOUNT, WHO'S GOT THE DISCOUNT?

Occasionally a buyer is faced with a plethora of discounts on a wide selection of parts. Some represent little more than a chance to increase inventory. Others offer a genuine saving to the company. Given the constraints of cash flow and maximums on tolerable inventory levels, what's a buyer to do? Twenty years ago, Plossl and Wight suggested a rather sophisticated method for sorting out such choices, and the logic is just as valid today as it was then. Figure 16–4 illustrates a simplified summary of this technique using a spreadsheet. The full technique can be programmed into a spreadsheet in less than an afternoon, and the interested Reader is encouraged to investigate the method.[8]

The column labeled "Additional $ needed" indicates how much addi-

---

[8] George W. Plossl and Oliver W. Wight, *Production and Inventory Control: Principles and Techniques* (Englewood Cliffs, N.J.: Prentice-Hall, 1967), pp. 163–69.

FIGURE 16–4 Analysis of Discounts Available

Product group: brass fittings   Buyer: J. Flavin

Vendor Name	Purchased Part	Planned Order quan	Quan. to get disc.	Cost w/o disc.	Cost w/ disc.	Additional $ needed	$ saved	($ saved)/ ($ needed)
Bell Brass	G77546	450	500	2.44	2.23	17.00	105.00	6.176
Biezemeier, Ltd.	J44249	58250	75000	0.45	0.39	3037.50	4500.00	1.481
Clare Closures	G77546	450	1000	2.44	2.10	1002.00	340.00	0.339
Clare Closures	H44568	2850	4000	1.25	1.20	1237.50	200.00	0.162
Bell Brass	H44568	2850	5000	1.25	1.18	2337.50	350.00	0.150
Bell Brass	G87654	675	1000	0.78	0.75	223.50	30.00	0.134

tional money (and inventory investment) is needed above the immediate needs (planned order quantity) to reach the next discount tier. The "$ saved" column shows the cost reduction on the total order if this tier is reached. The righthand column compares the dollars saved to dollars needed (similar to ROI). Finally, the chart was sorted by this last ratio to place the best discount opportunities at the top. This chart can be enhanced by adding a column to accumulate the additional investments thus indicating when the buyer has, in effect, run out of money to spend chasing discounts.

SUMMARY

Of course, purchasing decisions will never be reduced to a mere re-sorting of a spreadsheet column, but this type of analysis can bring needed insight to the mainframe-based purchasing support systems. It forces the discipline of quantifying the key performance criteria and clearly ranks the various vendors by these criteria. The trend is to smaller supplier bases and significantly more attention is given to each supplier. This attention often includes training of the supplier by the buying firm in the areas of statistical quality control, problem identification, problem resolution, and mistake-proof (poka-yoke) manufacturing methods. Both the training and the implementation of these concepts can often be most conveniently supplemented by microcomputers.

It is clear that the trend toward integration between supplying and buying plants will continue. Soon, virtually all of Ford's Body and Assembly Division suppliers will be on-line to Ford for direct computerized release processing. Next, this will be extended to suppliers of Ford's Engine Division. In the last three years the grocery industry has linked many manufacturers such as Kraft and Procter & Gamble with supermarkets and retailers for estimated savings of $300 million a year.[9]

Increasingly vendor capacities and processes will be made a part of the planning cycle of their clients. Within only a few years we will see computer-aided engineering systems that not only formulate the specs of a new product but also formulate the processes necessary to manufacture the needed parts. Furthermore, this system will load these product and process specs to the suppliers for use in their own computer-controlled workcells. Already, some firms in northern Europe have moved beyond

---

[9] Mitchell and Heywood, "Detroit Tries to Level a Mountain of Paperwork," p. 94.

just negotiating *price* with their vendors. Now they negotiate the vendor's *cost*. How efficient can the processes be made? If both supplier and buyer get better and better, then there is more profit to share, and both advance in the arena of world-class manufacturing excellence.

CHAPTER SEVENTEEN

Engineering

Over the last couple of years, the path trod by personal computer users has forked into two distinct tracks. The so-called power users, like the hot-rodding teenagers of yore, gladly spend much of their time customizing and reworking complex software to squeeze just a little more speed, a little more power, out of their machines. The second group more parallels the average commuter or shopper who asks only that his vehicle deliver him to his appointed destination with as little hassle as possible.[1]

With few exceptions, engineers tend to be "power users." The urge to tinker runs strong in the heart of every engineer, and this often manifests itself in continual tinkering with a design of a product. The acquisition of a PC may offer the opportunity to vent the urge to tinker on the PC, where the urge will do far less harm and may do some good.

AFTER ALL, ENGINEERS ARE PEOPLE, TOO

Most of the applications for which engineers employ micros are applications common to all micro users—spreadsheets, databases, costing, quality control reports, and so forth. A 1985 University of Michigan study entitled "A Methodology for the Detection of System Barriers to Engineering Productivity" reports that engineers spend only 19 percent of their time engaged in "applied engineering" (which we will discuss later in this chapter). The rest is spent in many of the same ways most manufacturing pros spend their time—word processing and documentation (30 percent), communication with others (23 percent), attending meetings (20 percent), scheduling work tasks (4 percent), and searching files (3 percent).[2]

---

[1] Erik Sandberg-Diment, *The New York Times*, December 9, 1986.
[2] C. H. "Pete" Link, "CAD Systems for Small Design Departments," *1986 APICS International Conference Proceedings*, pp. 472–74.

Spreadsheets, office automation, and databases have long been used by engineers for the above activities, tracking cost build-up, time studies, engineering changes, maintenance schedules, maintenance parts lists, and many other engineering activities.

QUALITY CONTROL

Elementary quality control (for example, at some food processing plants) can be maintained in a series of spreadsheets. Most spreadsheet packages can handle the modest volume of data in such limited SQC analysis and can calculate random samplings, variances, standard deviations, and the resultant graphs.

For those QC pros with more demanding requirements several firms sell beefy packages for statistical quality control. These packages include graphs of measurement distributions, calculation of control points (points well within the actual tolerances to assure satisfactory parts), analyses of deviations, random samplings, stratified random samplings, and many reports. Reports can be generated by operator, operation, shift, machine, part, date ranges, and type of material.

MICROS CAN SOLVE VARIOUS ENGINEERING CHALLENGES

A number of companies have discovered great utility in interfacing microcomputers to electronic equipment of many different types. This can include testing, weighing, measuring equipment, photoelectric cells, and so forth. We will suggest a few possibilities and examples from several industrial applications.

The impetus for suggesting and implementing such handy systems may stem from the shop floor itself, given keen awareness and support for the people on the shop floor. In more cases, though, such refinements seem to come through the engineering section.

Even so, this is only true to the degree that the engineers are alert to and involved in the shop floor, are willing (if not relishing the chance) to solve the actual gritty little problems out there, are listening to the descriptions of problems, and then applying the sorts of creative, innovative thinking that is suggested in the following examples. The intent of this section is simply to fuel the creative fires.

Microcomputers have been connected directly to electronic weighing scales. In one particular application delivery trucks are weighed as they cross the threshold of the warehouse. From a file of customers in the microcomputer, the name and address of the customer is brought up, and the empty weight is subtracted from the full weight. This net haul is extended by the price associated with that particular customer, and an invoice is created in a matter of a few seconds. This, in turn, is given to the truck driver who "hand delivers" it to the customer with the load at the time of delivery.

In another application the microcomputer stores a number of personnel ID numbers. As an individual moves his badge through an optical character recognition reader, or through a bar code reader, the microcomputer knows whether this individual is authorized to access a particular secure area and can then activate a bolt mechanism unlocking the door. The great flexibility here is that it can also keep track of the time that an individual is within that facility, and the number and identity of attempts to gain unauthorized access.

This can be very appropriate to control computer facilities or other high security areas where it is desirable to keep a list of these events. The micro can be placed on-line to actually allow the accumulation of this information to be periodically sent to a mainframe or to allow changes to be made. If, for example, a programmer has been dismissed, we would deny him further access to the computer room by removing his name from the list of approved employees.

The addition of such things as bar code readers, optical character recognition readers, sense switches, lock mechanisms, and weighing scales typically require special interface hardware and software to be added to the micro. Such a device may require an additional board or an external piece of equipment such as a program controller. A rather exotic application of the use of program controllers to accumulate dozens of inputs into a single microcomputer can be found in the chapter on production activity control (Chapter Fourteen).

TEST MONITORING AND DATA ACCUMULATION

A company in the southern part of the United States has developed interfaces between Unisys micros and a wide variety of testing equipment. The information can be converted from analog to digital form (that is from just a voltage level to a particular digital number, like 1.735). This test data is then fed into the microcomputer, permitting the micro to track and record the results of a wide number of simultaneous experiments or tests.

This particular firm operates a large laboratory themselves. This interface allows the engineers to monitor a wide variety of testing devices directly from the micro screen. Besides being a labor saver for the mellow engineer, it allows him to stay close to several experiments in a real-time environment. Also the information can be accumulated for spreadsheet and statistical analyses, charts, and graphs in the ongoing quest to cull meaning from data.

PC-BASED TEST MONITORING AT IKEDA BUSSAN

We observed microcomputers in a similar environment at the Ikeda Bussan vehicle seat plant and research facility in Yokohama, Japan. Here PCs are employed to record the actual stress exerted on seat belts and seat mounts as the seats were pounded with progressively more force. At the point that the seat actually ruptured, or at the point that the metal became deformed, the exact stress was recorded by the microcomputer. Then the information could be accumulated into statistical tables directly on the PC and sent to the laboratory mainframe system.

In the same way, resilience of springs, cushions, and fabrics could be tested through tens of thousands of unmanned iterations. The combination of robotic testers and microcomputer observers makes possible a wide variety of longitudinal tests not justifiable if human testing and observing were required.

PC CAN STAND FOR PROCESS CONTROL

The relationship between PCs and process control has two sides. On one side is the need to calculate optimal loads and sequences for batch process operations such as paint, industrial chemical, and some food processors. It is possible to define such processes as matrixes of constraints and apply linear programming techniques to arrive at the "solution vector." To nonengineering types, that means the most profitable schedule. This process usually involves some industrial-strength FORTRAN and a lot of computer humming.[3] Although it may mean waiting overnight for results, this is often within the reach of today's microprocessor—especially

---

[3] For examples, see Winfried Janicke, "Two Measures for the Variability of Multi-Purpose Batch Chemical Plants," *Hungarian Journal of Industrial Chemistry Veszprem* 11 (1983), pp. 59–62; see also *Computers and Chemical Engineering* 8, no. 6 (1984), pp. 339–43.

those based on 32-bit architectures (like the Motorola MC68000 micro-processor) and those that employ math coprocessors (like the Intel 8087).

The other side of process control involves the microcomputer directly in the minute-to-minute operations of the plant. The micros can be integrated into the batch control by extending their "hearing" through temperature, mix, viscosity, and flow sensors. Then their "reach" is extended by the addition of valve, temperature, and flow controls. In this manner micros can manage rather sophisticated confectionery manufacturing processes and similar operations. This is not unlike the integration of PCs into the energy and mechanical systems management of large buildings.

FISHING FOR GROUPERS AMIDST THE MURKY DEPTHS OF ENGINEERING FILES

Group technology (GT) offers significant improvements to two facets of engineering.[4] It offers a coding scheme to classify every part in the plant by its geometry, material, processes, and specifications. The group code may have from 8 to 30 digits, and a particular code may apply to several parts (ideally, no more than 30). For example, a brass bolt may be coded 37B45908—the 3 means that the part is essentially round; the 7 means it has two diameters (head and body); the B means it is brass; the 4 means it is threaded, and so forth. The number of digits depends on the number and complexity of parts being classified. Most companies can nicely classify several thousand parts with 15-digit codes.

The design of a new manufacturing part can involve $3,000 to $10,000 of engineering time and effort. As many as a third of these new part introductions may not be necessary since identical or similar parts already exist within the company. GT greatly accelerates the search for like items, since they will bear the same or similar group codes. One firm figured that designing a new part took 8 to 12 hours of engineering time but that designing a similar part from an existing one took 30 to 60 minutes.

Furthermore, GT can be applied to the process planning of the plant. In order to capitalize on the similarity of a family of parts, group cells may be developed which can be dedicated to the production of members of these families of parts providing greater manufacturing efficiencies. Naturally, standard process sheets can be automated as well to streamline the paperwork involved.

---

[4] Norm Raffish, "Group Technology: An Overview," *1985 APICS International Conference Proceedings*, pp. 536–38.

Xerox offers a GT program for PCs that can comfortably manage 10,000 to 15,000 part numbers. Several PC programs for GT are available for a wide range of classification demands. In fact, one archeologist is classifying bones with GT software! The advantage of PC-based GT software is partially the lower cost and, significantly, the interactive method with which the choices are presented to the engineer as the program proceeds along the decision tree representing the coding scheme. In some cases, the GT function can be integrated with the computer-aided design functions on the PC.

MICRO-BASED CAD

A major opportunity for increased engineering productivity is the arena of creating designs, blueprints, and specification drawings. Engineering departments have typically discovered that computer-aided design/drafting (CAD) can increase the productivity of such activity by 400 percent. Currently, about a third of all CAD is being done on microcomputers. By 1990 Daratech, Inc., predicts that 90 percent of CAD installations will use micros. Dataquest (a subsidiary of A. C. Nielson Company) predicts that by 1989 there will be a quarter million PC CAD/CAM workstations —out of a total of 2.8 million engineers in the United States.[5] International Data Corporation estimates that 25,000 CAD-equipped PCs left the stable in 1985.[6] The reason is simple. Today's PC can provide 70 percent of mainframe CAD functionality for less than 20 percent of the dollars.[7]

Mainframe CAD can run as much as $250,000 per workstation. Minicomputers can bring the cost per workstation to about half of that. Micro CAD can bring the cost to less than $20,000 per station. It should be noted that this enormous reduction in cost comes not without sacrifices. The response time between demanding keystrokes (zoom and scan, for example) can be quite frustrating if compared to dedicated mainframe systems. Also, most micros have screen resolution comparable to a TV set. This does not lend itself to relaxed viewing of densepack drafting. Moreover, storage can become a problem on PCs since one drawing may require a megabyte (just three years ago, the maximum available on a PC

---

[5] Norm DeWitt and David Burdick, "Personal Computer-Based CAD/CAM— Miracle or Mirage?" Dataquest newsletter, June 28, 1985.

[6] Barbara Darrow, "PC-Based CAD Comes of Age," *Design News*, August 19, 1985, pp. 88–91.

[7] Lester S. Shindelman and Carter C. Utzig, "Move over Mainframe: Make Way for the Micro," *1986 APICS Conference Proceedings*, p. 468.

was 10 megabytes). However, the comparison to the speed and convenience of manual drafting is favorable enough to have won many converts, and microcomputers are making advances daily to remove these bounds.

To the engineer that has never used a CAD station, drafting on a keyboard and mouse takes considerable time to learn. Indeed, some drafting tasks may take even longer on the PC. But as Barbara Darrow, associate editor of *Design News* reports: "Skeptics are silenced when they see CAD-produced crisp, neat drawings. Line weight—i.e., line width and density—is consistent and precise, vastly better than hand-drawn documents, and copies of identical or similar drawings are churned out."[8] Layered drawings, such as those for the various electrical, ventilating, and lighting systems of a building or ship, are easily accomplished.

Engineering management at Lawrence Livermore National Laboratory (LLNL) discovered that micro-CAD was thoroughly acceptable for their two-dimensional (2-D) drafting needs. Furthermore, they discovered that their engineers were spending about 60 to 70 percent of their time working in 2-D.[9] This not only underutilizes the costly 3-D workstations but requires the engineers to labor through a command set necessarily more complex to handle the 3-D environment. The engineers are now significantly more productive in the 2-D work through the use of micro-based CAD.

Links suggest several questions to consider prior to leaping into a $5,000 Personal Computer AT, a $2,400 off-the-shelf PC CAD package, a $4,000 cut sheet plotter, and another $2,000 for spreadsheet, word processor, and database programs.[10] First, one should ask:

1. What design functions should be automated?
2. What nondesign functions should be automated?
3. Can you plan a local area network, and then automate one step at a time?
4. Which expandable, available, and supportable CAD/office automation/communications hardware, system software, "environ-

---

[8] Darrow, "PC-Based CAD Comes of Age," p. 89.

[9] Gary S. Goldman, "Micro-Based CAD; A Production Tool for Manufacturing Engineering," *APICS Microprocessor Seminar Proceedings*, January/February 1984, pp. 74–83.

[10] Link, "CAD Systems for Small Design Departments," p. 473.

mental software," and applications offer the greatest benefit within the dollars available to invest?

5. Will the engineers/designers/draftsmen use the systems to do their work?

6. Are you convinced that automation of engineering tasks is essential to the long-term success and competitiveness of your company?

7. Are the rewards of so doing greater than the risks?

When those involved are clear on these issues, Link next suggests a useful 18-step checklist toward the acquisition and implementation of CAD systems in smaller design departments to which the author refers the interested Reader.

MICRO CAD CASE STUDY: ELECTRO CONTROLS

Electro Controls, located in Salt Lake City, Utah, is a privately owned manufacturer of automatic lighting control systems.[11] These systems have recently found popular application in office buildings and hotels where lights in certain areas need to go on, go off, or dim on schedule. These systems are customized for each site from standard components. The specifications for a site are developed from a working set of roughly 100 standard drawings.

Prior to installing the PC-based CAD, Electro Controls employed an engineering staff of six systems designers and six draftsmen. Drawings were produced through a manual process that included copying, combining, editing, and revising these standard sets as well as the creation of unique elements for a site. Then the company installed a CAD system of six networked PCs. Now, without the aid of draftsmen, the six systems designers can complete a design in about half the time required before. An average of 300 to 400 drawings are created per month.

The transition from the drawing board to the keyboard and joystick was considered easy due to the zoom features and visual orientation of the operation. Tim Hansen, systems designer for Electro Controls, notes that dimensioning the drawings had previously been the most problematic part of the work. With the largely automatic dimensioning of the PC CAD, designers with little drafting experience are now able to dimension components with the consistency and precision of skilled draftsmen.

---

[11] Goldman, "Micro-Based CAD," pp. 74–75.

SUMMARY

The 2.8 million engineers in the United States and the millions of their counterparts throughout the world will obviously make increasing use of microcomputers in the next several years. This will include the applications named above—office automation, CAD, CAM, process control, and GT. Also, more exotic applications loom on the horizon. Already one Michigan firm offers finite element analysis on microcomputers. Some software firms are experimenting with 3-D CAD on micros. A wide variety of micro-based expert systems are undergoing research and investigation.

Beside the applicational use of PCs, we must not overlook the great educational value of these powerful tools. This applies both to the traditional classroom setting for upcoming engineers and to the training activities of corporate engineering departments. The PC can also serve as a modestly priced testbed for experimenting with CAD or GT concepts prior to companywide commitment. At every turn the microcomputer is adding power and flexibility to the "technological toolbag" of the modern engineer.

CHAPTER EIGHTEEN

The Small Manufacturer

There are 148,000 manufacturers in the United States that employ between 20 and 100 workers. For many of these, computers were plainly beyond the reach of reason or justification until the advent of the microcomputer. The micro has opened new worlds of processing and reporting power to these smaller firms, but corresponding new cautions are also poised at the gate. This chapter explores briefly both aspects of micros for the small manufacturer.

It should be remembered that Chapters 1 through 8 are just as appropriate to the small firm as the large. The costs of the hardware and software are the easiest to measure. Beware! These are usually less than half of the total investment in a micro. While hardware costs have plummeted by roughly 18 percent per year (halving every four years) and software costs have fallen more slowly, the news on people costs is mixed. It is true that systems and operations costs are vastly less for the micro than for the mainframe. However, the big remaining cost will be employee time and effort—especially among the user community. This is often augmented by the cost of overcoming institutional inertia in implementing procedural changes. Before committing these people resources, the small manufacturer will certainly want to revisit needs definition, acquisition issues, systems implementation, software development/selection, and training. Since these were addressed earlier, they need not be repeated here, although a timely echo is sounded occasionally.

DISTINCTIVE CHARACTERISTICS OF SMALL MANUFACTURERS

Roughly 90 percent of the U.S. manufacturers with annual revenue of less than $25 million have not installed a computer-based *manufacturing* system although about half of them are doing some form of computer-based *accounting*. This relative lack of experience with computerized planning and control software creates particular problems in selecting and implementing any manufacturing system—unclear specifications, confusion among competing claims from vendors, and difficulty in training and supporting users.[1]

Often this inexperience combines with an ingrained predilection toward existing manual systems: "We've *always* had a card to check on-hand quantities and vendor performance. I want to see the cards created by this new-fangled computer." "Why can't we just use the new system for work orders and leave purchasing out of this? They've never been co-operative on this sort of thing before." Occasionally, this "nostalgia" is exacerbated by the scarcity of trained professionals with the time or training to manage the selection and subsequent implementation. If there are such personnel available there may also be a reluctance on the part of senior management to commit the time and money necessary to support such professionals in getting the job done.

All these challenges notwithstanding, the typical small manufacturer enjoys a number of advantages also. Top management is closely involved in daily operations. Communications among the management team are frequent; many responsibilities are shared. It may well be easier to reach and secure the commitment of senior management; the owner or CEO is not isolated by bureaucracy and staff minions. There may well be a willingness on the part of senior management to take an active leadership role in the decision and the implementation.[2]

BEWARE OF THE PITFALLS

Pendleton, Newman, and Kirk in several case studies have documented the following recurring pitfalls encountered by the small manufacturer attempting to install micro manufacturing systems:[3]

1. Misordering of priorities and planning—tendency to manage by firefighting, informal systems, and short-term plans.
2. Clouded view of current performance—unawareness of current performance or disbelief caused by inaccurate records, poor discipline, and disjointed subsystems.

[1] Scott Hamilton, "Microcomputer Systems for Small Manufacturers," *1986 APICS Conference Proceedings*, pp. 7–9.

[2] William E. Pendleton, "Successful Implementation of MRP II on a Micro," *APICS Microprocessor Proceedings*, January/February 1984, pp. 20–28.

[3] Ibid., p. 20; Art Newman and Steve Kirk, "MRP II Implementation of a Microcomputer: Case Studies," *APICS Microprocessor Proceedings*, January/February 1984, pp. 34–35.

3. Lack of discipline, procedures, controls, and performance measures.
4. Little attention to formal education and training.
5. Unrealistic expectations of the implementation schedule—"I want it all in six months,"—no recognition of the degree of change required, resistance to commit resources when tough sledding is encountered, failure to learn the lessons of earlier pioneers via consultants, books, training, and user groups.
6. Unproven, incomplete, or inflexible software and documentation—failure to *deeply investigate* actual installations among current users of proposed software; inadequate controls in the software; poor recovery, backup, and security procedures; inadequate documentation; unquestioning acceptance of the system vendor's assessment of needs and features; failure to clearly define actual needs; lack of integration among the modules.
7. Inflexible or inadequate hardware—insufficient disk storage to retain all needed data, difficult or nonexistent networking capabilities, inability to grow as needs and applications grow (for example, inability to support the desired number of users or inability to handle the volume of transactions generated by the firm as users get up to speed).
8. Failure of top management to lead—refusal to attend management education, disbelief in the benefits, reluctance to change, detachment from key decisions.
9. Failure to recognize incidental costs—although micro systems have brought the hardware and software costs from $150,000–$250,000 (minicomputer) to $20,000–$40,000 (micro), the people, time, and management costs have changed much less. This needs to be early recognized, and planned for to sustain steady resolve as the costs mount.[4]

CONSIDERATIONS IN THE SELECTION . . . AND IMPLEMENTATION

For the prudent, the foregoing list of pitfalls gives rise to a list of thoughtful considerations in the selection and implementation of micro manufacturing systems (see, for example, Meyer, above, and Boeder).[5]

---

[4] David A. Meyer, "The Micro MRP Decision: Evaluation and Selection Criteria," *APICS Microprocessor Proceedings*, January/February 1984, pp. 57–62.

[5] Steven M. Boeder, "Large System Benefits for the Small Manufacturing Environment," *1986 APICS Conference Proceedings*, pp. 32–36.

1. Misordering of priorities and planning. This can only be countered by clear leadership and sound plans. The systems plan should include all affected functional areas of the firm (marketing, purchasing, materials management, finance, and so forth), and it should include the various dimensions of the system (responsibility, justification, planning, control, environmental software needs, selection, education, and project management).

2. Clouded view of current performance. A clear-eyed audit of current systems and performance is needed. This serves several purposes. It establishes the key indicators of desired performance. It exposes and underscores the need for reliable data and associated controls. It documents current performance and serves as a baseline against which system successes can be measured. This builds encouragement and support as increasing resources are summoned.

3. Lack of discipline, procedures, controls, and performance measures. If the benefits are urgently, genuinely sought by senior management, it must be willing to develop and support the systems that will secure these benefits.

4. Little attention to formal education and training. This item and number 8 below sink more systems than any other pitfall on the list. (See Chapter 8 for helps and suggestions in this area.)

5. Unrealistic expectations of implementation schedule. To whatever degree possible, small manufacturers must assimilate the lessons of earlier pioneers via consultants, books, training, and user groups. Smaller firms just don't have the extra money lying around to reinvent the wheel or resolve each implementation problem. (It makes you wonder why bigger firms think that they have the money to do this!) They should challenge facile schedules with tough questions about who will execute detail tasks and how they will be accomplished; develop schedules with sufficient details and checkpoints to early detect signs of trouble; prepare for the unforeseen obstacles; and establish clear lines of responsibility for each element of the plan.

6. Unproven, incomplete, or inflexible software and documentation. Many considerations need to be included in this category such as controls, recovery, backup, security procedures, documentation, insightful comparison of company needs with proposed system features, availability of source code, and integration among the modules. However, much of this can be answered through a few thorough visits with current users of the prospective system. Since few people easily admit they have erred in judgment, superficial examination will uncover little but the good. To

overcome this, set up a meeting with a current user that also includes a trained manufacturing pro from your firm, or one who knows your firm well, and present a list of prepared questions such as: "How long have you been operational on X, Y, and Z module?" "What volumes of data (parts, suppliers, levels in the BOM) and weekly transactions (cycle counts, shop orders, purchase orders, balance inquiries) do you have?" "What reports or features would you most like to see added to the system?" "When a software bug is encountered, how is it handled?" "What training is required and supplied for the operators of X module?"

7. Inflexible or inadequate hardware. As in software, the same toughness is needed in hardware in questioning the vendor and current users. The recommendations (tested by actual user experiences) will be essential here. A small manufacturer with about 5,000 part numbers and corresponding transaction volumes can probably not get by on less than 20 MB of hard disk. A database of this size lends itself to tape backup. Everyone seems to need 640 KB or more of random-access memory these days, and at least one horsey matrix (or laser) printer. Check on growth capabilities and verify these through actual users.

8. Failure of top management to lead. The most important single criterion for success is committed leadership. This can be fortified by the establishment of baseline performance and progress tracking mentioned in number 2. It flourishes through executive education, a bias toward progress, regular and systematic involvement in getting the system operational, strong communications with the troops, and regular steering committee participation to oversee the project.

9. Failure to recognize incidental costs. Planning, regular involvement in justification and selection, and assimilation of the lessons of those who have installed similar systems (through user groups such as APICS and DPMA) all contribute to sound estimates of time scales and investments.

HAVING IT ALL: MRP II ON MICROCOMPUTERS

Several firms offer all the elements of what is usually classed as "MRP II" or "closed-loop" manufacturing planning and control systems. This broad term ideally includes production planning, master scheduling, material requirements planning, production activity control, and the associated elements of capacity planning and control. It may also include purchasing, sales management, accounting, costing, and engineering systems as well.

One of the most popular of these systems is offered by Micro-MRP, Inc., of Foster City, California. This system has reportedly been installed in more than 700 sites. Some of these sites include IBM training centers where it is used for managerial training as a simulator of an actual plant system.

One of the most comprehensive of this genre is AIMCS from Graftek in Colorado (a subsidiary of Unisys). The system not only includes the elements of MRP II named above but modestly extends to computer-aided design and manufacturing. One AIMCS site has the micro directly loading programs into a numeric-controlled machining center.

CASE STUDY: A FIRST-TIME COMPUTER USER

Bill Willson and two other enterprising young men started up Marbelite Corporation—a manufacturing firm in Novi, Michigan, in 1975. Their goal was to provide top-quality bathroom sinks, tubs, and accessories to builders, dealers, and retailers in the area. The industrial processes centered around molding and finishing operations. Growth was gradual and hard-fought during the first decade, but by the mid-80s the constant 12-hour days and 6-day weeks began to pay off in expanding reputation and consequent sales. By 1984 the company employed about two dozen workers and sported gross revenues of almost $1 million. In 1987 revenues will approach $2 million.

Such a success story warms the heart of the entrepreneur and challenges the mettle of the competitor. However, this success was coming at an increasing price in terms of maintaining control of the burgeoning operations. Bill was responsible for the molding and finishing operations in the plant. By now, this task typically amounted to 400 or 500 active customer orders in various stages of completion and another couple hundred internal orders. The nature of the operations required developing two complete schedules per day.

This was burying Bill in an avalanche of paper. Usually, six or seven hours of each day were lost to this scheduling task. Worse still, it was impossible to keep track of every contingency. On occasion, an order would be discovered at three o'clock that was due at the customer's site by the next day. Everyone scrambled to get the product out the door on time— and almost always did—but at the expense of all the other priorities in the plant.

The three partners agreed that their time was too valuable to forfeit it to the paper mountain. The time had come to *computerize*. They felt that the investment in a microcomputer would pay for itself in freeing their time for the widening demands of the business. A small software company in California had developed some programs that seemed tailor-made to their special scheduling and control needs. The company took the plunge into the uncharted waters of computerization with the same determination to succeed that had served their firm so well heretofore. They purchased a micro with a 80 CPS printer. Within a few weeks the critical applications of scheduling and materials planning were operative.

The schedules could now be maintained by a clerical assistant in about two or three hours a day. This freed Bill for the vital tasks of managing the shop and making the schedules come to life in the plant. The system generates reports on open orders, needed parts, inventory levels, and costs. No longer do 3 P.M. surprises jerk the plans around at the last minute. Every day the finishing department has a clear look at upcoming shipping demands. Many errors of omission and commission have been eliminated. The accounting functions were rapidly added to the system. The customer statements that used to require two or three days each month are now printed in half an hour.

Typical of the determination to triumph over every obstacle was their response to a printer problem encountered early on. The printer selected was incapable of pulling the thick multipart invoices through the print area. The operator remedied the situation by gently tugging on the emerging string of invoices to aid the forms tractors. A newer, faster, and stronger printer has provided the permanent solution. As Bill would say, "This didn't even merit the title *problem*. A problem is something that you don't have a program to correct. If you have a program to attack the situation, it's just another part of everyone's job. We're all involved in solving problems."

Altogether, the elapsed time from the decision to order the hardware and the software to the successful use of the scheduling and accounting applications was about six months. Two operators were trained by the software company. This training required about two weeks at a cost to Marbelite of about $1,000.

Asked about the future, Bill sees many more uses for the micro. He further volunteered that any manufacturer with sales above half a million could surely justify a system of this scale (about $18,000 counting hardware, software, and training). "In fact," he adds, "we should have done this before now."

CASE STUDY: A DIFFERENT "HOMEGROWN" APPROACH AND A MORAL

Peter Langford joined Standard Thomson as manager of manufacturing and planning in 1975.[6] Within two years it was clear that something beyond the current accounting minicomputer was needed to plan and control effectively. The obvious long-term answer was MRP, but some interim information handling was urgently needed. Peter took the rather unusual and courageous step of learning to program in BASIC and writing several applications himself. These included purchasing, order management, load planning, "what if" modeling, and a bill of material processor.

Peter and others in the company learned much about data processing and about the critical issues in making systems work—discipline, good data, relevance of systems to users' needs, and corrective feedback. When the company did eventually install an MRP system, these lessons greatly facilitated its success. Peter says, "We installed MRP in 11 months starting in November 1980. Many factors contributed to the relatively short time and achievements of benefits from the system. One was the participation of several APICS-certified practitioners. I am convinced that the experience and skills acquired with our micro made significant contributions which more than justified the expenditure of resources on our micro project."

CONCLUDING OBSERVATIONS ON THE TWO CASES

The second case was very early in the annals of micro lore. Today it would be hard to imagine writing such applications from scratch on a micro. However, the moral remains relevant today. The expenditure of effort in training (APICS certification illustrates this), analysis (of user needs, accuracy of data, and data processing issues), and commitment to better management through wise use of systems all remain indispensable ingredients in the recipe of success. The methodology of tackling the manageable and high-payback tasks first and pyramiding on each success multiplies this success.

Both cases illustrate management's willingness to get deeply, even

---

[6] Peter W. Langford, "The Micro Computer in Materials Management—A Stepping Stone to MRP," *APICS Microprocessor Proceedings*, January/February 1984, pp. 265–70.

intimately, involved with the details of systems selection, design, and use. Yet both cases also show management's recognition of the need to plan better and then execute these plans. Like good seeds in fertile soil, the micro solutions that grew up in this environment naturally bore the fruits of success for their owners.

Follow-Up Information

Lists of Lists—A Collection of Sources for Further Information

The following sources offer a wide variety of technical and general information to the interested Reader. In most cases each source pyramids into more sources. In this sense this section is lists of lists. The Reader is also referred to the useful compendium of knowledge in the Bibliography, Appendix C.

American Institute of Certified Public Accountants, "Report on the Study of EDP-Related Fraud in the Banking and Insurance Industries," EDP Fraud Task Force, 1984. Extensive report on the incidents and occasions of fraud, including measures to protect computer owners from fraud.

Applied Manufacturing Education Series (AMES). A series of six classroom courses—roughly 80 hours of instruction with 4 hours of video programs —teaching the application of manufacturing techniques to daily practitioners of these techniques. The courses include Overview, Master Planning, Material Requirements Planning, Capacity Requirements Planning, Inventory Management, and Production Activity Control. All modules have some Zero Inventory aspects, but these are especially well developed in the Production Activity Control course.

APICS (American Production and Inventory Control Society) *Dictionary*. Lists thousands of definitions of both computer-related and manufacturing words.

APICS Publications Guide. Lists dozens of publications describing various phases of manufacturing.

APICS International Conference Proceedings. List hundreds of presentations every year, including dozens on the use of microcomputers in manufacturing. The following may be of particular interest: 1984, 1985, and 1986. Also note the *1984 Microprocessor Seminar Proceedings,* January/February 1984.

APICS Training Aid on Microcomputers in Manufacturing. Home study course with software, instructional material, and questions for review. APICS

Training Aids also exist on most matters of manufacturing planning and control: master scheduling, forecasting, material requirements planning, capacity planning and control, production activity control, inventory management, cycle counting, zero inventory/just-in-time techniques, and so forth.

Computer Software Management and Information Center (COSMIC) in Athens, Georgia. All government-developed software (mainframe as well) is available free. This organization offers a service in searching out such software. Several other "matchmaking" services (that is, matching your software needs with most likely providers) are named in an article in *The Christian Science Monitor*, November 3, 1983, p. 21.

Data Decisions. An extensive reference series that includes microcomputer vendors, applications, communications, and so forth in several volumes. The series is updated monthly.

Datapro Directory of Microcomputer Software. A vast compendium, updated monthly, of information on applications (including manufacturing), vendors, user ratings, programming aids, office automation, and more. Datapro also publishes and updates a collection of articles and references entitled *Management of Microcomputer Systems*. They also issue *Reports* on microcomputer systems, office automation, and word processing and other reports on international aspects of these subjects and on the management of these functional areas.

Dow Jones-Irwin Technical Reference Guide to Microcomputer Database Management Systems (George F. Goley, IV). Published by Dow Jones-Irwin, 1987. Guide for experienced professionals to dBASE III Plus®, R:Base System V, and KnowledgeMan 2.

Dynamics Series by various authors. Published by Dow Jones-Irwin, 1987. Guides to popular software packages such as Reflex, Paradox, Symphony®, and Supercalc 4. Guides to DAC EASY, desktop publishing, and WordPerfect™ are also available from Dow Jones-Irwin.

Executive Support Systems: The Myth and Reality of Top Management Computer Use (John F. Rockart and David W. DeLang). Published by Dow Jones-Irwin, 1987. Describes the major ESS applications, successful installations, and analysis of the use and misuse of such systems based on studies at MIT Center for Information Systems Research.

General information about software, hardware, buying guides. A wide variety of magazines and services—*Business Software Review, Business Computer Systems* (for example, a listing of microcomputer database management systems is in the September, 1985 issue), *Computerworld, PC Week, PC World, Computer Buyers Guide and Handbook, 1987 Computer Buying Guide* (includes retail prices and likely available prices for the shrewd).

Manufacturing Planning and Control Systems, 2nd ed. (Thomas E. Vollman, William Lee Berry, and D. Clay Whybark). Published by Dow Jones-Irwin,

1987. Comprehensive study of the many elements of manufacturing applications and their implementation.

Production Activity Control (Steven A. Melnyk and Phillip L. Carter). Published by Dow Jones-Irwin, 1987. Techniques and methods of PAC and its integration to the other elements of manufacturing systems. This book and the preceding give a sound introduction and considerable detail on the development and operation of manufacturing systems in general and can be adapted for microcomputer-based systems.

Production and Inventory Control Handbook (2nd ed.) (James H. Greene, Ph.D., CFPIM Editor-in-chief in collaboration with 87 contributing experts). APICS 1987 McGraw-Hill Book Company. This is a vast collection of knowledge relative to virtually every facet of manufacturing.

Production and Inventory Management, quarterly journal of APICS, contains several articles on the subject. For example, see my article in first quarter 1985 on master production scheduling on microcomputers.

P&IM Review and APICS News. Often includes articles on micros in manufacturing. A special section, including introduction to systems, reviews of hardware and software (now a bit dated), illustrations of micro uses, and the tax incentives on micros, was published in the January 1984 issue, pp. 24–48. The regular feature on hardware and software often includes items of interest to micro users.

Society of Manufacturing Engineers (SME) publishes many useful works relative to the use of PCs in engineering. Two deserve special mention: *The Expanding Role of Personal Computers in Manufacturing* by Edward J. Heaton (1986); and *BASIC Programming Solutions for Manufacturing* by J. E. Nicks (1981).

World Conference of Production and Inventory Control (First), Vienna, Austria, May 1985 (available from APICS). "The Role of the Microcomputer in the Small Manufacturing Business" by Alan Patrick, pp. 38–42; "Master Planning on a Microcomputer" by Thomas H. Fuller, Jr., pp. 129–33.

Glossary of Acronyms and Related Terms

APICS. American Production and Inventory Control Society—62,000-member organization with affiliates in 17 countries dedicated to furthering the knowledge and practice of production and inventory management.

APMA. American Purchasing Managers Association.

B25. Unisys class of microcomputers—most often used in clusters and networks.

BASIC. Beginners' All-Purpose Symbolic Instruction Code—the most widely used programming language for novices (and some pros) on microcomputers. It is now taught to many school children (both of the author's children could write BASIC programs before they could see over the keyboard unaided by a stool).

CAD. Computer-aided drafting (or design or drawing)—uses mainframes or micros to record and develop engineering drawings.

CAM. Computer-aided manufacturing—ranges from simple programmable machine tools (such as NC lathes) to very complex networks of automation.

CAP. Computer-aided publishing—creates internal and external documents that include various font styles and graphic images.

DBMS. Database management systems—used to organize, enter, and report on names, numbers, dates, and so forth.

DP. Data processing—usually refers to the department.

FAS. Final assembly schedule—describes the particular configurations of major components needed to meet specific customer orders and relates these to daily schedules for the final assembly operations.

FORTRAN. FORmula TRANslation—a computer programming language oriented toward manipulating mathematical entities such as formulas, matrixes, vectors, and such. It is often used in engineering applications such as linear programming and CAD.

GT. Group Technology—a scheme for coding parts and processes to eliminate duplication and inefficiencies.

ISO. International Standards Organization—responsible for developing standards for PC communications and a wide variety of other standards.

KB. Kilobytes—1,024 bytes (bytes are characters and numbers)—usually used as a measure of internal memory.

LAN. Local area network—a cabling and software scheme to allow micros to talk to each other (and other programmable devices such as computers and robots).

MAD. Mean absolute deviation—the average of the absolute values of the differences between the actual sales and the forecasts.

MAP. Manufacturing Automation Protocol—General Motors has been making a noteworthy effort in the last two years, to develop a standardization of networking protocol that supports the OSI reference model and conforms to a number of standards set by the International Electronic and Electrical Engineering Society (IEEE). The standard is MAP.

MB. Megabytes—1,024,000 bytes (bytes are characters and numbers)—usually used as a measure of disk storage.

MIS. Management information systems—the avant-garde name for the DP department; recognizes the important difference between data and information.

Mouse. A hand-held input device that causes the cursor on the screen to follow the device's moves on the desktop; often used in CAD/CAM systems or in graphics applications.

MPS. Master Production Schedule—names the salable end items to be manufactured by time period.

MRP. Material Requirements Planning—a class of computer programs and techniques for determining part requirements.

MRP II. Manufacturing Resource Planning—a gathering of systems to support the planning and control of manufacturing resources. One element of this is MRP above.

MS-DOS. Microsoft Disk Operating System—the most widely used operating system in microcomputers today. It was written by Microsoft. Operating systems do all the nasty detail work we take for granted when using a computer such as loading and initiating programs, opening a disk file, interpreting input, and suchlike.

OSI. Open Systems Interconnection Reference Model—the standard access protocol and network architecture developed by ISO.

PC. Oh, come on! You know that this means personal computer. Since IBM has expropriated this generic moniker for its own line of such products, this has clouded the use of an otherwise fine label. Nonetheless, it is generally used synonymously with microcomputer.

Personal Computer AT. The advanced technology version of the Personal Computer XT which runs faster, has more memory, and costs more.

Personal Computer XT.   An extended version of the IBM Personal Computer that includes a hard disk and usually more memory.

PDN.   Public data network—a service offered by several companies available through ordinary phone lines. These can be used for sending mail across town or around the world. Many information retrieval services are also available through PDNs.

Phase Descriptors.   Used throughout the book as reference points for the progression from first experimentation forward to sophisticated applications of microcomputer technology:

Phase 1.   Experimental—early acquisition, may include some word processing, a few spreadsheets. Try different brands in the more adventurous departments.

Phase 2.   Individual—The users (several now) are quite competent at the above functions. The systems are all standalone—that is, they cannot directly share data or functions. Often, though, diskettes with such files are passed around.

Phase 3.   Departmental—The users within a department (or many departments) are now "within earshot." Disk files, printers, and plotters may be shared by local area networks (LANs). Joint applications may include office automation, databases, and scheduling.

Phase 4.   Organizational—The PCs become utilities. Most users of the organization are connected in the manner described in Phase 3. Most important, the organizational data is now part of the network. All planning and control functions are integrated in this network of mainframe and micro-size computers. Applications span the spectrum from memos to artificial intelligence.

PROM.   Programmable read-only memory—used in laser printers to store type fonts and in microcomputers to store commonly used instructions and operations.

SME.   Society of Manufacturing Engineers.

Bibliography—Sources and Additional Information

Aiello, Joseph L. "Successful Interaction between Purchasing and Production and Inventory Control." *1979 APICS Conference Proceedings*, pp. 234–35.

Alavi, Maryam. "Microcomputers & Small Manufacturing: A Strategy for Acquisition." *P&IM Review and APICS News*, January 1985, pp. 30–33.

American Institute of Certified Public Accountants. "Report on the Study of EDP-Related Fraud in the Banking and Insurance Industries." EDP Fraud Task Force, 1984.

Artes, Richard P., and John N. Petroff. "Solving Manufacturing Problems with a Personal Computer." *APICS Microprocessor Seminar Proceedings*, January/February 1984, pp. 211–18.

Austin, Sandy. "Data Options for Business." *Business Computer Systems*, September 1985, p. 81.

Barton, Terence E. "Is Your Forecasting System as Much Fun or as High Scoring as Pac-Man?" *APICS Microprocessor Seminar Proceedings*, January/February 1984, pp. 68–72.

Boeder, David M. "Large System Benefits for the Small Manufacturing Environment." *1986 APICS Conference Proceedings*, pp. 32–36.

Campbell, B. W. "The Planning Side of Success with Micros." *Data Communications Magazine*, October 1984; reprinted in *Datapro Research*, December 1984.

Chartier, Bruce A. "Microcomputers = Productivity Power." *P&IM Review and APICS News*, January 1984.

Chorafas, Dimitris N. *Office Automation, The Productivity Challenge*. Englewood Cliffs, N.J.: Prentice-Hall, 1982.

Clark, James T. "Selling Top Management—Understanding the Financial Impact of Manufacturing Systems." *1982 APICS Conference Proceedings*, pp. 265–72; reprinted in *APICS Material Requirements Planning Reprints*.

Cooper, Jeffrey H. "The Microcomputer—a Multipurpose P&IC Tool." *1984 APICS Conference Proceedings (Computers and Software)*, p. 4ff.

Darrow, Barbara. "PC-Based CAD Comes of Age." *Design News*, August 19, 1985, pp. 88–91.

De Lurgio, Stephen A., and Jiguang Zhao. "A Manufacturing Planning and Control System Simulator, Using Spreadsheet Programs." *1986 APICS Conference Proceedings* p. 53ff.

DeWitt, Norm, and David Burdick. "Personal Computer-Based CAD/CAM— Miracle or Mirage?" Dataquest newsletter, June 28, 1985.

Dowst, Somerby. "A Small Purchasing Operation Gets the Big Picture." *Purchasing*, March 14, 1985, pp. 65–67.

Dunn, Alan. "Distribution Management in the 1980s." *1986 APICS Conference Proceedings*, pp. 394–98.

Edwards, Chris. "Guidelines: Systems Investigation for Microcomputers." *Datapro*, November 1985.

Fey, Carol. "Working with Robots: The Real Story." *Training*, March 1986, p. 49ff.

Flavin, John P., and Thomas H. Fuller, Jr. "PDQ: Purchasing to Support Manufacturing, or Where's the Req?" *1986 APICS Conference Proceedings*, pp. 490–94.

Foss, W. B. *Business Quarterly, University of Western Ontario*, Summer 1979.

Goldman, Gary S. "Micro-Based CAD: a Production Tool for Manufacturing Engineering." *APICS Microprocessor Seminar Proceedings*, January/February 1984, pp. 74–83.

Hamilton, Scott. "Can I Really Buy My Manufacturing Systems from Retail Stores?" *1985 APICS Conference Proceedings*, pp. 693–95.

————. "Microcomputer Systems for Small Manufacturers." *1986 APICS Conference Proceedings*, pp. 7–9.

Hunter, Mike. "Inventory: Asset or Liability? *1986 APICS Conference Proceedings*, p. 261ff.

Iacocca, Lee. *Iacocca: An Autobiography*. New York: Bantam Books, 1984.

Janicke, Winfried. "Two Measures for the Variability of Multi-Purpose Batch Chemical Plants." *Hungarian Journal of Industrial Chemistry Veszprem* 11 (1983), pp. 59–62; see also *Computers and Chemical Engineering* 8, no. 6 (1984), pp. 339–43.

Jordan, Henry M. "Just-in-Time Performance Measurement." *First World Congress of Production and Inventory Control*, May 1985, pp. 43–45.

Langford, Peter W. "The Micro Computer in Materials Management—A Stepping Stone to MRP." *APICS Microprocessor Seminar Proceedings*, January/February 1984, pp. 265–70.

Lewyn, Mark. "1-2-3 gets 1 step easier." *USA Today*, October 6, 1986, p. 1.

Link, C. H. "Pete." "CAD Systems for Small Design Departments." *1986 APICS International Conference Proceedings*, pp. 472–74.

McKenny, James L., and F. Warren McFarlan. "The Information Archipelago —Maps and Bridges. *Harvard Business Review*, September/October 1982, pp. 109–19.

Metz, Richard. "Boeing's PC Practices." *Datamation*, January 15, 1986, p. 88ff.

Meyer, David A. "The Micro MRP Decision: Evaluation and Selection Criteria." *APICS Microprocessor Seminar Proceedings*, January/February 1984, pp. 57–62.

Miller, George J. "Software Selection: One More Time!" *1985 APICS Conference Proceedings*, p. 703f.

Mitchell, Russel, and Peter J. Heywood. "Detroit tries to Level a Mountain of Paperwork." *Business Week*, August 26, 1985, p. 94f.

Newman, Art, and Steve Kirk. "MRP II Implementation of a Microcomputer: Case Studies." *APICS Microprocessor Seminar Proceedings*, January/February 1984, pp. 29–36.

Orlicky, Joseph. *Material Requirements Planning: The New Way of Life in Production and Inventory Management.* New York: McGraw-Hill, 1975.

Paul, Horst J. "'Micro' MRP II User Audit Results: Is It Working?" *1986 APICS Conference Proceedings*, pp. 156–58.

Pendleton, William E. "Successful Implementation of MRP II on a Micro." *APICS Microprocessor Seminar Proceedings*, January/February 1984, pp. 20–28.

Perry, William E. *The Micro Mainframe Link: The Corporate Guide to Productive Use of the Microcomputer.* New York: John Wiley & Sons, 1985.

Piciacchia, Roy. "Microcomputer Applications in a Vertically Integrated Textile and Apparel Manufacturing Environment." *1986 APICS Conference Proceedings*, pp. 140–45.

Plossl, George W. *Manufacturing Control: The Last Frontier for Profits.* Reston, Va.: Reston Publishing (A Prentice-Hall company), 1973.

Plossl, George W. "Getting the Most from Forecasts," in *Forecasting*, 2nd ed. APICS, 1979.

Plossl, George W., and Oliver W. Wight. *Production and Inventory Control: Principles and Techniques.* Englewood Cliffs, N.J.: Prentice-Hall, 1967.

Rae, Sharon. "Micro DBMSs in Mainframe Shops." *Business Software Review*, December 1985, p. 41.

Raffish, Norm. "Group Technology: An Overview." *1985 APICS International Conference Proceedings*, pp. 536–38.

Rhodes, Wayne L., Jr. "Pulling It All Together." *Manufacturing Systems*, Summer 1984, pp. 14–18.

Rockart, John F. "Chief Executives Define Their Own Data Needs." *Harvard Business Review*, March–April 1979, pp. 81–93.

Sandberg-Diment, Erik. "Software for the Average User." *The New York Times*, December 9, 1986.

Schroer, Bernard J., J. T. Black, and Shou Xiang Zhang. "Microcomputer Analyzes 2-card Kanban System for 'Just-in-Time' Small Batch Production." *IE (Industrial Engineer) Magazine*, June 1984, pp. 54–65.

Scott, John Paul. "Micros and Manufacturing." *APICS Microprocessor Seminar Proceedings*, January/February 1984, pp. 252–58.

Shindelman, Lester S., and Carter C. Utzig. "Move over Mainframe: Make Way for the Micro." *1986 APICS Conference Proceedings*, pp. 467–71.

Skelton, Ron L. "The High-Tech Express." *Datamation*, December 1985, pp. 110–14.

Skinner, Wickham. *Manufacturing: The Formidable, Competitive Weapon.* New York: John Wiley & Sons, 1985.

Sullivan, Cheryl. "Computer 'Magic' — 30-Second Commute." *The Christian Science Monitor*, August 26, 1985, p. 1.

VanDeMark, Robert L. "The Path of Flow Dynamics of Network Distribution." *1986 APICS Conference Proceedings*, pp. 412–17.

Wantuck, Ken. "Measuring Labor Effectiveness in a Just-in-Time Environment." *1986 APICS Conference Proceedings*, pp. 310–11.

Wiener, Hesh. "Stalking the Wilds of the PC Market." *Datamation*, April 15, 1986, pp. 91–92.

Wight, Oliver W. *MRP II: Unlocking America's Productivity Potential.* Boston, Mass.: CBI Publishing, 1981.

INDEX